LIBERATION, METHOD AND DIALOGUE
Enrique Dussel and North American Theological Discourse

American Academy of Religion
Academy Series

edited by
Susan Thistlethwaite

Number 58
LIBERATION, METHOD AND DIALOGUE
Enrique Dussel and North
American Theological Discourse
by
Roberto S. Goizueta

LIBERATION, METHOD AND DIALOGUE
Enrique Dussel and North American Theological Discourse

by

Roberto S. Goizueta

Scholars Press
Atlanta Georgia

LIBERATION, METHOD AND DIALOGUE
Enrique Dussel and North American Theological Discourse

Library of Congress Cataloging-in-Publication Data

Goizueta, Roberto.
Dussel and dialogue.

(American Academy of Religion academy series ; no. 58)
Bibliography: p.
1. Dussel, Enrique D. —Contributions in liberation theology. 2. Liberation theology—History. 3. Theology, Doctrinal—North America—History—20th century. I. Title. II. Series.
BT83.57.G64 1987 230'.2'0924 87-28516
ISBN 1-55540-189-9
ISBN 1-55540-190-2 (pbk.)

Printed in the United States of America
on acid-free paper

CONTENTS

PREFACE

In a recent article appearing in *Sojourners* magazine, an anonymous Russian Christian emigre, living in the U.S., recounts a conversation he (or she) had with a fellow Russian Christian, "Yuri," who is still in the Soviet Union. In that conversation, Yuri offers consolation to his compatriot, now a naturalized citizen of the world's largest "Christian" nation. Yuri's words are quoted as follows:

> It is difficult for us, especially in the outreaches like Siberia and Central Asia. No Bibles, no churches—but we survive. With us, the choices are plain. But from what I know of you, the choices seem insidious. Materialism among us is an ideology. We can combat it. But with you, it seems to be a way of life. Your battle, it seems to me, is the harder to fight.

The Christian today is caught in a struggle—quite possibly to a nuclear death—between two empires, one bent on forcing its ideological atheism down the throats of its citizens, many of whom continue to offer courageous resistance, and the other finding it almost impossible to escape the seductive allure of its own practical atheism. The Christian finding him or herself in the aegis of either empire is confronted with two alternatives: spiritual death, or resistance (which may, in some cases, mean some form of martyrdom). Usually the choice does not present itself so starkly, but always it irrupts in our world when we least expect or desire it, calling us to grasp unashamedly our God-given freedom as human persons.

Nowhere has this choice confronted me, as an American citizen, more directly than in its human incarnation, the faces of those poor who, as "outside" the global power structure, represent an abiding challenge to the very foundations of that structure. This work is nothing more nor less than a part of my personal, life-long struggle to *choose*. Hopefully, it will contribute in some small way to our ongoing struggle, as a society, to choose.

In this dissertation, I examine the possibility of a liberative methodology grounded in and affirmative of the irreducibility of the human person to any system, or empire. I do this, first, by analyzing the Latin American liberative method of Enrique Dussel as a non-reductionist economic, historical, political, cultural, philosophical, and theological approach; secondly, by setting forth Bernard Lonergan's meta-method as an analogically liberative North American method; and, thirdly, by then suggesting how, as grounded in the irreducibility of the human person, these methodologies make important inroads in the direction of an "international division of theological labor" which would affirm the radical freedom of the person. I have undertaken this task in the humbling knowledge that no amount of writing, or reading, will advance human freedom unless these are the fruit of a life devoted to the cause of human liberation. Though this dissertation is no small task, therefore, the larger, far more significant task lies before me—and before *us*. It is in this light that the reader should proceed to the following pages.

Several comments need to be made regarding translation. Wherever I have quoted from a work in Spanish, I have myself done the translation into English. In the translations from the works of Dussel—and in a few other instances indicated in the footnotes—I have taken the liberty to use non-sexist language rather than render a more literal translation. Such non-sexist translation is fully consonant with the content and tone of Dussel's work. He himself has indicated that such a translation would not be problematic for him. In any case, I bear full responsibility for the accuracy, or inaccuracy, of the translations.

I would like to acknowledge a number of people without whose support this dissertation would still be *in potentia*. The Smith Family Scholarship Fund and the Fund for Theological Education, Inc., made it possible for me to approach this project with the necessary single-mindedness. The Theology faculty of Marquette University and the Religious Studies faculty of Loyola University in New Orleans have provided me with unstinting encouragement. I am grateful for the confidence they have shown in me. I owe a special debt of gratitude to Dan Maguire, Michael Fleet, Bob Masson, Sebastian Moore, Virgilio Elizondo, and Vernon Gregson, all of whom I am proud to call my colleagues, but even more proud to call my friends. I have been blessed with numerous other loving friends: Karen Wilhelmy, George Winzenberg, Marc Ellis, Maria Teresa and John Witchger, Lucy Edelbeck, Steve Price, Dennis Sylva, and many, many others. I am thankful to them and for them. Two very close friends deserve special mention. Tony Palese has been a constant source of both support and stimulation. His personal warmth and Christian witness have offered inspiration at those times when I most needed inspiration. Matt Lamb has been my dissertation director. Yet he has been, and is, so much more in my life: friend, confidant, colleague, mentor, role model. If I am a theologian today, it is because of Matt Lamb. Thanks are also due to Prof. Enrique Dussel for being so generous with his time and support. I know that I could never do justice to the breadth of his vision or the depth of his commitment.

Last, but certainly not least, I would like to express my gratitude to those who, as my most intimate co-travellers in this journey, have been daily reminders to me of the power of self-sacrificing love, my family. My parents, grandparents, and great grandparents have given me life—what more need be said? No words can express my gratitude for such a wondrous gift! And, what is more, they, along with my sister, Olga Mari, and my brother, Javier—have given me the gift of freedom. Despite their personal reservations about particular decisions I have made, they have never questioned my right to make those decisions. If I can understand what Prof. Dussel means by love of the Other as Other, it is because I was raised in a home where I experienced genuine Christian love and my personhood was never threatened. For this I will always be grateful. I would like to mention my entire family, but for a Latin like myself, such a listing could go on for many pages, so I will resist the temptation. I must mention, however, my brother Carlos Alberto. The brevity of his life on this earth belies the magnitude of his influence on the lives of his family and friends. His courage and spirit in the face of the suffering he encountered during his last days reflected that holy wisdom which has been revealed to the poor, the powerless, the children. His instinctive faith in God was truly remarkable. By rewarding him with eternal life, the Lord only confirmed what those of us closest to Carlos already knew: this was a most blessed child. To Carlos Alberto, to his living presence among us, and to all the children, in whose wisdom is our hope, I dedicate this dissertation.

Roberto S. Goizueta
Milwaukee, Wisconsin
April, 1984

INTRODUCTION

For almost a quarter of a century now, our hemisphere has witnessed the growth of the liberation theology movement. Originating in the experience of the Latin American peoples, it differs radically from most of the theology done in the academic centers of the West. For the first time since the Reformation we are witnessing a widespread pastoral and spiritual theological renewal grounded in grassroots communities, in this case, the over 100,000 *comunidades de base*. The experience of these communities has been one of oppression and poverty. Nevertheless, the centuries of suffering experienced by the Latin American people has not succeeded in quenching the flame of hope which, while often buried beneath the ashes of so many compatriots, has continued to burn as an inspiring testament to the faith of that people.

In the course of the last two decades, this faith has begun to find systematic, theological expression. The development of Latin American liberation theology over that period can be divided, following the schema of Juan Luis Segundo, into three major sub-periods: 1) 1962–1968, extending from the beginning of Vatican II (and, some would say, from the publication, in the same year, of Segundo's own *Función de la iglesia en la realidad rioplatense*) to the Medellín Conference; 2) 1968–1972, the period during which liberation theology was systematically formulated, e.g., in Gustavo Gutiérrez' *Teología de la liberación;* and 3) 1972–present, a period marked both by the maturation of liberation theology's understanding of itself and by a concomitant global response to the Latin American liberation movement, which response has often resulted in the persecution of the Latin American theologians themselves.[1]

The abovementioned book by Segundo represents the first attempt during this twenty year period to "reflect on praxis in the light of faith," from the perspective of the Latin American experience of oppression and exploitation. Beginning with an analysis of the contemporary situation in Uruguay and Argentina, and then moving to biblical exegesis as a cipher for interpreting that reality,

Segundo here lays out the rudiments of a Latin American liberative method.[2]

The second sub-period begins with the Medellín Conference, where the Latin American bishops for the first time made a collective attempt to apply the teachings of Vatican II to Latin America, and in so doing established guidelines for a critique of First World domination and for the development of a theology which would both reflect the Latin American experience of domination and effectively articulate the hope of liberation in the light of the Christian faith. The first theologian to accept this challenge in a thorough-going fashion was Gustavo Gutiérrez in his book *Teología de la liberación*. Its publication, the result of years of collaboration and dialogue with numerous other Latin American theologians, marked the climax of the second stage in the development of liberation theology.[3] This was the first book-length, systematic formulation of liberation theology and thus became, in Alfred Hennelly's words, the "Magna Carta" of the movement.

Finally, the third stage is the one now underway and the one which will essentially provide the context for our discussions in this work. During the last decade the liberation theology movement has experienced a great deal of both criticism and outright persecution while nevertheless, in the face of this adversity, continuing to grow and mature. This growth has been characterized by a more profound understanding of the themes of domination and liberation, a more explicit awareness of methodological issues, a greater self-criticism deriving from this methodological awareness, and a consequent complexification of the movement as the inevitable multiplication of nuances and emphases has begun to create different currents within the one movement.[4] The movement's maturation has occurred, moreover, in an increasingly global theological context, where the North American and European theological communities have felt free to offer their own input. These have found it impossible to ignore the goings-on to their south.

Contemporary Latin American liberation theology thus finds itself developing both internally, insofar as it attains a more profound self-understanding, and externally, insofar as its growth and consequent influence bring it into ever closer contact with the theological communities of the First World, who see themselves challenged to respond, whether positively or negatively, to the theological new kid on the block. It is to this double orientation that we will address ourselves in the remainder of this work: first, by examining the intellectual project of Enrique Dussel, one of the major contributors to liberation theology's methodological maturation; secondly, by suggesting the possibility of "analogical dialogue" between North and South.

The model we will be using for such a dialogue is one in which the foundations of Dussel's method find an analogue in the thought of the North American theologian-philosopher-methodologist Bernard Lonergan, the latter then emerging as a North American analogical—i.e., both complementary and critical—conversation partner with Dussel. As we will see, this type of dialogue differs radically from the types of dialogical critiques offered by other theologians, for, unlike these latter, analogical dialogue, while critical, is grounded in a fundamental methodological openness to the other's insights, which fundamental openness allows for a genuine complementarity. It will be our contention, moreover, that the critiques of theologians like Michael Novak, Dennis McCann, and Roger Vekemans not only do *not* contribute to effective dialogue insofar as they either seriously misinterpret or fail to appreciate the foundational import of liberation theology, but that they *would* be more open to such dialogue were they to fully appreciate the scope of Dussel's work.

The dissertation is divided into two major parts, the first comprising four chapters and the second two chapters. In the first we will present an analysis of the themes of domination and liberation as these become foundational in Dussel's method. This first part begins with a discussion of the dependency paradigm, for 1) it was in this context that the themes of domination and liberation first achieved social scientific and theological explicitation, 2) Dussel's project can be interpreted as an attempt to provide a theological and philosophical method grounded in the foundational *experience of dependency*, the reality to which dependency theories and liberation theology speak, and 3) Dussel's way of incorporating the dependency paradigm in that project itself becomes a refutation of the abovementioned critics' understanding of liberation theology as reductionist. Moreover, as we note below, Dussel's personal encounter with dependency theory represented a major turning point in his intellectual development.

The first chapter will be followed by an examination, in three chapters, of Dussel's anadialectical method as involving 1) the dialectical retrieval of Latin American history and Western philosophy, 2) the relation between the Totality, or the "system," and the Other, or the one who stands outside the system (this comprising the anadialectical method *per se*), and 3) the distinction between poiesis, or production, and praxis, or human interpersonal activity, as a methodological grounding for the relative priority of economic liberation discussed in the first chapter.

If Part I speaks to the internal, methodological maturation of liberation theology as a movement, Part II speaks to its growing external, global impact. Chapter five examines Bernard Lonergan's method as a North American analogue to Dussel's method and suggests ways in which the former can both complement the latter and contribute to its self-understanding (although Lonergan himself has never explicitly entered into dialogue with Dussel, or vice versa). Chapter six examines the critiques of liberation theology proffered by two key North American critics, Novak and McCann, and one European-born Latin American, Vekemans. The analysis of these critiques will serve both to clarify dialectically the *non*-reductionist character of Dussel's method—as well as those of other liberation theologians—and, as a counterpoint to chapter five, to show how the imposition of alien conceptual frameworks on liberation theology leads to serious misinterpretation, which in turn closes off any possibility of communication.

The need for such communication arises from two methodological exigencies: 1) Latin American liberation theology is intrinsically relational, i.e., the existence of oppressed peoples implies the existence of oppressors, and 2) the danger exists of attempting a wholesale importation of Latin American theology into North America in the same manner in which European theology has often been imported in the past, thereby forestalling the emergence of a *North* American theology of liberation.[5] By implicating North America as an oppressor and challenging the "academic" nature of most First World theology, Latin American liberation theology can offer what Hennelly calls an "'antienvironment,' that is, a distanced perspective from which to survey the western theological task and the role of the theologian in society," thereby impressing upon the North American theological community the need to take this global rationality seriously in the development of a North American theology.[6]

The task before us demands, therefore, an incorporation of the theological insights of Latin American theology (without superimposing our interpretative framework on them) while at the same time drawing upon the North American historical experience in order to embrace anew the liberative values present in our history—from the Declaration of Independence to contemporary Black and Feminist theologies. Latin American theologians can help us see how we have distorted "freedom" by making it a smokescreen for oppression.

An analogously liberative North American theology could thus develop alongside and in interaction with Latin American liberation theology. Our contention in this work will be that Enrique Dussel's Latin American liberative method, as "*ana*dialectic," intrinsically allows for such mutual development and is complemented in just such an analogous way by Bernard Lonergan's North American liberative method. This, then, is our thesis: Dussel's anadialectical method provides a comprehensive, non-reductionist methodological grounding for Latin American liberation and, moreover, one which, at its very foundation, is open to analogous expressions of the liberative orientation. Bernard Lonergan, in turn, provides such a methodological analogue within the North American context.

Enrique Dussel and the Struggle for Liberation

There exists a wide gulf between the theological context of the typical North American academic and that of the Latin American liberation theologian. If we North Americans are to even begin to appreciate Latin American liberation theology for what it is rather than imposing our own categories on it, therefore, we must start by appreciating the fact that, unlike most of us, the typical Latin American liberation theologian theologizes out of very personal experiences of political persecution. He or she knows little of "academic freedom." The experience of oppression is not an abstraction but a very personal reality, often taken on willingly, as the cost of solidarity with the poor.

If this fact is borne in mind, it becomes difficult to dismiss Latin American liberation theology as simply a "fad" or naive intellectualization. On the contrary, Latin American liberation theology shows itself as thoroughly "realistic" in that it emerges out of personal contact with the *reality* of oppression as this is experienced both by the poor and by the theologians themselves, which experience is then reflected upon and articulated in the Christian context of the basic ecclesial communities (*comunidades de base*). Consequently, far from representing an ephemeral fad, it promises to be around as long as systemic, global injustice continues unabated.

Before proceeding to an analysis of Dussel's intellectual project *per se,* therefore, it is important to take note of his own personal, concrete struggle with social injustice, for the struggle is the source of that project. What follows in the remainder of this introduction, therefore, is an account of his own personal journey in faith, which account is, unless otherwise indicated, taken from conversations with Dussel and from an autobiography which he graciously taped for my use.

Dussel divides his life thus far into four major periods: 1934–1959, 1959–1969, 1969–1975, and 1975–present. He was born in 1934 in La Paz, Argentina, "a small village of no more than 3,000 inhabitants and 150 kilometers from the city of Mendoza, next to the Argentine Andes."[7] Although he himself was not born into poverty (his father being a village doctor), such poverty was a part of his daily life, surrounded as he was by "women and men of the countryside, in extremely humble Indian or mestizo huts; a misery which saddened my childhood."[8] At that time, furthermore, Argentina was in the throes of the so-called "infamous decade," which had begun in 1930 and was characterized by military leadership and oppression. The injustice of this dictatorship made a lasting impression on Dussel.

Having left in 1940 for Buenos Aires, where his father would study medicine, Dussel returned home in 1942 and became involved in the Catholic Action movement, an association that would last for fifteen years (until he was 23 years old). During this time he assumed various leadership positions, eventually becoming president of the federation of students of the university in Mendoza and of his entire diocese. From 1954 to 1956 he became engaged in the struggle against populist Peronism in the name of Christian Democratic reformism. His studies at this time included the fine arts, which opened him to the possibility of a philosophy of production and theology of art, and, from 1953 to 1957, philosophy, which was then essentially *Thomist* philosophy. It was during these years that he was first sensitized to the "problem of analogy," which would eventually lead to the development of the anadialectical method.

In 1957 Dussel left Argentina for Spain to undertake doctoral studies in philosophy. During the next two years he produced a three volume 1,200 page dissertation on Jacques Maritain's notion of the common good, which work essayed a defense of Maritain's position "against the most conservative elements of Thomism." In the dissertation, Dussel defends the rights of the person vis-a-vis the common good.

The vacation periods in 1957 and 1958 proved to be, for Dussel, of the most profound personal significance. Having always had a special devotion to St. Francis of Assisi, and harboring a deep desire to experience radical poverty in his own life, he left on a journey to the Holy Land. As he had little money at the outset of his trip, he was forced to beg alms for food and shelter. Arriving in Nazareth, he met Father Paul Gauthier, a French worker priest who would have a great impact on Dussel's life.

Gauthier invited him to return to the Holy Land for a longer stay and so, after finishing his doctorate in Madrid, Dussel returned to Israel to work with the French priest. Thus ends what Dussel calls the first major period of his life (1934–1959) and begins a second period (1959–1969). This latter included, then, two years (1959–1961) during which Dussel worked as a carpenter and a fisherman and lived on an Israeli kibbutz.[9] Traveling throughout the Holy Land, he sought out the holy places of Christianity and read through the Gospels in the context of the physical surroundings in which they were inspired. He learned Hebrew and became engaged in ongoing discussions and reflections within Gauthier's community on the meaning of evangelical poverty. Their rule of life in the community was Isaiah 61:1: The Spirit of the Lord is upon me, for He has anointed me to preach good news to the poor . . .

Along with the other members of this small community in Nazareth, Dussel and Gauthier were indirectly involved in introducing the theme of "the poor" at Vatican II. They entered into a series of discussions with the Bishop of Nazareth, with Dom Helder Camara, and other prelates, who then took their common concerns to the Council. The intellectual fruit of these years is reflected in Dussel's first book, *El humanismo semita,* written in 1961:

> In that book one can already see the theme of dialogue, the theme of "the Other." The Other is not yet "the poor," and the Other and the poor are not yet conjoined to the problem of analogy or of the analectic. But they are present there.

In 1961 Dussel returned to Europe, this time for four years of theological study in France, primarily at the Institut Catholique, and two years of historical studies at Mainz, Germany with Lortz. While in Paris he remained in close contact with the worker priest movement. In 1964, while in Germany, he wrote *Hipótesis para una historia de la iglesia en América Latina*, which would later be influential in the development of a Latin American theology. Still in Germany, he matriculated at Münster, studying the European conciliar theology there with Pieper and Ratzinger. In 1965, Dussel received his licentiate in theology and, in 1967, his doctorate in history. Although having done most of his historical work in Mainz, he received this doctorate—his second—from the Sorbonne, where he devoted his dissertation, *Les évécques hispano-américains defenseurs de l'indien (1504–1620)*, to the theme of the poor as this related to the defense of the Amerindians during the time of the colonial episcopacy:

> This was for me a fundamental thesis, because from there I began to have a much more profound vision of the origin of our Latin American Church and of the struggle for the poor: the historical poor, the Indian.

He then wrote *El humanismo helénico*, which was meant to offer the Hellenistic world view as a contrast to the Semitic world view examined in his first book. In *El humanismo helénico*, Dussel analyzes the individualism and dualism of Hellenistic thought, which, he argues, is incapable of accounting for the unitive corporality characteristic of the Semitic world view. Following upon *El humanismo semita* and *El humanismo helénico*, Dussel wrote a third book in the "trilogy," this last one entitled *El dualismo en la antropología de la cristiandad*. This work engaged him for a number of years upon his return to Argentina, where he would eventually become professor of philosophical anthropology and, beginning in 1969, professor of philosophical ethics at the National University of Cuyo.

At this point it is important to emphasize again that Dussel's absence from Argentina during the decade from 1957 to 1967 was personally enriching in that it served to deepen his understanding of earlier experiences with poverty and oppression in Argentina. He was able to see the oppression of his people "from outside," from the European centers of power.[10]

Dussel's return to Argentina in 1967 was "difficult, since the military had come to power in 1966." Almost immediately upon his return, he was invited by the Latin American Pastoral Institute (IPLA) in Quito to give a series of lectures in Church history there. As Dussel describes it, his entrance into IPLA was of great significance for him. Given the opportunity to travel throughout the continent and "to live the concrete anguish of thousands of Christians," he was able to avoid the danger of limiting his experience of the Latin American reality to that of a small corner of Argentina.[11]

It was not until December, 1969, however, that Dussel entered into a third major period of his life. The turning point was a conference of sociologists which he attended in Buenos Aires during that month. A theme of discussion at the conference was dependency theory. Here Dussel first came to fully appreciate the importance of dependency theory for Latin American theological reflection.

At about this same time, he was also engaged in an in-depth reading of the works of the philosopher Emmanuel Levinas. The confluence of this exposure to Levinas and the exposure to dependency theory provided Dussel with an initial theoretical framework for synthesizing his experiences in Europe, the Holy Land, and Latin America.

The themes of analogy and analectic had already begun to take shape in 1969 in the course of his own reading as well as in discussion with Juan Carlos Scannone and other Argentine theologians. Along with Levinas' writings, particularly influential in this regard were Lakebrink's *Hegels dialektische Ontologie und die thomische Analektik*, L. Bruno Puntel's *Analogie und Geschichtlichkeit*, Erik Przywara's *Analogia entis*, and J. Yves Jolif's *Comprendre l'homme*. By early 1970, therefore, he had already discovered the possibility of an ethics of liberation grounded in an analectics of the Other (see chapter three below).

After the Argentine "*cordobazo*" in 1969, moreover, Dussel and his colleagues were finding themselves more involved in political questions. Politics entered their reflection as a central theme and, influenced by Marcuse, they developed a greater sensitivity to the expressly political dimension of "the Other" as over against "the system." It was during this period, the spring and summer of 1970, that Dussel finished the first volume of his *Ethics*, which would later be expanded to become a seminal, five volume work in ethics and methodology.

In 1971 Dussel gave a series of conferences, on "history and the theology of liberation," to 900 directors of religious schools and members of religious orders (which conferences would later be published in English under the same title). In 1972 he attended the conference of Latin American theologians in El Escorial, where "there were some interesting discussions on the theme of 'class' and 'the people'." While not denying the significance of class as a category, the Argentines at the conference (including Dussel) influenced as they were by Peronism, insisted on the categorical priority of "the people" (over against the Chileans, e.g., Pablo Richard, and some of the Peruvians).

The years 1971–1974 were Dussel's most prolific. In the course of these years he published approximately twenty books and articles. The significance of these accomplishments was overshadowed, however, by an event that occurred on October 2, 1973: an attempt on Dussel's life. At 2:30 A.M. on that day he was awakened by a tremendous explosion in his house. Assuming at first that there had been a gas explosion in the kitchen, he soon discovered that the source of the destruction was a bomb that had been placed at his doorstep. He described his immediate reaction to the destruction of his house and the attempt on his life:

> Before that overwhelming scene, still covered with smoke, I simply reacted by saying "Lord, I am not worthy," because I was aware that the blessing which says "Blessed are those persecuted for justice's sake" applied to me. At the same time my heart prompted me to say "Father, forgive them for they do not know what they are doing."

Dussel knew that his commitment to the poor in the *comunidades de base* and in the university had led to this assassination attempt.[12] His life, and that of his family, would never again be the same. Whether he liked it or not, he was personally implicated in the global struggle between the oppressed and their oppressors.[13] When, in his later exile in Mexico, he turned to those books which had survived the explosion, their charred pages—and the occasional errant doornail that had found a resting place among the thoughts of Hegel or Kierkegaard—would serve as constant reminders of that struggle, from which not even Hegel or Kierkegaard are immune.

The following months in Argentina were marked by widespread persecution and fear. Finally, having been blacklisted and expelled from the National University of Cuyo, Dussel and his family went into exile in Mexico in 1975. Upon arriving in Mexico,he wrote *Filosofí de la liberación*, which he calls "a testament to this period." Here now began Dussel's fourth major period, his exile in Mexico (1975–present). This period has been characterized, in his intellectual development, by an increased criticism of populism and a more in-depth reading of Marx. Through his reading of Marx, he has been able to enhance his understanding of the relationship between praxis (human interpersonal activity) and poiesis (production). This, in turn, has given him a new perspective on religion and, particularly, on worship as service to God mediated by poiesis, that is, mediated by the offering of the fruits of production to the neighbor and, through him or her, to God (see chapter four for a further elaboration of this point).

With the Sandinista victory in Nicaragua, this new perspective took on historical concreteness. For the first time, Christians had played a key role in a successful socialist revolution on Latin American soil. In numerous visits to Nicaragua and El Salvador, Dussel has been able to further develop his thought along these lines. More and more, he now finds himself looking to the experience of the Churches in Nicaragua and El Salvador as current historical examples of the liberation movement which provides the grounding (remember the charred pages!) for a Latin American liberation theology. It is the course of this movement that will determine the course of Latin American liberation theology.

Dussel's story is not unique among Latin American theologians. It is characterized by an ongoing, personal confrontation with injustice, out of which confrontation emerges a theoretical framework for understanding and responding to injustice. If contact with dependency theory marks an axial point in his life, for instance, it is only because he had already experienced the *reality* to which the dependency paradigm speaks. The same can be said for the philosophical and theological categories which, though originating in Europe and the Middle East, provided him with an initial vocabulary for talking about the Latin American reality. He would then be able to reformulate those categories by "thinking" them in the material context of that reality.

Having presented a glimpse into some of the personal experiences out of which Dussel's intellectual project has been born, we will now turn to an examination of the project itself. This analysis will move from 1) the dependency paradigm as an initial framework for understanding Latin American sociohistorical praxis, to 2) the dialectical retrieval of the Western intellectual tradition as an entrance into philosophical and theological categories which will then 3) be further developed in the light of Latin American history, ultimately allowing for the formulation of 4) a *Latin American* liberative method. Ending the analysis in Part I with a discussion of Dussel's latest work on praxis and poiesis, we will thus repeat

Dussel's own journey, which has taken him from his earliest confrontation with poverty in La Paz to his current position as perhaps the leading Latin American methodologist, and certainly the most prolific liberation theologian.

NOTES

/1/ Alfred T. Hennelly, *Theologies in Conflict: The Challenge of Juan Luis Segundo* (Maryknoll, N.Y.: Orbis, 1979) p. 25; personal conversations with Enrique Dussel.
/2/ Hennelly, pp. 59ff.
/3/ Ibid., pp. 26–27.
/4/ Ibid., p. 25.
/5/ Ibid., pp. 15–16.
/6/ Ibid.
/7/ Enrique Dussel, "Supuestos histórico-filosóficos de la teología desde América latina," in *La nueva frontera de la teología en América latina*, ed. Rosino Gibellini (Salamanca: Sígueme, 1977) p. 176.
/8/ Ibid.
/9/ Ibid., taped autobiography of Dussel.
/10/ Dussel, "Supuestos histórico-filosóficos," p. 176.
/11/ Ibid., p. 177, taped autobiography of Dussel.
/12/ Dussel, "Supuestos histórico-filosóficos," p. 177.
/13/ Ibid.

PART ONE

CHAPTER ONE

FROM DEPENDENCE TO LIBERATION; THE EMERGENCE OF A PARADIGM

An Initial Interpretative Framework

As the paradigm which provided Enrique Dussel's initial social scientific framework for interpreting the Latin American historical reality, dependency theory played an important role in the development of his thought.[1] Though, as we will see later, he offers a critique of the dependency paradigm, his anadialectical method nevertheless incorporates both the economic specificity and the interdisciplinary dialectical openness of that paradigm. Dussel, however, further develops the themes of domination and liberation characteristic of the dependency paradigm by drawing out their methodological implications, thereby providing a foundation for a multidimensional, interdisciplinary hermeneutic of domination and liberation.

In this chapter, therefore, we will analyze the development and basic tenets of the dependency paradigm as the first systematic, social scientific attempt to articulate the Latin American experience of domination. In so doing, moreover, we will pay special attention to the manner in which the proponents of the dependency paradigm frame the relationship between economic and social aspects of domination. This will allow us both to see how the dependency paradigm differs from its more economistic ancestors and to present its more comprehensive approach to the issues of domination and liberation as an initial "open dialectic" which will later become methodologically explicitated in Dussel's anadialectical method and in his formulation of the praxis-poiesis (action-production) relationship. We will examine further the emergence of liberation theology as an ideological component of that comprehensive approach, which component will furnish Dussel's immediate theological context. As Dussel himself indicates, an adequate understanding of that context is not possible without an understanding of the relation between liberation theology and the categories of the dependency paradigm.[2]

From an Economics of Development to a Political Economics of Liberation

Its ability to encompass the whole range of modes of human domination is perhaps the major advance of liberation thought in general. The recognition of the need for liberation has emerged only gradually, however, insofar as the initial attempts to deal with global injustice have been limited by their partial, economistic understandings of and approaches to injustice. The massive alienation engendered by such well-intentioned programs as the ill-fated Alliance for Progress has led many to question both the applicability of economic growth-oriented development models and the belief that *the* root cause of global inequality is Third World economic stagnation and underdevelopment.[3]

Concomitantly there has emerged a movement to integrate *qualitative* as well as quantitative criteria in order to better account for the "social" variables of what now comes to be known as *human* development.[4] Even within most of these revised models, however, "development," in its late capitalist *economic* formulation, continues to be the primary goal of all economic systems.[5] While these "revised growth models" already begin an appropriation of qualitative criteria of development, in practice they tend to "subordinate value judgments about human goals to the achievement of economic growth."[6] The more "humane" growth models still fail to escape the economism inherent in human and economic development insofar as 1) Euro-America is considered *the* model of development, and 2) that model stresses economic growth as the foundation for human development.[7] Modern capitalist patterns of development are seen as "inevitable, given the demonstration effects and technological penetration of modern societies throughout the world."[8] Economic growth remains the primary means of achieving development; what is needed is an amelioration of the negative side effects attendant to economic growth.

The relegation of these "side effects" to the periphery of the model has resulted, however, in a development which, while sometimes raising per capita GNP's, has often *increased* the marginalization of popular majorities.[9] Even the revised development model, in its manner of framing the "side effects" of capitalist development, thus fails to account for 1) the *double* oppression of most Latin Americans at the hands of both foreign elites and local elites who appropriate for themselves the benefits of development and 2) the complex *interpenetration* of foreign and local capital. In short, the liberal capitalist understanding of development overlooks the *inherent* ambiguity of all economic growth. Massive inequality is not merely a side effect of economic growth, but is *generated* by it.[10] But if this is the case, then the very nature of that process and not just its effects comes into question.

This fundamental questioning represents a crucial epistemological break. "Equitable growth" is recognized as a self-contradictory term—at least as formulated within the dominant capitalist models. Consequently, any genuine development must emerge from outside those models. Because of this externalization of development-as-goal, it now relinquishes its central, normative role to "liberation," which is seen as better expressing the *dis*continuities between the previous models and the current Latin American struggle to chart an autonomous course in history.[11] *Liberation* becomes the goal.

In the liberation paradigm, development is by no means eschewed, but transformed. No longer is Third World underdevelopment understood in isolation from First World development, but the former is understood as its inevitable corollary and consequence.

"Equity" is no longer seen as an external, desirable or even necessary *corollary* to growth, but as an internal, determinative or constitutive element of true growth itself. The marginalization of equity considerations inherent in capitalism, where economic and civil societies are severed, is rejected in favor of a reintegration of infra- and superstructure, quantitative and qualitative criteria, growth and equity, and economic society and civil society as implying one another. Hence, liberation as a category moves away from the dualism of development theories and toward a non-reductionist, non-fragmented understanding of human development.

The three stages of the post-1950's evolution of economic thinking, from the advocacy of strictly economic growth, through the incorporation of qualitative equity goals, to the formulation of a liberation paradigm, have been elaborated upon by a variety of scholars.[12] Most scholars favor the revised development model.[13] This fact is of importance in that it signifies that, at this historical juncture, the indigenous liberation movement emerging in Latin

America must concern itself not only with the struggle against direct oppression, but also with a more benign danger, namely, that of cooptation and consequent premature integration into an existing global economic system that will encourage "development" as long as the system itself remains secure.

If the notion of liberation is to survive, therefore, its advocates must be able to articulate it in a way that avoids both economistic reductionism and a reformism which would leave the existing global structures essentially untouched. This will be our concern in the course of this work. In the remainder of the present chapter, we will analyze the basic outlines of the dependency paradigm, drawing out some of its methodological implications regarding non-economic forms of domination, in hopes of moving toward an interdisciplinary, dialectical framework for dealing with the issues of domination and liberation. Such a framework, we will argue later, is presented by Enrique Dussel.

The Dependency Paradigm

Liberation-as-goal expresses a belief in the causal link between underdevelopment and dependence, and in the inherent inability of conventional development approaches to break the bonds of dependence.[14] While most dependency theorists do not deny the significance of aggregate economic growth in their definition of underdevelopment, they broaden this definition to include such variables as economic inequality and high expenditures for luxury goods, i.e., the *nature* of that growth.[15] The point at which *dependencistas* distance themselves most radically from conventional economists, however, is in the fundamental role the Latin Americans ascribe to and the emphasis they place on the symbiotic nature of the relationship between dependency and underdevelopment. The definition of underdevelopment comes to be expressed in more comprehensive terms as "lack of control" by nationals over the social, political and cultural life of their nation"—control being usurped by foreign and local elites.[16] This broader definition is already suggesting the notion of dependence and pointing to the possibilities of an interdisciplinary understanding of that notion.

Such a definition of underdevelopment leads directly then, to a consideration of dependence. This latter in turn will eventually lead to the realization, not that dependence is the result of underdevelopment (as Prebisch and the advocates of import substitution would have it), but that, on the contrary, underdevelopment is the result of dependence: "no country was ever in an original state of *under*development, although it may have been *un*developed."[17] "Underdevelopment" is, by definition, a *relational* term.

As a term describing the relation between one nation, or region, and another, dependence (i.e., what defines *under*development) involves essentially two elements: subordination and integration.[18] In other words, the phenomenon of dependence impacts not only *inter*national relations (colonial analysis) but also *intra*national structures (class analysis):

> This dependence is the result of the historical development and contemporary structure of world capitalism, to which Latin America is subordinated, and the economic, political, social and cultural policies generated by the resulting class structure, especially by the class interests of the dominant bourgeoisie. It is important to understand, therefore, that throughout the historical process dependence is not simply an "external" relation between Latin America and its world capitalist metropolis but equally an "internal," indeed *integral* condition of Latin American society itself, which is reflected not only in international and domestic economics and politics but also has the most profound and far-reaching ideological and psychological manifestations of inferiority complexes and assimilation of metropolitan ideology and "development" theory.[19]

Thus, inasmuch as dependence involves not only market relationships but, most fundamentally, power relationships, it embraces the whole of a nation's life. What first becomes visible in the economic sphere permeates the political, cultural, ideological, etc.

Dependence involves *subordination*. The term "subordination" is carefully chosen, for dependence does not refer to some sort of "interdependence" between nations, the existence of which must be taken for granted in virtually any international relationship, but rather to the assimilation of one nation, or region, within another's sphere of influence to such a degree (and the degrees of dependence vary) that the development or lack thereof, of the former is governed, controlled and determined by the development of the latter.[20] Samir Amin offers an illustration of the difference between interdependence and dependence:

> When the iron ore of Lorraine is eventually worked out this may create a difficult reconversion problem for the region, but it will be able to overcome these difficulties, for an

> infrastructure has been formed on the basis of the mineral, which would be imported from elsewhere. But when the iron ore of Mauritania is worked out, that country will go back to the desert.[21]

The structures of international dependence are, thus, understood only when national and regional economies are viewed from the perspective of "the structure of the world economy as a totality," thereby revealing how development/underdevelopment "are not different stages or states of a productive system, but rather are functions or positions within an international system of distribution and production."[22] Underdevelopment is, hence, the result of an international division of labor:

> The situation of underdevelopment came about when commercial capitalism and then industrial capitalism expanded and linked to the world market nonindustrial economies that went on to occupy different positions in the overall structure of the capitalist system . . .: some produce industrial goods; others, raw material. This requires a definite structure of relations of domination to assure an international trade based on merchandise produced at unequal levels of technology and cost of labor force.[23]

Moreover, through the penetration of national structures by external dominant forces (the most salient examples of which are modern multinational corporations) these international structures of domination are internalized and replicated in urban-rural and class relationships at the national level.[24] The logic of the global system thus extends into the national dependent economies. The relationship between external and internal forces of dependence has provided the context for much disagreement among dependency theorists. There is general agreement, however, that this question is perhaps *the* crucial one in dependency theory and the one that distinguishes it from those paradigms that focus primarily on either the internal (e.g., national class struggle) or the external (e.g., theories of international markets).[25]

As an integral element of the dependency paradigm, the internal-external relationship manifests itself in three major "contradictions" at the national level: 1) a horizontal contradiction in the form of internal, sectoral, economic disarticulation ("a lack of internal structural interdependence between many of the most important elements of the economic system"); 2) a vertical contradiction in the form of class struggle (as the local ruling classes become "denationalized"); and 3) a spatial contradiction in the form of geographical disarticulation and dependence of the "oppressed and backward hinterland" on the relatively advanced capital cities.[26]

While some sectors of dependent economies (e.g., mineral producing sectors, or export oriented agriculture) become increasingly integrated with the world economy, other sectors fail to participate in the capitalist dynamic—the latter postulate being a corollary of the former.[27] What results is an "internal disarticulation" characterized by an "absence of inter-dependence between the economic functions of a system."[28] While dependent economies may participate in a larger capitalist system, the phenomenon of external articulation-internal disarticulation functions to divest the dependent economies of the dynamism characteristic of the capitalist mode of production (as it exists in the metropoli), thus altering the "manner of functioning of that mode of production" within the dependent economies.[29] Consequently, what determines the existence of dependence in the context of horizontally related sectors and their modes of production is their disarticulation "in such a way as either to discourage growth, or to transfer the benefits of growth abroad."[30] The lack of interdependence among economic sectors prevents the emergence of an independent, autonomous entity.[31]

This horizontal disarticulation is accompanied, secondly, by a vertical contradiction in the form of class divisions and class struggle. Through the "coincidence of interests between local dominant classes and international ones" and the consequent "symbiotic relationship" between the two, alliances are formed which serve to internalize external interests while, at the same time, denationalizing segments of the local bourgeoisie.[32] As Cardoso and Faletto point out, the confluence of external and national dominant interests represents more than a mere envelopment of the latter by the former. If that were the case, the internal-external dialectic would be dissolved and underdevelopment could simply be ascribed to imperialism. On the contrary, if dependency is to have any meaning beyond a circular identification of dependence and non-autonomy ("dependent countries are those which lack the capacity for autonomous growth and they lack this because their structures are dependent ones"), then an analysis must be made of the internal reproductions of the structures of dependence through class interests and relations.[33]

The economic analysis necessary would need to attend to, moreover, a third contradiction, or internal mode of dependence:

spatial (Frank's term), or geographical disarticulation. This particular contradiction peculiar to capitalist underdevelopment has been analyzed to a great extent by Frank. He argues that there exists a *chain* of dependency that extends from the metropoli of the center, to regional metropoli, to national metropoli, to local centers, all the way down to "large landowners or merchants who expropriate surplus from small peasants or tenants, and sometimes even from these latter to landless laborers exploited by them in turn."[34]

Given these different modes of economic dependence, it is ultimately the historical situation that must determine *which* mode of dependence should take tactical precedence at any particular time.[35] Yet normative precedence cannot be accorded any one of the modes without thereby distorting the nature of dependence, not only through reductionism, but also through ignorance of the web of interpenetrations that characterizes dependency. Such a distortion would in turn obstruct the emergence of a comprehensive, and thus effective, liberation struggle at the strategic level. By analyzing each aspect of dependence as a distinct—though dialectically related and hence not separate—dimension of dependence one can also avoid a reification of "dependency" (beyond a mere categorial, or analytical normativity), which would again impose a conceptualistic straightjacket on historical realities which are seldom completely black or white. (E.g., though Peru and El Salvador are both "dependent" nations, the nature and degree of their dependence varies in accordance with the differing alignments of the modes of dependence in each country.)[36]

Neither can any one mode of economic dependence, i.e., external, internal horizontal, internal vertical, or internal spatial, be reified. Its inherently dialectical nature would be lost, thus distorting not only the dependency paradigm as a whole, but also the particular reified mode. Were this the case with respect to horizontal disarticulation, for instance, sectoral articulation would be sought as a means of fostering dynamic economic growth, but, quite possibly, at the expense of the poorer classes, both urban and especially rural. Furthermore, in this instance economic growth would presumably be *capitalist* growth, the *nature* of which would need to be questioned by the issues brought out most acutely in the other three modes of economic dependence.[37]

There is, however, one element which is *common* to the dependent groups in each mode of dependence. That element is *the poor*. Historically, the poor classes and, in Latin America, especially the rural poor have experienced the weight of oppression, or domination, in every one of its manifestations. Consequently, while "dependence" must be valued as analytically normative, with each of its modes carrying tactical value according to the particular historical situation, only the historical poor carry *absolute value*.

The dependency paradigm can provide, then, intermediate categories which aid in the specification of the historical poor, for the poor are oppressed as members of dependent nations, disarticulated sectors, lower classes, and economically backward rural communities. Tactical decisions made to favor one mode over another at a particular historical juncture will, therefore, be both effective against dependence and underdevelopment, and normatively desirable to the extent that they are aimed at the liberation of the poorest segments of the dependent group in any particular mode of dependence.

Social Domination

The fact that dependence refers to both market relationships and broader *power* relationships reflects the recognition that the reality of dependence embraces all areas of society.[38] This is so, not because the economic process somehow impinges on social processes from the outside, but because the economic process is itself intrinsically social and all areas of social life are, at the same time, intrinsically bound to the economic process.[39] This recognition represents a third moment in the evolution of the notion of dependence, which: 1) was born out of the ECLA economists' perception of international economic imbalance (the "Prebisch thesis"); 2) reached maturity in the various expositions of the dependency theorists; and 3) now finds further methodological explicitation along the interdisciplinary lines already adumbrated by those dependency theorists (e.g., Frank, Furtado). Despite the inseparability of the economic and the social in concrete historical situations, however, care must be taken to avoid the latter's being subsumed into the economic process as its epiphenomenon. Some scholars sympathetic to the insights of the dependency theorists have thus sought to emphasize the need for analyses of political, cultural, and ideological domination (the three major manifestations of what we refer to as "social domination").[40]

One possible framework for an analysis of the reciprocal relationship between economic domination and social domination in its three manifestations is furnished by the so-called cultural or political Marxists. Some fascinating work has recently been done in this area by Ellen Meiksins Wood.[41] Against economistic or reductionist Marxists, she argues that the positing of any *real* separation of the material infrastructure and the superstructure represents not only a misreading of Marx but, in effect, an enbourgeoisfication of Marx.[42] Such a separation—beyond mere distinction—of infra- and superstructure implies the same fragmentation of social life which, in capitalism, is typified by the schizophrenic split between civil and political society.[43] Marx, on the other hand, insists that "a productive system is made up of its specific social determinations."[44] The relation of social processes to the economic process is not "merely reflective" but "organic:"

> The distinction between "organic" and "merely reflective" connections is especially significant. It suggests that any application of the base/superstructure metaphor that stresses the separation and enclosure of spheres . . . reproduces the mystifications of bourgeois ideology insofar as it fails to treat the productive sphere itself as defined by its social determinations and in effect deals with society "in the abstract."[45]

The economic process (person-nature) is always at the same time a social process (person-person).[46]

Much as the separation of economic growth and equity issues, even if only to argue for the necessity of ensuring equitable *effects* of economic growth, distorts reality by implying that the struggles for economic growth and for equity are related only as cause to effect, so too does the separation of the economic and the social (i.e., political, cultural, ideological) distort reality by implying that, in the real world, these "exist" on separate planes, from which they relate to each other externally. Such a conception is not only an ahistorical abstraction, but a reification: what are, in truth, organically related *aspects* of *one* historical process are objectified and accorded their own proper spatial "domains," from which they relate externally, as objects, to other equally objectified levels of a now dehistoricized reality. The practical result of this abstraction and reification is that struggles for liberation will inevitably be partial and ideological (i.e., obfuscatory) inasmuch as they will overlook the inherently social *nature*—not "effects"—of the economic struggle, and vice versa. All of these struggles are, above anything else, *human* struggles. The only historical agent is the human being suffering domination. If not grounded in the essential unity of the person and his or her historical struggle, therefore, any dialectic will remain abstract and distortive of historical reality. The person then becomes but one more "moment" of the dialectic.[47]

For political or cultural Marxists, "culture" and "ideology" are key dimensions of this one process:

> By culture we mean the general set of values, attitudes, beliefs, sensibilities, and practices that structure the way of life of a people. . . . An ideology, on the other hand, refers to the set of perspectives and judgments with which a person or group defines its social relationships and political options. It differs from . . . culture by virtue of its greater explicitness and structure. Ideally, at least, an ideology consists of explicit and systematically structured normative values, analytical judgments, and strategic orientations.[48]

These ideological structures are usually elaborated most extensively and systematically by intellectual elites and leaders of a movement. Among "followers," we find a variety of more diffuse, symbolic, cultural representations.[49]

Domination as a category, then, must be able to account for not only economic, but also political, cultural and ideological oppression because all are mutually implicit and organically-related (because *human*) aspects of one historical reality of domination. The liberation struggle must encompass all these dimensions, while according tactical precedence to some over others in given historical situations.[50]

However, economic dependency retains a five-fold "priority:" an epistemological priority, inasmuch as it is the most palpable aspect of domination;[51] a descriptive or statistical priority, inasmuch as the *economically* poor are the common denominator among the various aspects of domination; a teleological priority, inasmuch as, because it is the economically poor who suffer acute oppression in all its guises, it is *their* liberation which must be the end of liberation movements; a normative priority, inasmuch as, because liberation of the economically poor is *the* criterion of liberation, they (*not* the dependency paradigm itself, or any other analytical category) provide the "absolute value" for the liberation process; and only then, a causal priority, inasmuch as, because of its epistemological, statistical, teleological, and normative priority, economic liberation is presupposed by any liberation project as its *sine qua non*—though not as leading "automatically" to other manifestations of liberation.

(The causal priority is, hence, not absolute but relative, since the aspects of domination do not relate unidirectionally but organically-dialectically).

Political Domination

Far from being a "mere reflection" of the economic process, then, a nation's political institutions and practices represent the political manifestation of the one historical process. As such, not only are they partially defined and conditioned by the economic process, but they also help define that process (especially, for instance, when there is no hegemonic class and a situation of "praetorian politics" exists).[52] A nation's "political institutions and dynamics provide the channels into which . . . materially rooted experiences, sentiments and energies . . . flow and take form."[53] These channels may be expanded or constricted as the result of the material and other conjunctural forces operative at a particular place and time, but they are never "determined." Otherwise, the historicity of the political process, which involves flesh-and-blood, conscious human beings, would be placed in jeopardy.[54]

In practice, political domination supports and is supported by economic domination through either direct intervention or cooperation. These two arenas are affected by the interplay between international and national forces, all of which have some stake in repressing sentiments for social change that may be surfacing among dominated groups. That stake is *power*, defined in both economic and political terms. Such power is primarily economic but also political insofar as a nation's political structures and practices contribute, either positively or negatively, to the development of class consciousness and a historical class project. As the history of Latin America shows, the nature of that contribution is contingent upon a whole host of conjunctural variables (different levels of intra-class political and economic consciousness, disagreements as to political strategies, the availability of political options and alliances, the presence or absence of a hegemonic class, etc.).[55]

The most subtle means used by Latin American dominant groups to maintain power is that of cooptation. Such cooptation can take, and has taken, numerous forms: "classless" populism (Peronism), bureaucratic technocracy (Brazil), or various other corporatist models which seek a vertical integration, and hence neutralization, of competing interests (the Mexican PRI, "progressive" military regimes, etc.).[56] All of these forms of cooptation represent attempts, by local elites, to consolidate their power through the favorable structuring of political institutions.[57] These elites, however, need not be economic elites, but may be bureaucratic elites who function as the political arm of a larger ruling elite (if not as members of the ruling *class*, either through ideological cooptation by the ruling class or through a coincidence of interests). These political elites, then, may have group interests proper to them as state functionaries.[58] Finally the picture is further muddled by the entrance of foreign economic interests and their success, or lack thereof, in establishing alliances with local elites, thereby giving further support to and benefiting from the local politics of cooptation.[59]

If the alliances of dominant elites are unable to successfully coopt competing interest groups within the existing political structures, thereby failing to establish hegemony, if the ruling alliances are thus exposed to revolutionary pressures from below, there is typically a turn to the more explicitly repressive measures of direct intervention, or, as Alfred Stepan calls it, *exclusionary* corporatism (still "corporatism" since the ultimate aim remains that of forging "a new state-society equilibrium").[60] Political domination now takes on a more expressly militaristic dimension as the military is increasingly called upon, or feels itself called upon, to crush any budding resistance, thus becoming direct participants in the political arena.[61] At times, the coincidence of local and foreign interests may even invite *foreign* military intervention and occupation as a means of repressing challenges to existing power relationships.

An analysis of the political aspect of domination must incorporate, then, not only evaluations of the conjunctural factors operating to either increase or decrease the politicization of the economic process, thereby, conversely, either decreasing or increasing the relative "autonomy" of political structures, but it must also incorporate empirical studies of the impact that those factors—be they in the form of particular class alliances, degrees of class consciousness, or strategic alternatives—have on the historical manifestations of political domination in the course of its evolution. This becomes necessary because to understand the development of political domination it is necessary to analyze its articulation to economic processes within the larger, organic historical process. In other words, what applies to the various dimensions of economic dependency also applies to political domination: i.e., to understand the evolution of one aspect of domination it is necessary to analyze the significance of that aspect in the overall system of domination. The paths of domination, whether in the form of cooptation or direct intervention, are forged, or forsworn, not as abstract alternatives, but as concretely delimited by both "material," strictly economic factors (national and foreign) and the ability of dominant elites to form political alliances and develop political structures which will maintain the close bond between economic and political domination.[62] The history of Latin American corporatist regimes has shown the importance of maintaining hegemony through political structures as a means of consolidating political and economic power.[63] Yet that hegemony is in no way "automatic" and has, from time to time, been defended by recourse to more interventionist methods. The less "automatic" that hegemony, the more exposed become the structures of political domination, and hence the more openly repressive they become.[64]

Cultural Domination

Here we must ask: what is *Latin American* culture? and how has Latin America experienced cultural domination as an external and/or internal force? Studies abound concerning the applicability of the term "culture" to Latin America, a continent composed of twenty-five countries.[65]

While certainly exhibiting national and regional variations, it is possible to posit, as many historians do, that there does exist a "Latin American culture:" the national cultures of Latin America "can only be said to possess distinct personalities within a limited scope manifesting a certain consistency which could be legitimately designated by the name 'culture.'"[66] Latin American nations, therefore, stand somewhere between the historical cultural coherence of some of the European nations and the cultural fragmentation of, for instance, a South Africa.[67]

As a backdrop to an examination of the cultural aspect of domination in Latin America one is thus presented with a complex of subcultures which nevertheless comprise an essential unity. In his preface to *Latin America*, William Lytle Schurz states the thesis well:

> In this book I have endeavored to consider Latin America as a unit. I have not ignored the factors of differentiation, which often are very great but yet not sufficient to break the essential unity that causes a Colombian and a Uruguayan to meet the same situation in much the same way. To have treated the twenty republics in any other way would only

> have created in the reader's mind the confusion that comes from an effort to follow the separate fortunes of the Saxon kingdoms of early England or the city-states of medieval Italy.[68]

This essential unity presents, therefore, a framework within which the individual national or regional cultures can be studied as functional parts of a whole, exhibiting in different "shades, grades, and levels" the structures of the whole.[69] While several fine works exist which attempt expositions of the set of attitudes, etc. that comprise this "whole,"[71] the cultural attitudes will concern us here only insofar as they 1) foster domination and obstruct liberation, and 2) reflect, or function as a foil to, Euro-American cultural domination.

Like all germinal cultures, Latin American culture did not spontaneously generate, but has "for four centuries . . .. manifested secondary and marginal characteristics of European culture," while at the same time becoming "consistently more autonomous."[71] The degree and nature of this autonomy have varied, however, at different levels of Latin American society, becoming, in some instances, almost non-existent as European culture loses its "secondary and marginal" character and becomes more dominant.[72] While European cultural characteristics, reflecting centuries of political and economic colonization, remain prominent as cultural "standards" among national elites (especially in the so-called "Latin America of the Atlantic"), for instance, other levels of Latin American society have not succumbed to such a thoroughgoing Europeanization, but, instead, continue to embody a complex of myths, value systems, symbols, and religious structures which reflect the historical clash between and mixture of European (primarily Spanish and Portuguese), Amerindian, and African cultures, out of which clash has been born the mixed culture we refer to as Latin American culture.[73]

Yet, despite the often underground survival of this multi-racial Latin American culture, Latin America still often perceives itself as inferior to a European culture which it dutifully strives to emulate.[74] The phenomenon of foreign cultural domination cannot be understood, therefore, as resulting from the insertion of European culture into a Latin American cultural vacuum, since no such vacuum exists. An interpretation must be sought elsewhere: in the articulation of not only economic and political domination, but now also of cultural domination with these two aspects discussed earlier. Again, all are part of the one process of domination:

> Hispano-Indian America was subjected first to Spanish power only to pass from this state of political servitude to being the economic colonies of the factories and markets of the British Empire, completely under its economic and even political control, an empire which was later inherited along with a network of power more efficient and closed by the United States of America. We have been dependent and are underdeveloped for this reason, and consequently we are countries with a culture of domination.[75]

This foreign cultural domination has been achieved through cultural penetration of local elites. Economic and political domination feed on and are fed by cultural domination. These represent three dimensions of power and are, consequently, three interconnected means used by local power elites to defend both foreign interests and their own interests (whether through a coincidence of interests or through domination of the latter by the former) against popular movements seeking to assert Latin American independence in all three areas. The internal-external dialectic of domination remains the same and functions in the same way precisely because, while embracing different spheres of social life, it is incarnated in the same dominant historical groups. Insofar as the Europeanized national groups continue to serve as local conduits for a European culture seen as somehow the "measure" of all cultures they will continue to forestall the further development of a genuinely Latin American culture which does not sense the need to look elsewhere for its cultural standards. Liberation from cultural domination can, in turn, come only when the Latin American people are no longer

> taught . . . the culture of the oppressors without the knowledge passing through the filter of a self-conscious awareness of domination that is being exercised by means of . . . imported cultural structures.[76]

Ideological Domination

While culture and ideology are closely connected, the two are distinguished by virtue of the latter's "greater explicitness and structure."[77] Ideology is thus the systematic articulation and explicitation, in cognitive and normative categories, of "the general set of values, attitudes, beliefs, sensibilities, and practices" that structure social life, and the "analytical judgments and strategic orientations" derived from these.[78] Ideological domination occurs when a wedge is inserted between a people's social life ("the general set of values . . .") and their ability to articulate systematically their lived values, which wedge usually takes the form of an ideology seeking to impose its own symbols and cognitive categories (e.g., when European theology, or any system of *knowledge*, imposes itself on Latin American religion, or practical *consciousness*). This disjunction impacts upon both culture, insofar as the dominated culture is unable to become reflectively self-conscious and thus aware of domination, and ideology, insofar as the repression of cultural self-consciousness prevents the emergence of an authentically Latin American philosophy, theology, etc.[79] Cultural domination engenders ideological domination by robbing this latter of its symbolic and mythic "material," substituting a foreign set of symbols and myths; ideological domination fosters cultural domination by substituting foreign cognitive and normative categories, thus suppressing the emergence of a "self-conscious awareness of domination that is being exercised by means of the . . . imported cultural structures."[80] (What is said of cultural domination relative to ideological domination also applies to political and economic domination. These latter also rob ideology of its "material," only in these cases what is stripped from the dominated groups is their political and economic autonomy.)

The dominant political and economic systems thus concomitantly import a dominant ideology. This ideology is not merely a passive reflection of the dominant political and economic systems, but also functions as an oppressive force in its own right insofar as it supplants what would have been a native ideology and coopts the value systems of dominated groups, thereby suppressing the emergence of a "self-conscious awareness" of economic, political and cultural domination. By thus distinguishing, for purposes of analysis, between culture and ideology, then, one is able to further emphasize the inseparability of ideology from the concrete, historical system of domination as a whole. Ideology is neither a mere reflection nor an independent entity, rather it is an intrinsic element of an organic system of domination whose dimensions are dialectically related.

Conversely, ideology is an intrinsic element of the *liberation* process. It comes as no surprise, therefore, that in Latin America, the struggle against domination has had an ideological dimension, not only in the form of the social scientific dependency paradigm, but also in the form of philosophical and theological movements seeking to articulate, in broader terms, the newly emerging "self-conscious awareness of domination." In so doing, these movements are providing cognitive categories for that awareness. By recovering and developing the *liberative* elements of ideology in the light of the Latin American experience, they hope to prevent further ideological penetration which would obstruct the formation of self-conscious awareness not only by filling an ideological vacuum, but also by coopting native value systems, myths, and symbols and turning them into ideological tools of oppression.[81]

Liberation Theology

One attempt to give systematic expression to the incipient self-consciousness of dominated groups in Latin America is what has come to be known as liberation theology. This major articulation of the Latin American experience incorporates the analyses of dependency theorists, but more explicitly extends their critique of dependency to the ideological dimension, arguing that the theological methods of the metropoli have for centuries claimed a universality which has served to mask their true partiality (in both senses of the word) and, in so doing, has denied the authenticity of the theological experiences and reflections of dominated groups. Liberation theology—and philosophy—seeks to recapture those experiences and give them a role as truly authentic hermeneutical ciphers for the interpretation of Scripture, the Christian tradition, and human existence.

While the recognition of the injustices of the Latin American situation had already begun by the time of the first meeting of CELAM (when Dom Helder Camara was consecrated bishop of Recife and Olinda) and had, with the official sanction of Vatican II, continued to spur a great deal of grassroots activity aimed at remedying those injustices, liberation theology as such received its major ecclesiastical, institutional impetus from the Medellín Conference in 1968. There the Conference of Latin American Bishops (CELAM) met to formulate a corporate response, from their Latin American experience, to the promulgations of Vatican II. Taking as their hermeneutical starting point, not "revealed doctrine," but the historical experience of the Latin American people, they put forth for the first time in the history of the Church a thoroughgoing critique of systemic, structural domination as an abominable sin and expressed the hope of their people—much as Moses had done in the Exodus—for liberation from these "sinful social structures." For such a liberation to come about, they continued, profound changes would have to be made and paths opened beyond the equally violent and closed options of capitalism and communism.[82]

Despite ongoing attempts to muffle the cries of the Latin American people—attempts largely financed from abroad and finding supporters among conservative Latin American bishops at, for instance, the Sucre Assembly of 1972—the dynamic of Medellín has proved unconquerable and, at the 1979 Puebla Conference, the Church again took up the themes of Medellín and decried the injustices of domination in Latin America.[83] At Puebla, for the first time in the history of the Latin American Church, hundreds of ecclesiastical voices from all over the world joined the dialogue and cautioned against deviation from the path begun at Medellín:

> The explanation for this worldwide reaction was that the decisions made in the Puebla Conference would affect, directly or indirectly, the orientation of the Church on other continents. Also, the Christian population is shifting toward Latin America. In 1975 America surpassed Europe in the number of Christians, and Latin America will soon contain over half of all the Catholics in the world.[84]

Though at certain points lacking the forcefulness of the Medellín Document, the Puebla Document gives clear ecclesial expression to the Latin American people's growing self-awareness as a dominated people; their poverty is "not a passing phase [as posited by development theory]. Instead, it is the product of economic, social and political situations and structures, though there are also other causes for the state of misery."[85] The Church, in turn, must be not only *for* the poor, but also *with* the poor and *of* the poor. In this document, the indigenous peoples and Afro-Americans are for the first time singled out as "the poorest of the poor," oppressed at the hands of economic, political and cultural elites.[86] Likewise for the first time, the role of women in the Church is treated (a subject to which we will return later, when we discuss the advances represented by Enrique Dussel's extension of the notion of domination to include sexual domination).[87] In short, then, Puebla represents a reiteration—in the face of opposition—of the major liberation themes of Medellín.

If Medellín was the Church's first institutional acknowledgement of the necessity of a Latin American liberation theology, Gustavo Gutiérrez's *Teología de la liberación,* first published in 1971, was the initial attempt to present a systematic exposition of such a theology. That book became the standard-bearer for a Latin American theological movement.

The theology of liberation (although there is no one monolithic "theology of liberation" the use of the singular here includes an acknowledgement of that fact, despite the essential methodological and historical unity that characterizes the different currents and emphases of "liberation theology") is rooted, according to Segundo Galilea, in three basic assumptions about the present juncture in Latin American history:

> (1)The present situation is one in which the vast majority of Latin Americans live in a state of underdevelopment and unjust dependence; (2) viewed in Christian terms, this is a "sinful situation;" (3) hence it is the duty of Christians in conscience, and the church in its pastoral activity, to commit themselves to efforts to overcome this situation.[88]

The first assumption involves the recognition that unjust dependence is "one of the basic causes for the present misery and poverty of our peoples—though not the only cause." Such dependence is most patently socioeconomic, but at a more subtle level, also political and cultural. While liberation theology can, at a later methodological stage, incorporate the findings of the dependency theorists, therefore, its *starting point* is not the dependency paradigm itself—or any other theoretical paradigm—but quite simply, "the concrete fact of dependence." Its starting point in actual historical experience allows liberation theology to effect such an incorporation without, however, identifying itself absolutely with any one theory or paradigm.[89]

The second assumption posits that this injustice is not simply a violation of human rights, but is an offense against God. Moreover, this sin is not simply located in particular individuals, but is concretized in the structures of society. Here is where—at this second stage—we enter the realm of social scientific theory as a critique of those structures, and theology proper as a critique of those structures as not only *unjust* but also *sinful*.[90]

Finally, the third assumption, dependent on the first two, represents "an appeal to the conscience of individual Christians and the church." This plea for concerted Christian action against injustice, while involving the political component indicated in the second assumption, is, however, primarily a call to evangelization—not an individualistic evangelization, but one which will seek both individual and social conversion as organically and dialectically related necessities.[91]

Each of these assumptions finds elaboration in Gutiérrez' book (and, as we will see, in the subsequent development of liberation theology). Thus, for instance, Gutiérrez formulates not so much a new content for theology—though this is present—as a "*new way* of doing theology": the privileged locus of theological reflection is the experience of domination, or oppression, which, through an ongoing dialectic with the Scripture texts, yields a new Scriptural hermeneutic, which in turn contributes to historical praxis. Beginning with the *fact* of domination, he then moves to a reconceptualization of the Christian notion of sin. This move to a critique of social sin is mediated by the dependency paradigm. It is here, in the move from the fact of injustice to its articulation in both Scriptural and social scientific categories, that the current notion of liberation finds meaning as an attempt to express the *conflictual* nature of sociohistorical processes as well as the imperative that human beings be allowed to assume conscious responsibility for their own destiny. The demand for Christian action, as found in the third assumption above, is then based on implications found in the prior stages of the hermeneutic: namely 1) if sin is structural, then, insofar as the Church belongs to those structures, it is implicated in that sin, and 2) therefore, the Scriptural call to liberation is addressed to the Church itself, as a participant in social sin. The role of the Church, however, is not one that exists in isolation from, or "above" the temporal realm. That role plays itself out within humankind's "single vocation to salvation" as the "sacrament" of that salvation. Hence, the historical process of liberation and the salvific process are mutually implicit dimensions of one historical process.[92]

As liberation theology—with Gutiérrez' work providing an excellent example—arises out of and articulates the experiences and yearnings of committed Christians at the grassroots level of local Christian communities, the further evolution of these grassroots movements, with its attendant new experiences and exigencies, has elicited a concomitant evolution within liberation theology as it seeks to respond to the new demands. Consequently, the early ground-breaking work of Gutiérrez and others has but provided the basic features which Latin American scholars, including Gutiérrez himself, have subsequently been developing in a number of directions, thus leading to a real enrichment of the liberation theology movement.[93]

Alfred Hennelly has furnished a helpful breakdown of some of the major currents of contemporary liberation theology by focusing on the central thematic concerns of the theologians. Thus, for instance, he points to Segundo Galilea as one scholar who has sought to articulate a *spirituality* consistent with the demands of liberation. The Brazilian Franciscan, Leonardo Boff, on the other hand, has concerned himself primarily with questions of *Christology*. Others, such as Juan Luis Segundo, Ignacio Ellacuría, and Raül Vidales have concentrated on the articulation of a liberation *methodology* in contradistinction to the methodologies of the metropoli. Finally, there are a number of liberation scholars who cannot be said to belong to any one of these major currents, because of either the breadth or the specificity of these scholars' thematic concerns. It is important to note, however, that, in *all* of the above cases, the breakdown reflects differences in *emphases*. Moreover, given the inherent fluidity of the liberation theology movement, any one scholar's *own* particular emphases may change in the course of his or her intellectual development.[94]

These different emphases also suggest different methodological emphases. After all, if, as Gutiérrez and other liberation theologians aver, the central distinguishing characteristic of liberation theology is that it represents a "*new way* of doing theology,"[95] then it is precisely in the area of methodology that many of the key ideological battles will be fought. Consequently, it comes as no surprise that, as liberation theology has matured, it has increasingly turned to critical reflection on its methodology.[96]

Essential to that reflection has been the belief that, given the organic interrelations of the economic, political, cultural, and ideological structures of domination, the effectiveness of a liberation movement will largely depend on its ability to attack those structures both in themselves and in their interdependence. A Latin American liberative method must reflect and affirm this fact. If the former is the exclusive emphasis the power structures will remain intact at their base, that is, at the point where they participate most fundamentally in the dominant power relationships which root all the other dominant structures as well. If the latter is the exclusive emphasis the danger will arise of ignoring the quite concrete modes of domination, and thereby of inadvertently struggling for a "liberation" which, because lacking in specific practical determinations and criteria, will be unhinged from its practical moorings and will, thus, remain at the level of abstraction.

Consequently, the need for a dialectical and organic approach to liberation appears at the levels of both theory and praxis. The liberation theologians' "vertical" (strictly a graphic, not a "real" term) praxis-theory, or praxis-ideology, dialectic is thus complemented with "horizontal" dialectics in the spheres of both theory (ideology) and praxis (economics, politics, culture). In other words, liberative praxis incorporates all the various aspects of human praxis and liberative ideology incorporates the various intellectual disciplines. Such a "horizontal" dialectics serves to safeguard liberation theory and praxis against both partiality on the one hand and premature abstraction on the other; the correlative dangers appearing as, in the first instance, reductionism, and, in the second, conceptualism.

We have seen how the dependency paradigm, as multi-dimensional, both safeguards the relative priority of economic liberation and relates it intrinsically, or organically, and dialectically to non-economic aspects of domination. As a liberative ideology born out of the experience of oppression, liberation theology plays a major role in the relationship. A Latin American liberative method thus needs to explicitate the conditions of the possibility and the methodological exigencies of the relationship. It is to an analysis of this task, as embodied in the intellectual project of Enrique Dussel, that we now turn.

NOTES

/1/ See Introduction *supra:* While "dependency theory" is the common term, henceforth we will opt for the term "dependency paradigm" in recognition of the fact that there is no *one* "theory" of dependency: see Ian Roxborough, *Theories of Underdevelopment* (London: MacMillan, 1979) pp. 35ff.
/2/ See Introduction, *supra.*
/3/ Denis Goulet, *The Cruel Choice: A New Concept in the Theory of Development* (New York: Atheneum, 1975) pp. xii–xv, 60–84. In its 1966 report, the Cambridge Conference observed that "paradoxically . . . the 'Aid and private enterprise' school [and, *a fortiori,* the exclusively private enterprise school] shows more faith in the power of purely economic factors to promote economic growth and alter society than the so-called 'socialists' who hold that traditional social and political structure has the power to determine and frustrate economic growth." Cambridge Conference Report, "Obstacles to Progress," in *Developing the Third World: The Experience of the Nineteen-Sixties,* ed. Ronald Robinson (London: Cambridge University Press, 1971) p. 43.
/4/ Goulet, pp. xii–xv, 60–84; see also David Morawetz, *Twenty-Five Years of Economic Development 1950–1975* (Washington, D.C.: The World Bank, 1977).

/5/ Goulet, pp. xii–xv, 60–84; Roxborough, pp. 27ff., 42ff. For an example of this approach, see Raúl Prebisch, *Change and Development: Latin America's Great Task* (Washington, D.C.: Inter-American Development Bank, 1970).
/6/ Goulet, pp. xiii–xiv, 60–84.
/7/ Ibid., pp. xii–xiv.
/8/ Ibid., p. xiv.
/9/ Peter Evans, *Dependent Development: The Alliance of Multinational, State and Local Capital in Brazil* (Princeton: Princeton University Press, 1979) esp. pp. 94–100; Albert Fishlow, "Some Reflections on Post-1964 Brazilian Economic Policy," in *Authoritarian Brazil: Origins, Policies and Future*, ed. Alfred Stepan (New Haven: Yale University Press, 1973) esp. pp. 104–5; Andre Gunder Frank, *Capitalism and Underdevelopment in Latin America: Historical Studies of Chile and Brazil* (New York: Monthly Review Press, 1969) esp. pp. 205–8; José Serra, "The Brazilian 'Economic Miracle,' in *Latin America: From Dependence to Revolution*, ed. James Petras (New York: John Wiley and Sons, 1973).
/10/ Goulet, pp. 215–330.
/11/ Ibid., pp. xiv–xv.
/12/ See, e.g., Goulet (We have generally followed Goulet's account); Gustavo Gutiérrez, *A Theology of Liberation: History, Politics and Salvation*, trans. and ed. Sister Caridad Inda and John Eagleson (Maryknoll, N.Y.: Orbis, 1973) pp. 21–42, 81–99.
/13/ See Goulet, p. xiii.
/14/ Evans, pp. 25–34; Thomas Weisskopf, "Dependency as an Explanation of Underdevelopment: A Critique," March, 1976 paper prepared for presentation at the sixth annual meeting of the Latin American Studies Association, Atlanta, Georgia, p. 3.
/15/ See, e.g., Weisskopf, p. 7; Sanjaya Lall, "Is 'Dependence' a Useful Concept in Analyzing Underdevelopment?," *World Development* 3 (1975) 799-810.
/16/ Weisskopf, p. 7; see also Andre Gunder Frank, "The Development of Underdevelopment," in James D. Cockroft, Andre Gunder Frank and Dale L. Johnson, *Dependence and Underdevelopment: Latin America's Political Economy* (Garden City, N.Y.: Doubleday, 1972); Dale L. Johnson, "Dependence and the International System," ibid., pp. 71–74.
/17/ Cockroft, Frank and Johnson, Introduction, p. xi. Fernando Cardoso and Enzo Faletto define *un*developed countries as "economies and peoples . . . that do not have market relations with the industrialized countries." As an economic category, undeveloped countries are "fast disappearing." Fernando Henrique Cardoso and Enzo Faletto, *Dependency and Development in Latin America*, trans. Marjory Mattingly Urquidi (Berkeley: University of California Press, 1979) pp. 16–17.
/18/ Weisskopf, p. 3; Frank, "Economic Dependence, Class Structure, and Underdevelopment Policy," in Cockroft, Frank, and Johnson, p. 19.
/19/ Frank, "Economic Dependence," pp. 19–20; see also Frank, *Capitalism and Underdevelopment*, p. xv.
/20/ Theotonio dos Santos cited in James Petras and Thomas Cook, "Dependency and the Industrial Bourgeoisie: Attitudes of Argentine Executives

Toward Foreign Economic Investment and U.S. Policy," in Petras, ed., p. 143.
/21/ Samir Amin, *Unequal Development: An Essay on the Social Formations of Peripheral Capitalism* (New York: Monthly Review Press, 1976) p. 239.
/22/ Philip J. O'Brien, "A Critique of Latin American Theories of Dependency," in *Beyond the Sociology of Development: Economy and Society in Latin America and Africa*, eds. Ivar Oxaal, Tony Barnett and David Booth (London: Routledge and Kegan Paul, 1975) pp. 7–27.
/23/ Cardoso and Faletto, p. 17.
/24/ Frank, "The Development of Underdevelopment" and "Economic Dependence," in Cockroft, Frank and Johnson; Frank, *Capitalism and Underdevelopment*, pp. 145–50, 16–17; Roxborough, pp. 50ff.; Evans, pp. 29, 50–54.
/25/ Roxborough, pp. 50ff.
/26/ Ibid., pp. 45ff.; Cardoso cited in Gutiérrez, p. 94; Frank, "The Development of Underdevelopment;" Evans, pp. 28–30.
/27/ N. Girvan cited in Roxborough, p. 50.
/28/ Brewster quoted in Roxborough, p. 50.
/29/ Roxborough, pp. 66–67.
/30/ Ibid., p. 68.
/31/ Girvan cited in ibid., p. 50.
/32/ Cardoso and Faletto, p. xvi; Lall, p. 801.
/33/ O'Brien, in Oxaal, Barnett and Booth, eds., p. 24.
/34/ Frank quoted in David Booth, "Andre Gunder Frank: an Introduction and appreciation," in Oxaal, Barnett and Booth, eds., pp. 67–8; Frank's studies of Chile show the varied ways in which "relations of exploitation (between classes) produce the effect of inter-regional [at the national level] transfers of capital which in turn contribute to uneven development within Latin American countries." Ibid., p. 79.
/35/ See Enrique Dussel, *Método para una filosofía de la liberación: Superación analéctica de la dialéctica hegeliana* (Salamanca: Sígueme, 1974) p. 225.
/36/ Lall, pp. 802–3.
/37/ Ibid., pp. 807–9.
/38/ See n. 19; cf. Michael Novak, *The Spirit of Democratic Capitalism* (New York: Simon and Schuster/American Enterprise Institute, 1982) pp. 306–7. Novak here mistakenly criticizes dependency theorists for claiming that the *only* kind of social power is economic power.
/39/ O'Brien, p. 13; Samuel L. Parmar, "Self-Reliant Development in an 'Interdependent' World," in *Beyond Dependency: The Developing World Speaks Out*, eds. Guy F. Erb and Valeriana Kallab (New York: Praeger, 1975) pp. 8–17.
/40/ Michael Fleet, *The Rise and Fall of Chilean Christian Democracy* (forthcoming) chapter one.
/41/ Ellen Meiksins Wood, "The Separation of the Economic and the Political in Capitalism," *New Left Review* no. 127 (May–June, 1981) pp. 66–95.
/42/ Ibid., pp. 66–75.

/43/ Ibid., pp. 66, 69.
/44/ Ibid., p. 69.
/45/ Ibid.
/46/ Ibid., p. 72.
/47/ Ibid., pp. 68–75.
/48/ Fleet, p. 12.
/49/ Fleet, pp. 12–13. Here we use "ideology" in its broader, neutral sense as over against the negative, reflexive notion of ideology propounded by economistic Marxists.
/50/ Dussel, p. 225.
/51/ See Segundo Galilea, "Teología de la liberación y nuevas exigencias cristianas," in *La nueva frontera de la teología en América latina,* ed. Rosino Gibellini (Salamanca: Sígueme, 1977) p. 167.
/52/ Fleet, p. 16; Roxborough, pp. 112–17.
/53/ Fleet, p. 16.
/54/ Ibid.
/55/ Ibid., pp. 14ff.; Roxborough, pp. 112ff.
/56/ Alfred Stepan, *The State and Society: Peru in Comparative Perspective* (Princeton: Princeton University Press, 1978) pp. 46–113.
/57/ Ibid.
/58/ Roxborough, p. 121.
/59/ Stepan, *The State and Society,* pp. 56, 230–47.
/60/ Ibid., p. 74.
/61/ Alfred Stepan, "The New Professionalism of Internal Warfare and Military Role Expansion," in *Authoritarian Brazil,* ed. Stepan, pp. 47–65.
/62/ Fleet, pp. 14ff.
/63/ See Stepan, *The State and Society.*
/64/ For an analysis of the relationship between ideological hegemony and political domination, see Antonio Gramsci, *Selections from the Prison Notebooks of Antonio Gramsci,* eds. and trans. Quintin Hoare and Geoffrey Nowell Smith (London: Lawrence and Wishart, 1971) esp. pp. 55–60, 206–76.
/65/ See, e.g., Glen Caudill Dealy, *The Public Man: An Interpretation of Latin American and Other Catholic Countries* (Amherst, Mass.: University of Massachusetts Press, 1977); Enrique Dussel, *A History of the Church in Latin America: Colonialism to Liberation (1492–1979),* trans. and rev. by Alan Neely (Grand Rapids, Mich.: Eerdmans, 1981); Enrique Dussel, *Desintegración de la cristiandad colonial y liberación: Perspectiva latinoamericana* (Salamanca: Sígueme, 1978); Pedro Enríquez Ureña, *Historia de la cultura en la América Hispánica* (México: Fondo de Cultura Económica, 1959); Leopoldo Zea, *América en la historia* (México: Fondo de Cultura Económica, 1957).
/66/ Dussel, *The Church in Latin America,* p. 28.
/67/ Ibid., p. 27.
/68/ William Lytle Schurz quoted in Lawrence S. Graham, "Latin America: Illusion or Reality? A Case for a New Analytic Framework for the Region," in *Politics and Social Change in Latin America: The Distinct Tradition,* ed. Howard J. Wiarda (Amherst, Mass.: University of Massachusetts Press, 1974) p. 232.

/69/ Dussel, *The Church in Latin America,* pp. 28, 31.
/70/ See n. 65.
/71/ Dussel, *The Church in Latin America,* p. 28.
/72/ Ibid., p. 29.
/73/ See José Juan Arrom, *Certidumbre de América: Estudios de letras, folklore y cultra,* segunda edicíon ampliada (Madrid: Editorial Gredos, 1971).
/74/ Dussel, *The Church in Latin America,* p. 28; Dussel, *Método,* pp. 279ff.
/75/ Augusto Salazar Bondy quoted in Dussel, *The Church in Latin America,* p. 136.
/76/ Dussel, *The Church in Latin America,* p. 136.
/77/ Fleet, p. 12.
/78/ Ibid.
/79/ Dussel, *The Church in Latin America,* p. 136.
/80/ Ibid.
/81/ Dussel, *Método,* p. 258.
/82/ Dussel, *The Church in Latin America,* pp. 125–6; Samuel Silva Gotay, *El pensamiento cristiano revolucionario en América Latina y el Caribe* (Salamanca: Sígueme, 1981) pp. 63–4.
/83/ Dussel, *The Church in Latin America,* pp. 224ff.; for an excellent collection of papers relative to the Puebla Conference, including the official English translation of the final Puebla document itself, see John Eagleson and Philip Scharper, eds., *Puebla and Beyond: Documentation and Commentary,* trans. John Drury (Maryknoll, N.Y.: Orbis, 1979).
/84/ Dussel, *The Church in Latin America,* p. 231.
/85/ Eagleson and Scharper, eds., p. 128 (The Final Document of Puebla, para. 30); Dussel, *The Church in Latin America,* p. 234; Arthur McGovern, *Marxism: An American Christian Perspective* (Maryknoll, N.Y.: Oris, 1980) p. 202.
/86/ Eagleson and Scharper, eds., p. 128 (The Final Document of Puebla, para. 34); Dussel, *The Church in Latin America,* p. 234.
/87/ Eagleson and Scharper, eds., p. 128 (The Final Document of Puebla, para. 9); Dussel, *The Church in Latin America,* p. 234.
/88/ Galilea, p. 167.
/89/ Ibid.
/90/ Ibid., pp. 167–8.
/91/ Ibid., pp. 168, 170.
/92/ Gutiérrez, pp. 15, 36–7, 72, 84ff., 301; Alfred T. Hennelly, *Theologies in Conflict: The Challenge of Juan Luis Segundo* (Maryknoll, N.Y.: Orbis, 1979) pp. 27–9. See Chapter 6, *infra,* for a more detailed analysis of the relation between salvation and liberation relative to the critiques of Latin American liberation theology as "reductionist."
/93/ Hennelly, p. 30.
/94/ Ibid., pp. 30–36.
/95/ Gutiérrez, p. 15.
/96/ Hennelly, p. 33. As an example of such reflection, see Enrique Dussel, et al., *Liberación y cautiverio: Debates en torno al método de la teología en América Latina* (México: Comité Organizador, 1975).

CHAPTER TWO

FROM A CLOSED TO AN OPEN DIALECTICS: TOWARD A LIBERATIVE RETRIEVAL OF THE WESTERN INTELLECTUAL TRADITION

An Overview of the History of Dialectics

If the dependency paradigm provided an initial social scientific framework for Dussel's understanding of the Latin American historical experience, his dialectical retrieval of the Western philosophical tradition provided initial foundational categories for a methodological grounding of both the dependency paradigm and liberation theology. As we have seen, the confluence of these two factors (i.e., the dependency paradigm and the dialectical retrieval of the Western intellectual tradition) in Dussel's personal development opened him to the possibility of what would later become the Latin American "anadialectical method."[1] Having examined the basic features of the first factor, we now turn to an analysis of the second factor. It is important to note, in this regard, that our main concern here will be to establish the role of the Western intellectual tradition in the development of Dussel's method. Consequently, we will prescind from a critique of his *interpretation* of that tradition and, likewise, from an analysis of his interpretation vis-a-vis other interpretations. Such a task would require another book, and one of a very different nature.

In his interpretation of the Western tradition, Dussel focuses on the notion of dialectics and demonstrates its susceptibility to antiliberative understandings of reality. He *also* demonstrates, however, the openness of certain aspects of the tradition to the possibility of liberation.[2] Therein lies Dussel's "dialectical" retrieval of the "dialectical" tradition.

According to Dussel, the problem of dialectics is one which has been engaged, either explicitly or implicitly, by the great philosophers of the Western tradition and which posits "a radical and introductory method . . . or way, a movement towards what things are."[3] While the problem has been framed differently in different epochs, depending upon the particular categories available to the thinkers of each epoch, what is common to all the variants of dialectics is that they

> part from a *factum* (from a *fact*), from a limit *ex quo* or point of departure . . . [and move] in one or another direction, depending upon the sense of being (the sense determines the direction) and, because of it, the point of arrival, the *towards-which* (*ad quem*) of the dialectical movement, will be very different.[4]

This *ad quem* has traditionally been conceived in two basic ways: as "being which im-poses itself (e.g., Aristotle)," or as "subjectivity which posits being (Kant)."[5]

The shift from pre-modern to modern dialectics is characterized by a progressive involution of the dialectic: beginning with Descartes and culminating in Hegel the *ad quem* becomes internalized in the ego, with the result that "the ego is no longer merely the measure of all things [as in Descartes], but, as the absolute, *is* all things insofar as the totalizing ego embraces all entities in its drive towards absolute self-consciousness."[6] A critical analysis of this process of involution is thus necessary as the foundation for a restructuring of dialectics in the form of a post-modern, Latin American, open dialectic, or *ana*-dialectic of liberation.

Pre-Modern Dialectics

The first "way" opened by dialectics is that which leads to "being which im-poses itself." "Being" here is understood as "the concealed and dis-covered, like the invisible visible in the appearance, or like that which acts in presence." This is the common conception of the dialectic from the pre-Socratics to Plato and Aristotle.[7]

In the pre-Socratic lists of opposites and in the practical dialectics later characteristic of the sophists' debating style the groundwork had already been laid for the development of Platonic and Aristotelian dialectics. Plato rejected the sophistic dialectic as merely a rhetorical technique and, thus, was unconcerned with "what things are." Dussel maintains that, for Plato, dialectics is "the supreme moment of thought," through which one arrives at "the final intellectual level or intuition (*noein*) of the Ideas," and, consequently, in which one is able to function only after having practiced "inferior levels of knowing." Dialectics, then, "*follows upon*" all other scientific studies as their culmination (this, as we will see later, in contradistinction to Dussel's dialectic, which, as foundational, is *prior* to the sciences).[8]

Plato's dialectic is one of *ascension* to increasingly higher levels of knowing. After Plato, Plotinus begins the process of *involution*, a process involving the "descent" of the dialectic ("what in Latin will later be translated as *explicatio*") in such a way that the dialectic as a whole, as *the* Whole, becomes both *ex quo* and *ad quem* in the "ascending or unifying movement of the plurality in the One."[9] The One, the Whole, is now definitively reified:

> The One is the point of departure and arrival; from which one descends and towards which one ascends; the many is the opposite, appearance, the material, the corporeal, evil.[10]

Like the Platonic dialectic, the Plotinian dialectic is positive ("insofar as *gnosis*"), but in its positing of the "negativity of multiplicity as necessary to recover by ascension the initial simplicity of the fragmented One," the Plotinian dialectic is already foreshadowing, in Dussel's view, the Cartesian, Kantian and Hegelian dialectics. For Plotinus, individuation is defined in a negative sense, as the fragmentation of the Whole, which fragmentation must, then, be overcome in the "*return* to the One."[11]

Platonic and Plotinian dialectics both find a counterposition, however, in Aristotelian dialectics. Deviating from the Platonic opposition to the rhetorical dialectic, Aristotle first posits dialectics as the art of questioning and refutation (of what is false, or non-being). Dussel concludes that, as such, the Aristotelian dialectic is "the art of *dis-covering* the truth of being; it is a dis-covering of what is covered." The starting point of this dialectic is the *a priori factum*, the "everyday" which, in the form of "common sense" (i.e., the concrete world which we inherit, or, in Paul Ricoeur's terms, the "ethical-mythical nucleus") is received as a given. The *factum* of the Platonic dialectic follows upon the everyday, since this is perceived as negative and downgrading relative to the highest form of knowledge (dialectics). The Aristotelian *factum*, the starting point of the dialectic, is, on the other hand, located precisely in the everyday (*doxa*), which is understood existentially and from which (*ex endoxon*) the dialectic proceeds. For Aristotle the negation of the naive, absolutized everyday *precedes* all demonstrative, apodictic, or scientific knowledge and, as a form of wisdom, undergirds all forms of knowledge. In Aristotle, then, the "man on the street" regains the stature which he had lost in Plato and which he will again lose in modernity, with the Cartesian depreciation of the "world as ambiguous horizon."[12]

Because of his or her *fundamental* wisdom the dialectician can question the different sciences without necessarily being well-versed in scientific knowledge:

> Because of this, Aristotle tells us, "Socrates only questioned and never answered, because he confessed to knowing nothing;" in effect, he knew nothing ontically of the intramundane, but he had an ontological wisdom of the foundation of the ontic which is like knowing nothing (he knew nothing of the entities scientifically, but he had a dialectical or ontological knowledge).[13]

While dialectical knowledge implies questioning, as in the sophists, here this questioning is not merely a rhetorical technique but an art whose goal is the dis-covering of the truth of being. The Aristotelian dialectician puts forth a dialectical critique of common sense in order both to negate what the received world (the *a priori factum*) contains that is false *and* to dis-cover what it contains that is true. As a critique of the foundational *factum*, the dialectic is here primarily an inductive process that grounds all deductive knowledge.[14]

This critique takes the form of a juxtaposition of contradictory opposites given in the everyday, which juxtaposition will reveal being by pointing beyond the ambiguity of the everyday, showing the impossibility of the identity of being and non-being. Unlike scientific knowledge, therefore, dialectical knowledge parts from an ambiguous *factum* which posits, not one self-evident axiom or principle, but two contrary possibilities. As foundational, Aristotelian dialectics puts into question precisely that which science accepts as self-evident. Its pre-thematic, existential comprehension of *being* (the horizon of dialectics) grounds any systematic comprehension of particular *entities* in their relation to the horizon of being.[15]

Dussel goes on to explain that, therefore, Aristotelian dialectics is not only a *method* of dis-covering being, but is also a fundamental ontology of being which opens up an ultimate horizon against which all systematic knowing takes place. In positing this ultimate horizon, Aristotelian dialectics reveals itself as *primarily* neither ascending nor descending, but *negative*, since it "negates the absolutizing determination which makes of the everyday entity something closed, enclosed, absolute." The ultimate horizon thus makes possible the passage from the naiveté of appearance to a dis-covering of being, a passage not possible for philosophy *per se* or the sciences, since these simply represent *modes* of being in the world.[16]

According to Dussel, Aristotelian dialectics effects this passage by making possible the separation, against the ultimate horizon, of what is false and absolutized in the *factum*, which presents itself as ambiguous, from what is a true comprehension of being—also in the *factum:*

> The task of dialectics will be the passage from the ontic or everyday comprehension which implicitly includes being in the mere appearance to the fundamental comprehension of being, discarding what is false, what is non-being.[17]

This fundamental comprehension is not deductive but existential inasmuch as it points to the principles presupposed by deductive knowledge "but does not originate in them;" rather, it "originates in the everyday," whose first "principle" is that of the impossibility of self-contradiction, i.e., being cannot be non-being.[18]

The Aristotelian dialectic, therefore, is both unifying, insofar as it identifies reality with being (what is real cannot not-be)—thereby relegating what is outside the Whole to the "status" of non-being—and subversive, insofar as it effects a radical critique of the everyday. Only through this critique, that is, through negation, is one able to make progress towards a comprehension of being. Moreover, such comprehension, because existential, is always nevertheless incomplete, or asymptotic.[19]

Modern Antecedents of the Hegelian Dialectic

Beginning with nominalism, argues Dussel, the "facticity of existential understanding" is rejected in favor of consciousness-as-subjectivity as the starting point of the dialectic. Thus begins the progressive involution of the dialectic in modernity: the dialectical movement is now not "from the *factum* towards being, but from the *factum* towards consciousness." (As we will see, the German idealists will tend to equate "consciousness" with "knowledge." Consequently, this involuted consciousness takes on conceptualist, cognitive features defined by their deductivism. Such an understanding of consciousness contrasts sharply with the notion of consciousness-as-praxis characteristic of, for instance, Bernard Lonergan's dialectics, which we will explore in chapter 5.) According to Dussel, an understanding of this key shift in the Western interpretation of dialectics is indispensable for an appreciation of the work of Hegel later on.[20]

For Dussel, the first seminal modern thinker is Descartes. In the French philosopher's thought the everyday cannot be the starting point of the dialectic since, because the everyday always includes what is false, it is incapable of yielding certitude.[21] Since our senses are often in error, what we receive through them, i.e., the everyday, is also often in error. Consequently, Descartes concludes, the dialectic must be grounded in a starting point whose locus is completely outside the sensual or corporeal: i.e., in the soul, the consciousness, the ego. Dussel characterizes this Cartesian move as that establishing a dualism in which the external world is idealized vis-a-vis the now reified ego:

> This unattenuated radical dualism was the disintegration of being in the world and the reduction of that world to the mere abstract spatiality of a machine called the body, a realm alien to the soul or *cogito*.[22]

With Descartes, the *cogito* becomes the all-inclusive reality. There is still an ascension and a descent, but, unlike those found in Plotinus, the *ex quo* and *ad quem* are both intra-*subjective:* the Plotinian Whole becomes egocentric. Likewise, the facticity of the external everyday, where, as Dussel points out, Aristotle found the supremely human, i.e., being, is reduced to mere intra-subjective ideas, from which the material world is *deduced*. Consciousness is reduced to subjectivity, subjectivity to knowledge, and knowledge to perception. Aristotelian induction is replaced by Cartesian deduction. Whereas Aristotle's starting point was being itself, that of Descartes—and all of modernity—is the ego.[23]

With Immanuel Kant the dialectic attains a new level of sophistication. As a key element in his philosophical project, the dialectic is understood by Kant in a negative sense, as "critique." The foundational doubt inherited from Descartes is explicitated in the Kantian assertion of the inherently dialectical, or internally contradictory nature of reason. For Kant, then, dialectics makes visible the limits of reason:

> Because of this, the transcendental "Dialectic" encloses its positivity in its own proper negativity; in Hegel, on the other hand, the dialectic will be a supreme mode of knowing and positive by negation. The Kantian dialectic denies the system; the Hegelian dialectic is the system itself.[24]

According to Kant, one is fooled not so much by one's senses, as Descartes would have it, as by reason insofar as it claims knowledge of ideas (things in themselves cannot be known, only believed in). As in Descartes, the dialectic remains intra-subjective, but becomes more complex as a result of Kant's inclusion of praxis as intrinsic to the egocentric dialectic: the Kantian ego is an active ego. The return to the empirical, and hence the completion of the dialectical circle, takes place, for Kant, through the moral action of a free and active subject.[25]

If Kant posits the impossibility of a purely rational system, J. G. Fichte becomes the first modern thinker, according to Dussel, to develop a dialectical system as such, taking as his point of departure what he ironically sees as a latent system within Kant's thought, especially within Kant's development of the notion of unconditioned subjectivity. It is this Kantian notion which, avers Dussel, undergirds the Fichtean "absolute Ego," which in turn becomes the starting point of the Fichtean dialectic.[26]

Arguing against the Kantian skepticism concerning the possibility of knowledge of things in themselves, Fichte proposes that one *can* know the *noumenon*, but, because operating within an idealist worldview, he still envisions that knowledge as taking place intra-subjectively: the subject-object relation is, for him, an exclusively immanent relation (within consciousness) inasmuch as the absolute, unconditioned Ego, the *eines jeden Ich selbst*, embraces both the finite and the infinite, both the facticity of the "external" world and the subjectivity of the ego. According to Dussel, the foundation of the Fichtean dialectic is an act whereby "the Ego gives to itself everything that can be an object [the not-Ego]; at its base, it is an act by which the object is given to the Ego by the Ego." The absolute Ego's pure act of positing itself as the philosophical unconditioned is the only possible starting point of the Fichtean dialectic since the everyday-as-*factum* finds its locus in the external world of being, which world is finite and, as such, incapable of embracing the infinite. Only in the pure act of the self-positing Ego do the infinite and finite worlds meet.[27]

Dussel maintains that with the Fichtean subordination of being to the unconditioned, absolute subject in the self-positing Ego the triumph of idealism is secured. As he points out, the Fichtean dialectic is completely immanent inasmuch as it is based upon "neither a synthetic nor an antithetic judgment but upon an absolute thesis:" the absolute Ego. The only synthesis is that of the negation of the negation (i.e., the negation of the not-Ego's negation of the absolute Ego's infinity—this latter taking place through the process of determination), which synthesis is merely a revestiture of the Ego as absolute and unconditioned. For this reason, Dussel denies the applicability of the term "synthesis" to the Fichtean dialectic, arguing that, because "there is no real novelty, only a development of what is already given," the movement is more truly analytic than synthetic, leaving nothing to transcendence. The "synthetic" Ego of Fichte, the negation of the negation, prefigures Hegel, however, insofar as it already points to the totalization of the Absolute at the negation-of-the-negation stage of the dialectic even beyond the originary thetic (Ego) stage.[28]

Dussel continues his analysis of the Western dialectical tradition by examining F. G. Schelling's expansion of the Fichtean dialectic to include the dialectics of nature. Schelling's absolutization of nature, or the universe, foreshadows, asserts Dussel, the work of Marx and Nietzsche, especially the material dialectics of the former and the supremacy of cultural production posited by the latter.[29] The idealism of the Fichtean absolute Ego is taken a step further in Schelling's Absolute. Schelling's neo-Platonic understanding of the universe as absolute presents a more coherent—and involuted—subjectivism insofar as it does away with the not-Ego altogether, stipulating that, as Dussel indicates, the not-Ego itself be

> assimilated into the movement of interiority, because, since the Ego is the starting point, it does not even need the not-Ego to move dialectically: the Ego knows the Ego and is pure self-consciousness.[30]

Once the Ego is posited as knowing *itself as object*, the not-Ego is no longer necessary:

> From the thing *known* in Descartes' idea, one moves on to the thing *believed* by Kant, from there to its disappearance in the purely antithetical not-Ego interior to the Ego, to its annihilation even as not-Ego in the pure immanence of the absolute Ego, which knows itself as self-consciousness. The involution is complete.[31]

Moreover, the self-knowing Ego represents the ascendancy of knowing over being since, as Schelling asserts, "self-consciousness . . . is not a mode of *being* but of *knowing*." *Contra* Aristotle, Schelling's goal is not being but knowledge. Nevertheless, Hegel's absolute reduction of being to knowing is not yet fully attained; in

Schelling's system being retains a certain "opacity" as "suppressed liberty." However, there is still no mistaking the fact that the Ego-as-pure-act is its *cognitive* self-production.[32]

In Dussel's view, then, Schelling's work at this point (later Schelling will offer a critique of Hegel which will present different methodological possibilities) represents the elimination of the thing-in-itself and the not-Ego, and, consequently, of the everyday world. The full involution of the dialectic will wait until Hegel, however, to find a comprehensive, systematic exposition.[33]

The Hegelian Dialectic

Hegel's is a positive dialectic whose aim is absolute knowledge. The dialectic reveals that fundamental unity which is both prior to what are given to our understanding as *apparent* contradictions and eliminates those "contradictions" in the negation of the negation, or identity of non-identity.[34]

In contradistinction to both Fichte and Schelling, Hegel locates the dialectical starting point in *empirical* categories, but, unlike Aristotle, he does so only negatively, in order to achieve absolute, coincident self-consciousness, or self-knowledge. Unlike Fichte, who prescinds from the ontic realm to ground his dialectic, Hegel acknowledges the significance of the ontic as a necessary moment in the dialectic. According to him, Fichte's subjective starting point too easily dismisses the objective moment. Both of these moments are in turn comprehended—in what Dussel sees as a key Hegelian revision of Schelling—in the Absolute.[35]

The ontic starting point, the everyday, must be negated, however, inasmuch as it represents "merely natural consciousness." The everyday world contains an infinite number of determinations, or limitations. Liberation occurs, then, only when these negations are themselves negated ("*omnia determinatio est negatio*"). The dialectical starting point in "natural," or "non-coincident" consciousness must be negated in order to make progress towards total coincidence of consciousness, at which point no further possibilities of novelty exist.[36]

As Dussel emphasizes in his analysis of Hegel, this drive towards coincidence is, further, not merely logical but is, even more, "the real process of consciousness, of the spirit as humanity, as absolute: God as subject."[37] Coincident self-consciousness thus represents the final identification of being and knowing inasmuch as consciousness is "an act of self-manifestation" (through the mediation of determined entities) which, because the object of its knowing cannot lie outside itself, posits the existence of those objects as identical with the thinking of them: "the concept is the very actuality of the object as known" and "the actuality of the concept . . . [is] the actuality of consciousness as consciousness and the being of the object."[38] The subject-object tension is thus dissolved:

> The being of consciousness as consciousness is knowing; the being of the object as object is its being known.[39]

According to Dussel, an appreciation of the inherent circularity of the Hegelian dialectic, whose completed movement is always but a neo-Platonic "remembering," is of central importance in an analysis of the Hegelian dialectic. (Here Dussel alludes to the etymology of *erinnerung* as signifying both a remembering and the internal [-inner] origin [er-] of something.) The Absolute is prior to its determinations and can only know itself through those determinations. Consequently, any progress in self-consciousness is always both intra-subjective and circular. It is intra-subjective because the determinations are posited by consciousness and absolute subjectivity is defined by self-conceptualization. It is circular because the determinate mediations, as negations of infinity, are the means toward absolute coincidence in the return to the genetic Absolute. This point of return is not now, however, indeterminate "nothingness," rather it is the *positive* negation of negations (these latter reflecting finiteness and, hence, limits to absolute self-consciousness). The intra-subjective totalization of the Absolute in the Hegelian system is simply "the eternal reversion of the Absolute to itself." Fundamental unity (uniformity in this case) is both the beginning and the end of the Hegelian dialectic.[40]

Critiques of the Hegelian Dialectic

In what he calls his "post-modern" project, Dussel ventures a critique of the Hegelian tradition, not only as this tradition finds expression in Hegel's own total system but also as it later becomes expressed in the "anti-Hegelian critiques . . .—from Schelling to Sartre."[41] This is by no means to say that Dussel sees nothing of value in Hegel's work, which the Argentine describes as nothing short of brilliant; rather, Dussel's own critique will issue in a dialectical sublation of Hegel, within which the German thinker's work will be viewed from a different "horizon of comprehension." Even more, Dussel will draw upon the post-Hegelian Europeans' critiques of Hegel.[42]

The first modern critique of Hegel is put forth by the mature Schelling, who outlived Hegel and was called by the Prussian state to hammer the final nails into the coffin of Hegelianism, a system already quickly becoming discredited in the wake of Hegel's death. It is in this "post-Hegelian" critique that Schelling offers what amounts to a significant development of his earlier, pre-Hegelian, involutive dialectic. By accusing Hegel of confusing "ontology with logic, reality with mere possibility," Schelling paves the way for a positive expansion of the dialectic towards a "beyond-being."[43] This beyond-being cannot be fully comprehended by the concept.

It comprises a real exteriority, experienceable *a posteriori:* "Existence is a 'prius' that had been left aside by Hegel at the level of consciousness."[44] The direction taken here by Schelling's critique represents a major advance, argues Dussel, in that it already points to the possibility of revelation from beyond the identification of thinking and being characteristic of the involutive, egocentric Totality. For Schelling, God is the source of being and reason. God *reveals* being from beyond the ontological horizon. The Idea is not God. On the contrary, reason is grounded in existential faith, which is in turn expressed in the "history of the symbology of peoples (mythology)."[45]

Schelling's critique is followed by Feuerbach's, which, according to Dussel, presents two major objections to the Hegelian system, asserting that: 1) the exclusively temporal Hegelian dialectic, in overlooking spatiality, is unable to account for physical coexistence over and above temporal succession; and 2) as the "absolute self-alienation of reason," the Hegelian dialectic overlooks sense experience. Having rejected the inherited, divinized ontology of Hegel, Feuerbach looks beyond the totalized concept to the sensorial, material, spatial. The *factum*-as-everyday now returns as the starting point (however, no longer merely negative, as in Hegel) and the anthropological, or the human, becomes foundational. The primacy of reason, of the concept, gives way to the primacy of material human existence.[46]

Feuerbach's critique of Hegelian idealism is taken a step further by Karl Marx, who identifies reality not with materiality *per se*, but with what-is-produced:

> For Hegel, the real is thinking and what is thought; Schelling proposes to go beyond the ontology of the identity of

> being and thinking and discovers the transversality of revelation; Feuerbach goes beyond the ontology of being as thinking, opening himself to the realm of sensoriality, affectivity, the I-thou, person-person relationship. Now Marx goes beyond the Feuerbachian ambit . . . describing the real as the produced, the labored upon; and the abstract I-thou, person-person relationship as that of master (capitalist), exploited.[47]

In positing the historical priority of the forces of production, Marx supersedes the passive anthropology of Feuerbach and inverts Hegelian idealism by maintaining that philosophy is ideologically conditioned by its material base: knowledge is not an *a priori* of historical reality, nor is it identified with that reality.[48]

Beyond this basic insight into Marx's critique of Feuerbach and Hegel, however, Dussel's understanding of the actual scope of that critique has undergone a significant development over the course of the past decade. In the early 1970's Dussel claimed that, while giving them new content, Marx was still bound to the Hegelian categories and was, thus, still a product of the "age of ontology."[49] By 1983, however, Dussel would assert that "in Marx, the concept and category of exteriority was clearly expressed."[50] Referring to Marx's *Paris Manuscripts*, especially the second manuscript, Dussel contends that

> Marx explicitly indicates that, for the political economy, the person *as such*, i.e., the worker *before* working and, above all, before being a salaried worker, is *nothing*.[51]

Even more fundamentally than "what-is-produced," reality is the person as exterior to any system. The realm of exteriority is the person as "nothing" to the Totality, the system, the Whole. In other words, for Marx, "the worker as such can . . . irrupt in the Totality of Being from the *reality* of his or her exteriority as Other." Prior to being a serf, a salaried worker, etc., the person is "living labor." As living labor, the person is independent of and outside any system. A person becomes an entity only when he or she enters the system as—in the case of capitalism—a salaried worker, i.e., as a mere "moment" of capital. He or she then becomes but an instrument, or commodity for the system. Consequently, the *un*employed are "nothing" for the system and, as such, are a symbol of exteriority.[52]

Dussel points out that, for Marx, the instrumentalization of the person in the capitalist system results in the fetishization, or idolatrous worship of that system as Absolute. Marx's critique of capitalism is thus, above all, a *religious* critique. (Marx repeatedly employs Biblical language, particularly that of the Old Testament prophets, to denounce the divinization of Capital.) Dussel emphasizes that Marx's famous assertion that "the criticism of religion is the premise of all criticism" cannot be understood apart from its anti-*fetishistic* context:

> How could the slaves rebel with Moses against the Pharaoh if they did not criticize his divinity, if they did not reject the (fetishistic) religion? How could the Christians preach about a more just reign to the oppressed poor of the Roman Empire if they worshipped the Emperor as God? Weren't the Christians accused of being "atheists" of the Roman gods—and they effectively were—and weren't they, because of this, taken to the amphitheatres?[53]

Insofar as Marx defends the untotalizability of the person over against the capitalist instrumentalization of the person, then, his anti-fetishistic critique is, as Dussel concludes,

> identical to the antifetishistic (antipolitical) critique of the prophets of Israel, the early Christians, and . . . the Christians who commit themselves to the process of liberative revolution in all of Latin America, especially in Central America.[54]

Though Marx *was* an atheist, he never formulated a comprehensive *theory* of religion. Such was not his concern. According to Dussel, what Marx *did* formulate was a *critique* of *dominative* religion. Insofar as Marx did not have a *theory* of religion, therefore, his critique of dominative religion (parallel to the Judaeo-Christian critique) does not contradict, but rather is open to a *Christian* theory of religion.[55]

Dussel further detects a development of Marx's defense of exteriority in some of the German socialist's later work, particularly in chapter 43 of the third volume of *Capital,* where Marx writes about the realm, or reign of freedom (*Reichtum der Freiheit*):

> In that text [Marx] again treats the theme of exteriority, but not as the prior subjectivity of living labor, rather as objectivity beyond any finality which the system can propose. There, then, is where he says that the reign of freedom is beyond all the possibilities and all the horizons of the material conditions of production.[56]

Marx's affirmation of an "absolute exteriority" is what allows him to judge all systems as the exteriority's (the reign of freedom's) non-realization. While he affirms the exteriority of living labor as a "real" moment, then, Marx does not understand the absolute exteriority of the reign of freedom as historically "real," or realizable in history, even in the "communist" stage.[57]

It is with the discovery of Marx's notions of "living labor" and "reign of freedom" as pointing beyond the ontological horizon that Dussel's understanding of the Marxian critique of Hegel has, in the last few years, taken a new turn, one which perceives in that critique a rejection of the closed Hegelian ontology. As Dussel indicates, this understanding of Marx makes it possible to critique, from a Marxian perspective, the extant socialist systems, particularly the Soviet system. Insofar as these attempt to carry forward a total planning of society, they also—along with capitalist systems—impede the historical expression of the exteriority, or independence intrinsic to the person, who is never completely totalizable. While their means are different, both the capitalist system and the Soviet system have the same end.[58]

Following Marx, the European critique of Hegel finds further expression in the work of Kierkegaard, Husserl, and Heidegger. In contradistinction to Hegel's understanding of concrete, determined, differentiated human existence as a negation of being, Kierkegaard locates human existence outside the grasp of the concept and counts human existence as the determinative criterion of the individual's stance in relation to the revelatory Other (still an exclusively theological category in Kierkegaard), who is beyond reason. That stance cannot be fundamentally rational, but only existential.[59]

The return to the everyday as the starting point of the dialectic is continued by Husserl. If one remembers, explains Dussel, that, for Aristotle, the dialectical method was principally "a way of passing from the everyday (*ta endoxa*) to that realm where being reveals itself as distinct from the false and non-being," one notices the same kind of movement in Husserl's thought, where "phenomenology as the 'first philosophy' is, in its entirety, a doctrine of method, the dialectical method within the metaphysics of modernity."[60] Unlike Marx, however, Husserl is still functioning within the Hegelian ontology. Also, in contradistinction to Kierkegaard's theologically open dialectic, Husserlian phenomenology remains a mode of involution. On the other hand, argues Dussel, Husserl's analyses of the different horizons—from that of the immediate everyday to that of pure, phenomenological, or transcendental subjectivity—already suggest the possiblity of a "'new' post-modern dialectic."[61]

The path to a post-modern dialectic is further opened by Martin Heidegger, whose dialectic, while originating in the everyday, moves outward (through the various intermediate horizons), to the ultimate, ontological horizon of being, which grounds the ontic, there to reaffirm the *factum*. The ontological foundation of the ontic lies outside subjectivity (the person is not the producer of being, but its steward). Dussel paraphrases the Heideggerian objection to the Hegelian position in this way:

> If the human being were the manifestation, as finite spirit, of the absolute Spirit without discontinuity (metaphysically: by emanation, since in Hegel there is no creation), the human being would be, as finite subjectivity, the same absolute Subjectivity: being would issue from itself as the first-born in itself or as auto-indeterminateness.[62]

Dasein would then be relegated to functioning in the role of one more intramundane entity among many others. In contrast to Hegel, Heidegger locates the starting point of the dialectic at precisely the *most* "determined" level, i.e., the human being as untotalizable. The *ad quem* is, then, the fundamental ontological horizon, which posits and manifests itself in the intermediate horizons and which is, hence, a reminder of human finiteness.[63]

As a fundamental ontology, therefore, the Heideggerian dialectic affirms the inherent finiteness of the person, whose dialectical movement from the everyday towards the ultimate horizon is accompanied by a hermeneutic which, because the everyday is posited by and within the ultimate horizon, is always ongoing. Consequently, a coincident identity is not a possibility:

> Never, for the human being, will there be an identity between thinking and praxis, between the existential and existentiell. The Hegelian dream of identity has been overcome.[64]

The notion of an open-ended dialectic finds further elaboration and development in the work of Jean Paul Sartre. The French philosopher grounds his affirmation of the impossibility of a closed, totalized dialectic (such as Hegel's) in the inherent historicity of the person (who can never place him or herself at "the end" of history), which historicity is in turn grounded in the inherently open-ended character of history.[65] Like history, the dialectic is ongoing. Consequently, Sartre emphasizes that it is necessary

> to establish irrefutably against Hegel that history is still in process, that being remains irreducible to knowing and, at the same time, that it is necessary to preserve the dialectical movement *in being* and *in knowing*.[66]

The next philosophical figure whom Dussel cites as moving towards a more open-ended dialectic is the Spanish existentialist Xavier Zubiri. For Dussel, Zubiri's major significance lies in his extension of the scope of the open dialectic to include physico-biological reality, which is in continuous evolution and, as such, always exceeds the grasp of our theoretical comprehension.[67] This reality, moveover, is not simply, as in Heidegger, the "objectivity of the entities in the world," but also, more specifically, the entities as "'already' *constituted* in their own proper structure," this latter definition already implying an order prior to the entities-as-concrete-reality—not only as entities *per se*.[68] Consequently,

> reality is not . . . a mode of being, but rather, on the contrary, *being* is something grounded in reality.[69]

This, insists Dussel, is not to fall into the Kantian trap of the unknowable *noumenon*, but rather to affirm that, while things in themselves are intelligible, that intelligibility is always "finite, progressive, dialectical:"

> The thing preserves an immense degree of exteriority, which ambit announces that history as future is still possible.[70]

After his treatment of Zubiri, Dussel comes to the end of his prefatory study of the Western dialectical tradition with an analysis of the thought of Emmanuel Levinas, whose work, as we indicated in our Introduction *supra*, has been a major influence in Dussel's own project. Levinas' notion of "the Other" represents, for Dussel, a major advance beyond Heidegger. While in the Heideggerian ontology the Other, as the ultimate horizon, is always present in the world as the backdrop against which the entities are prehended (i.e., the Other is always "with" us), in Levinas' thought the comprehensibility, and *in*comprehensibility of the Other is made more explicit on the basis of three key insights: 1) the European philosophical tradition has naively assimilated the Greek notion of being as "what-is-seen" (*idein:* "to see"); 2) the basis of the I-thou relationship is language; and 3) therefore, reality is "what-is-*heard*" from *outside* the Totality, or the ontological horizon which gives meaning to "my" world. "What-is-heard" issues from one who is revealed in his or her word and is not embraced by "my" Totality.[71]

For Levinas, then, the Other is always beyond my comprehension because he or she always exists outside my horizon of meaning, my Totality, or my "world." My comprehension of the Other can never encapsulate him or her as "what-is-seen" but will always be indistinct, as "what-is-heard." The voice of the Other breaks into my Totality as something alien to it. At the same time, that voice, as the expression of the Other's exteriority, demands justice. It demands that the Other be affirmed as other than I. I cannot relate to another person as I relate to a mere object, which I can "know."[72]

Levinas presents his ontology as a critique of the entire phenomenological tradition. That tradition, he argues, subordinates the inter*personal,* and hence *ethical* relation to the relation with the "*being of the entity*" (a cognitive, impersonal relation). Justice is, in turn, subordinated to liberty, since "liberty would oppose itself to that justice which imposes obligations with respect to an entity that refuses to yield."[73] For Levinas, on the other hand, liberty is inconceivable apart from justice, since justice demands that the Other be allowed to express him or herself as *unique*.[74]

Still influenced by the Greek notion of being, Heidegger subordinates the entity to being and, in so doing, makes violence an inevitable consequence whenever an entity refuses to submit. Dussel explains:

> If being is presence or "what-is-seen" its consequence is violence. Because the Other is embraced in a Totality, in a system in which he or she already has his or her place and his or her meaning "in" *my* world.[75]

The Other as "what-is-heard," however, is always beyond my Totality and exterior to my world. The dialectic is always open to that exteriority. The word of the Other as mystery thus represents the unforeseeability of history. The Other is true novelty to the givenness of my world.[76]

Toward A Latin American, Post-Modern Dialectic

Far from rejecting the Western tradition as a whole, Dussel essays a dialectical retrieval of that tradition in order to open the possibility of a *Latin American* liberative method (hence Dussel's interpretation of the Western tradition from the explicit perspective of Latin American historical praxis, adopting and adapting those aspects of the tradition which speak to the Latin American reality). Such a method would proffer a critique of the dialectical tradition, which critique, however, would not annihilate but sublate: "it would be a contradiction for a work on dialectics not to use a dialectical method."[77] Thus, a Latin American liberative method would, from its perspective outside the main currents of European history, find much of value in, for instance, the mature Schelling's affirmation of the possibility of revelation from beyond the identity of being and thinking; Feuerbach's anthropologically-grounded rejection of Hegel's divinized ontology; Marx's economic critique of the passive materialism of Feuerbach and his development of the notions of "living labor" and the "reign of freedom;" Kierkegaard's theology of the Other; and the whole of Levinas' thought, though still European and ambiguous with respect to the concrete history of Latin America as exteriority.[78]

The various advances on Hegel's closed dialectic reveal, according to Dussel, three levels of dialectics: 1) the dialectics of nature (e.g., Zubiri); 2) the historical dialectic (e.g., Sartre, Levinas); and 3) the dialectical method as a fundamental ontology. This last level, *qua* theory, always *follows upon* the first two, since, *contra* Hegel, being always exceeds knowing. A Latin American method would reject the totalitarianism of a deductive ("from being to the entity") method and, instead, take as its starting point that finiteness which characterizes the untotalizable person as always external to the totalized Absolute, as what-is-heard, not what-is-seen, and as a being always open to an unforeseen future.[79]

Dussel's method, as an "initiation into philosophy" will recover the "Aristotelian intent" of an externally-directed dialectic. His method is grounded in the first two levels of dialectics. Choosing to prescind—because of his essentially historical concern at this point—from an analysis of the dialectics of nature as such (which dialectics he accepts from Zubiri), Dussel grounds the Latin American dialectic in a "dialectics as existential history, as Latin American *praxis*."[80] Thus, for instance, one finds the Amerindian world clashing with the sixteenth century Spanish world "to constitute the Hispanoamerican 'world' of *colonial* Christianity." This colonial world, in turn, relegates the Amerindian to the level of slave, with the conquistador fulfilling the role of master. The nineteenth century witnesses the dethroning of the colonial masters by the bourgeoisie *criolla*. This historical dialectic, Dussel contends, is the *a priori factum* of a Latin American liberative method, whose elaboration will in turn symbolize—at the theoretical level—the dawn of a new age in Latin American history, one of liberation.[81]

Such a method eschews, then, both the conservatism of those who are content to languish in the unchallenged everyday of the status quo and the "unhinged radicalism" of those who, inattentive to the *a priori factum*, the conditions of the possibility of liberation, put forth programs which are abstract and utopian in the worst sense.[82] Dussel explicitly delineates these conditions of possibility:

> aa) A profound and real knowledge of the Latin American experience (Amerindian, colonial and present). In this sense Sartre shows in the *Critique of Dialectical Reason* how, for example, "Valery is a petite bourgeois intellectual . . . but every petite bourgeois intellectual is not Valery. . . ." bb) An adequate knowledge of the movement named after the "utopian socialists," who formulated for the first time in Europe an interpretation of the structures of their time . . . . cc) A clear discernment between the *existential* and historical *intention*, of for example a Marx, and the conceptual formulation which, after Hegel, could not but be expressed from the perspective of the horizon of the modern, *European* ontology of the twentieth century.[83]

The correlative implications of the above minimal conditions of possibility are as follows: aa) an aversion to ideological constructs which make of concrete human beings abstract "symbols" (as in some forms of conceptualist, totalitarian Marxism, where human relations are understood not as between historical, concrete persons, but as between abstract universals); bb) an openness to alternatives beyond those presented by bourgeois neo-colonialism; and cc) an appreciation of the fact that, while the *intentions* of the Latin American liberation movement may be similar to those of other liberation movements and their intellectual proponents, it will be necessary to "conceptualize the interpretative scheme in another way," for "mere imitation is to fall into utopianism, alienation, and cultural colonialism." Dussel reminds us that, for example, Thomas Aquinas and Marx would not have been Thomist or Marxist in Latin America.[84]

It is because the Latin American philosopher or theologian is first of all a Latin American, his or her theory grounded in Latin American praxis, that a methodology of Latin American liberation will be a *Latin American* methodology.[85] That methodology is a second step, following upon an ethical conversion, in justice, to the Latin American Other in his and her concrete history. A comprehensive Latin

American, liberative, interpretative framework follows upon the open, dialectical (or, as we will examine in greater detail in the next chapter, *anadialectical*) liberation *movement* which seeks the liberation of the "negated being" of the Latin American. The articulation of such a framework is Dussel's intellectual task.[86]

In the next chapter we will follow the course of that articulation, beginning with the *a priori* Latin American historical dialectic, which will then lead to the development of a Latin American methodology of liberation grounded in Latin American historical praxis and incorporating, but going beyond, the social scientific and philosophical categories we have examined above.

NOTES

/1/ See Introduction, *supra*.
/2/ See Introduction, *supra*.
/3/ Enrique Dussel, *La dialéctica hegeliana: Supuestos y superación o del inicio originario del filosofar* (Mendoza, Argentina: Editorial Ser y Tiempo, 1972) p. 10.
/4/ Ibid.
/5/ Ibid.
/6/ Roberto S. Goizueta, "Liberation and Method: The Analectical Method of Enrique Dussel," in *The Pedagogy of God's Image: Essays on Symbol and the Religious Imagination* ed. Robert Masson (Chico, CA: Scholars Press, 1982) p. 114.
/7/ Dussel, *La dialéctica hegeliana*, p. 13; Enrique Dussel, *Para una ética de la liberación Latinoamericana*, 2 vols. (I–II), *Filosofía ética latinoamericana*, 3 vols. (III–V) (I–II: Buenos Aires: Siglo Veintiuno, 1973; III–V: México: Edicol, 1977–80) 1:33.
/8/ Dussel, *La dialéctica hegeliana*, p. 14.
/9/ Ibid., p. 15.
/10/ Ibid.
/11/ Ibid.
/12/ Ibid., pp. 16–17; Dussel, *Método*, pp. 19, 27–29; Dussel, *Etica de la liberación*, 1:81–83; Goizueta, pp. 115.
/13/ Dussel, *La dialéctica hegeliana*, pp. 20–21.
/14/ Ibid., pp. 21–22; Dussel, *Etica de la liberación*, 1:40–41.
/15/ Dussel, *La dialéctica hegeliana*, pp. 22–24; Dussel, *Etica de la liberación*, 1:43.
/16/ Dussel, *La dialéctica hegeliana*, p. 25.
/17/ Ibid., p. 28.
/18/ Ibid., pp. 28–29.
/19/ Ibid., pp. 29–30; Dussel, *Método*, p. 31; Goizueta, pp. 115–16.

/20/ Dussel, Método, p. 33; Dussel, *La dialéctica hegeliana*, p. 32; Goizueta, p. 116.
/21/ Dussel, Método, p. 34; Dussel, *La dialéctica hegeliana*, p. 32; Dussel, *Etica de la liberación*, 1:108; Goizueta, p. 116.
/22/ Dussel, *La dialectica hegeliana*, p. 34.
/23/ Ibid., pp. 35–36.
/24/ Ibid., p. 38.
/25/ Ibid., pp. 36–43; Dussel, *Método*, p. 41; Dussel, *Etica de la liberación*, 1:57; Goizueta, p. 116.
/26/ Dussel, *La dialéctica hegeliana*, pp. 43–46; Goizueta, p. 116.
/27/ Dussel, *La dialéctica hegeliana*, pp. 46–49; Dussel, *Etica de la liberación*, 1:110.
/28/ Dussel, *La dialéctica hegeliana*, pp. 49–55; Goizueta, p. 117.
/29/ Dussel, *La dialéctica hegeliana*, p. 56.
/30/ Ibid., pp. 57–58. Here, "interiority" is interpreted in a subjectivist, conceptualist manner. See chapter 5 *infra* for an analysis of how this notion of interiority differs from that of Bernard Lonergan.
/31/ Dussel, *Método*, p. 56.
/32/ Dussel, *La Dialéctica hegeliana*, pp. 59–61.
/33/ Ibid., p. 63.
/34/ Dussel, *Método*, pp. 72–73, 112; Dussel, *Etica de la Liberación*, 1:36, 57, 111–14; Goizueta, p. 117.
/35/ Dussel, *La dialéctica hegeliana*, p. 76; Goizueta, p. 117.
/36/ Dussel, *La dialéctica hegelina*, p. 80; Dussel, *Etica de la liberación*, 1:57, 2:18–19; Goizueta, pp. 117–18.
/37/ Dussel, *Método*, p. 84.
/38/ Dussel, *La dialéctica hegeliana*, p. 81.
/39/ Ibid., pp. 81, 95.
/40/ Ibid., pp. 86–111.
/41/ Ibid., p. 123.
/42/ Ibid.
/43/ Dussel, *Etica de la liberación*, 2:157; Dussel, *Método*, pp. 121–27; Goizueta, p. 118; Dussel, tape recorded autobiography, April, 1983.
/44/ Dussel, *Método*, pp. 121–27; Goizueta, p. 118; Dussel, tape recorded autobiography, April, 1983.
/45/ Dussel, *Método*, pp. 121–27; Dussel, tape recorded autobiography, April, 1983.
/46/ Dussel, *Método*, pp. 129–36; Goizueta, pp. 118–19; Dussel, tape recorded autobiography, April, 1983; Feuerbach's understanding of the opening to the Other as, above all, an *erotic* opening to the woman-Other will later influence Dussel's own understanding of the Other (see chapters 3 and 4 *infra*).
/47/ Dussel, *Método*, p. 139; Dussel, *Etica de la liberación*, 2:158; Goizueta, p. 119.
/48/ Dussel, *Método*, pp. 144–45; Dussel, *Etica de la liberación*, 2:46–47, 120.
/49/ Dussel, *La dialéctica hegeliana*, p. 126; Dussel, *Etica de la liberación*, 1:116, 2:49–50.
/50/ Dussel, tape recorded autobiography, April, 1983.

/51/ Ibid.
/52/ Ibid. See also Robert C. Tucker, ed., *The Marx-Engels Reader,* 2nd edition (New York: W. W. Norton, 1978) pp. 252–61.
/53/ Enrique Dussel, "La religión en el joven Marx (1835–1849)," *Los Universitarios* 205 (December, 1982) 25–31.
/54/ Ibid.
/55/ Ibid.
/56/ Dussel, tape recorded autobiography, April, 1983.
/57/ Ibid.
/58/ Ibid.
/59/ Dussel, *Método,* pp. 149–54; Dussel, *Etica de la liberación,* 2:159; Goizueta, p. 120; Dussel, tape recorded autobiography, April, 1983. According to Dussel, Kierkegaard's notion of faith as "absurd" sets the Danish philosopher apart from Schelling, who understands faith as the ground of reason. Dussel will take Schelling's side on this issue.
/60/ Dussel, *La dialéctica hegeliana,* p. 127.
/61/ Ibid., p. 128; Dussel, *Etica de la liberación,* 1:58–59.
/62/ Dussel, *La dialéctica hegeliana,* pp. 132–33; Dussel, *Etica de la liberazción,* 2:55.
/63/ Dussel, *La dialéctica hegeliana,* pp. 133–34; Dussel, *Etica de la liberación,* 1:98–99.
/64/ Dussel, *La dialéctica hegeliana,* p. 135; Dussel, *Etica de la liberación,* 1:86, 100–02.
/65/ Dussel, *Método,* pp. 164–67; Dussel, *La dialéctica hegeliana,* pp. 137–38; Dussel, *Etica de la liberación,* 1:48; Goizueta, p. 120.
/66/ Jean Paul Sartre, quoted in Dussel, *La dialéctica hegeliana,* p. 139.
/67/ Dussel, *Método,* pp. 169–70; Dussel, *La dialéctica hegeliana,* pp. 141–45; Goizueta, p. 121.
/68/ Dussel, *La dialéctica hegeliana,* p. 143.
/69/ Ibid., pp. 143–44.
/70/ Ibid., p. 144.
/71/ Dussel, *Método,* pp. 171–72; Dussel, *Etica de la liberación,* 2:160–61; Goizueta, p. 121.
/72/ Dussel, *La dialéctica hegeliana,* pp. 146–47; Dussel, *Método,* p. 172.
/73/ Emmanuel Levinas, quoted in Dussel, *La dialéctica hegeliana,* p. 147.
/74/ Dussel, *La dialéctica hegeliana,* p. 147–48.
/75/ Ibid., p. 148.
/76/ Ibid., pp. 148–49; Dussel, *Método,* pp. 173–74; Goizueta, p. 121.
/77/ Dussel, *La dialéctica hegeliana,* p. 151.
/78/ Dussel, *Método,* pp. 176–81; Dussel, *Etica de la liberación,* 2:89–92, 156–62; Goizueta, p. 122.
/79/ Dussel, *La dialéctica hegeliana,* pp. 152–55.
/80/ Ibid., p. 156.
/81/ Ibid., pp. 156–57.
/82/ Ibid., p. 158; Dussel, *Método,* p. 203; Goizueta, p. 126.
/83/ Dussel, *La dialéctica hegeliana,* pp. 158–59.
/84/ Ibid., pp. 159–60.
/85/ This is not to say, however, that one is a "Latin American" theologian

merely by birthright. As we saw in chapter 1, the national intelligentsia can be penetrated by foreign culture, ideology, etc. In the following chapter we will see how one can be "Latin American" only if he or she is in solidarity with the historical aspirations and project of the Latin American Other, as "exteriority." A "Latin American" method must be grounded in Latin American praxis.

/86/ Dussel, *La dialéctica hegeliana,* p. 161.

CHAPTER THREE

A LATIN AMERICAN ANADIALECTICAL METHOD

A Latin American Dialectics of History

Drawing upon some of the insights gained in his dialectical retrieval of the Western intellectual tradition, Dussel is now able to expand and revise those insights in the light of *Latin American* historical praxis. In order to take this key methodological step, he develops a Latin American dialectics of history, which dialectics will then help clarify the historical underpinnings of his anadialectical method.

Both the dialectical retrieval of the Western tradition and the Latin American dialectics of history thus mediate between Latin American historical praxis and Dussel's anadialectical method. Along with the preceding examination of Dussel's retrieval of the Western intellectual tradition, therefore, an analysis of his interpretative framework for understanding the Latin American experience, or everyday, is a necessary preface to an analysis of his anadialectical method.

One thing that must be made clear at the outset, for instance, and a stipulation which Dussel himself explicitly makes in his *Historia de la Iglesia en América Latina* and *Desintegración de la cristiandad colonial y liberación,* is that, precisely because historical dialectics is not concerned primarily with the sequential, "objective" account of historical events as such (though these, of course, are important) but with the attempt to derive meaning from those events *in the light of* the present experience of a people, his historical analyses are not undertaken in isolation from theological, epistemological, etc., considerations, but inform and are informed by those considerations:

> Within the horizon of the everyday the historian begins to study his or her topic, which is historical events. He or she

> should be able to express that historical fact after discovering its meaning. Otherwise one succumbs to the naivete of thinking that he or she is effecting an "objective" and scientific interpretation, valid for all times. . . . If we are Latin Americans, Latin America constitutes our everyday horizon of comprehension. . . . The *meaning* of the event, which is the object of our study, is thus grounded in a certain horizon. One must take explicit account of that horizon in order also to describe later the discovered meaning of the event.[1]

That horizon of comprehension, moreover, is also *Christian*.[2]

Unless and until history has meaning, it cannot constitute the self-comprehension of a people.[3] This statement is premised upon two methodological principles: 1) "*pure* objectivity is impossible in any science;" and 2) "non-subjectivity is impossible." Because of the inherently perspectival nature of knowledge, objectivity can be said to exist only within given perspectives. Dussel denies that this amounts to "relativism," if by that word is meant, not that human beings are finite (an axiomatic statement, yet one whose implications are often overlooked), but that human beings are incapable of discovering truth. Truth is indeed absolute . . . *for everyone situated in a given horizon of comprehension*.[4]

Just as all knowledge is perspectival, so too is it "subjective" inasmuch as it is conditioned by all sorts of historical, sociological, and psychological considerations. This is not to imply that such subjectivity must be eliminated (since it *cannot* be), but rather that there must be an explicit methodological mediation between subjectivity and objectivity.[5]

Dussel speaks here of a "historification of objectivity," or a "methodological subjectivity." Much like Ricoeur's "transcendental subjectivity" these aim at transcending vulgar subjectivity in order to be able to treat the historical object scientifically, with the awareness, nevertheless, that all description is, at the same time, interpretation.[6]

The historian who expects to exempt him or herself from these contingencies cannot but proffer a vulgar, acritical interpretation of history, despite the fact that his or her method may have been impeccably "scientific." One need not deny the exceptional professional talent of the scores of "scientific" historians who have for centuries graced European and North American halls of academe to be struck by the fact that, despite the hundreds of histories issuing from those halls, the history of the poor, oppressed, dominated remains largely undocumented. The same observation can be made of Latin American historians themselves, since a Latin American birth certificate is no assurance that what issues from one's pen will indeed be a *Latin American* history:

> Almost always [in Latin America] history was written by the cultural elite, who, on its part, is culturally dependent. We have been educated in universities, in seminaries, in Europe, or under its influence, and all of this has given us a certain view of reality.[7]

Dussel argues that, for the most part, Latin American history, as presented by this cultural elite, has been written from three perspectives: 1) the anecdotal; 2) the liberal anti-conservative; and 3) the "revisionist, traditionalist, antiliberal and apologetic." The first perspective simply concerns itself with the documentation of historical events and was especially prevalent during the period of colonial Christianity. The second appears in the 19th century and results in an ideologization of history (still characteristic of much of Latin American education) in which the liberal status quo is accepted and propounded as embodying the "truth." Finally, the third perspective, the most prevalent, differs from the second in that it makes no normative claims at all, but instead puts itself forward as "objective." As it turns out, however, this perspective is also ideological inasmuch as its so-called scientific method serves to obscure the fact that its descriptions are also interpretations.[8]

Dussel opts for a fourth perspective: the explicitly Christian critical perspective. As the *a priori* of his historical dialectical project, however, his perspectival option, while going beyond the other three, nevertheless dialectically sublates them:

> It is necessary to recover the contributions . . . of the notable studies of the colonial era . . . and at the same time it will also be necessary to take into account the liberal description and not disregard what many of them have done for the present constitution of our nationalities.[9]

As *Christian*, this perspective will take a critical attitude, but one informed by Christian criteria. Among these criteria there is, in turn, only one which is absolute: "outside the established Totality, outside any organized system ('the flesh') are the vulnerable *poor;* the poor are already Jesus."[10] By "poor" Dussel means those who are outside the "system" and whose values are, therefore, *dis*values for those in power:

> The poor person is poor because he or she does not share in the reigning value of the system; if the value of the system in the Middle Ages is honor, he or she has no honor; if the supreme power in the system is money, he or she does not have it; if in the future society the system has technology as its supreme value, he or she will be a person without technology.[11]

The Latin American present, with its blatant injustices and inequality, thus serves as both starting point and horizon of comprehension for Dussel. Situated in this horizon, he seeks to interpret history from the perspective of those suffering injustice. Given that starting point and horizon of comprehension, Dussel undertakes a dialectical study of the history of Latin America, focusing on the history of the Latin American Church. The study is dialectical in that it seeks the meaning of the present by situating the present in relation to the preceding eras of both Latin American history and Latin American pre-history (i.e., the history of humankind as a whole) in such a way as to reveal the continuities and discontinuities of meaning, or the dialectical movement of the ultimate horizon of comprehension. As indicated above, this method is both critical, in that the dialectic prevents a reification of the present everyday, and Christian, in that the existential meaning of history is sought not merely as an end in itself, but as the only way open to us to discern the revelation of a God who has chosen to become revealed *in history*.[12]

The task of the dialectical historian, then, is not so much one of recounting historical events in all their detail, hoping thereby to present an "objective" picture, as it is one of searching for the existential *meaning* of past events as a way of enriching the meaning of the present. Because his or her primary concern will be to discern horizonal shifts in history, the focus will be on those events which prove to be significant as meaning-constituting events in a particular place and time. This historian's primary aim is not a photographic portrait but an x-ray of history.[13]

Historical Stages of Domination and Liberation: A Hypothesis

After undertaking this "x-ray" of history, the historian, like the scientist, may then put forward a hypothesis regarding the meaning of that history. Concomitantly, he or she may establish a periodization of history by demonstrating, through the analysis of their essential characteristics, the validity "of establishing limits for each of these periods." As a "problematization" of a method, this hypothesis is not a finished history, but a framework for later, more detailed analyses.[14]

In *Historia de la Iglesia en América Latina* and *Desintegración de la cristiandad colonial y liberación* Dussel puts forth such a framework within which to discover the meaning of present-day Latin American Christian experience in the light of the dialectically related historical eras from which that experience emerges. In Dussel's framework, present-day Latin American Christianity can be situated, as it were, in the center of two concentric circles, the inner circle representing the history of Latin America and Latin American Christianity, and the outer representing "universal history," or Latin American pre-history:

> There are many who say that we [Latin Americans] were "born" in 1809–1825, as if there our nation appeared and emerged out of nothingness (*ex nihilo*). . . . There are others who go back farther, to the 16th century. . . . As long as we are unable to situate Latin America within universal history, we will be like the water that falls from the sky without knowing its origins.[15]

Universal History

Universal history, the broadest framework, refers to the history of humankind as an essential methodological factor. The possibility of Christian meaning, i.e., of God's revelation in the present, is dependent upon the historical emergence of humankind, which "transforms . . . the great biological evolution into history; and within that human history the revelation of God emerges." Far from contradicting the belief in a creator God, therefore, evolution *presupposes* a creator God since it was "first necessary to desacralize the cosmos so that the cosmos would be a creature." The cosmos desacralized, God is free to become revealed in the course of human history, i.e., in the course of the evolutionary process.[16]

Dussel divides universal history into three stages, with their order being determined more by cultural features than by chronology. These stages are: 1) the neolithic, 2) the Indo-European, and 3) the Semitic.[17]

According to Dussel, the neolithic stage is characterized by "a great urban revolution in which human beings, thanks to agriculture and pasturing, can become concentrated in cities." Urbanization in turn leads to the increasing and rapid complexification of social and productive processes. The first great example of this stage of cultural progress, avers Dussel, was the lower Mesopotamian culture of the fourth millenium B.C.E., followed by the burgeoning Egyptian culture in the next millenium, then the Hindu, etc.[18]

The corresponding Latin American neolithic cultures do not appear, however, until approximately 300–900 C.E., with the emergence of the Aztec Teotihuacan empire and the Inca Tiahuanaco. By studying the documents that have come down to us from this time period—documents which, Dussel insists, should be studied with the same intensity as we study, for instance, the pre-Socratics—we can obtain a glimpse of the "cosmovision," the horizon of comprehension, which characterized this particular era of Latin American pre-history. This point of entry into pre-history provides a different horizon within which to view the conquest of the New World—now from the perspective of the poor, the Other, whom the Europeans cannot allow to exist outside the European horizon of comprehension and are, therefore, either "pacified" or killed outright.[19]

The second, Indo-European, stage is exemplified by "the cultures which, in the Euro-Asiatic continent, undertake invasions from the North."[20] Originating around 4,000 B.C.E., in the areas north of the Black and Caspian Seas, these Indo-European cultures move progressively south, until, by about 2,000 B.C.E., all of the other major world cultures are "subjected to the dominion of others."[21] The cultures spawned by this Indo-European expansion all share, with local variations, a certain world view, one to which Dussel ascribes the following traits: an anthropological dualism, an ahistoricism, and a panontic Totality ("the divine is what is eternal and unique, and that is being: the Totality"):

> Paradoxically, then, the anthropological dualism becomes a monistic tension in ontology.[22]

The third stage, the Semitic, while originating in the Arab desert rather than in the northern steppes, is to a great extent chronologically simultaneous with the Indo-European stage. Culturally, however, it differs markedly from the Indo-European and, thus, must be distinguished. Dussel contends that, in contrast to those of Indo-European cultures, the common traits of Semitic cultures are: a unitary anthropology and intersubjective bipolarity; an ethos of liberty, or liberation (the origins of evil are found not in the body, or in materiality, but in free will); an identification of perfection with "commitment" (intersubjectivity replaces solitary contemplation as the locus of salvation); an historical consciousness.[23]

A highpoint of the Semitic stage is marked by the emergence of Christianity, whose history can itself be divided into three stages: the Palestine apostolic community; the Mediterranean expansion (resulting in the Hellenization—Byzantium—and Latinization—Rome—of Semitic Christianity); and universal expansion. Despite the vestiges of the Mediterranean expansion, evident mostly in Europe and North America, Christianity as a whole now finds itself in the midst of this last, post-Vatican II stage. Unlike the Mediterranean expansion, which witnessed the absorption of Semitic Christianity into Greek and Latin culture, the universal expansion phase now underway attempts a genuine openness to other cultures. Like the Christian martyrs of the early Mediterranean expansion period, who dared to raise their voices against the worship of false gods, the Third World Churches are today taking prophetic stands against the idolatry of money, political systems, cultures, etc. The stages in the history of Christianity, therefore, are not clear-cut and decisive, but represent the sometimes tentative outcome of monumental clashes between world views and horizons of comprehension, as a result of which clashes the contending world views are transformed.[24]

A History of Latin American Christianity

If the stages of universal history represent a Latin American pre-, or proto-history, Latin American history as such does not begin, Dussel maintains, until 1492, with the meeting of East (Dussel includes American Indians among those cultures exhibiting an oriental world view) and West on Latin American soil. The result of this clash is a culture which is "neither Amerindia nor Europe, but is something distinct."[25]

This new, "distinct" geographical and cultural reality soon becomes a victim, however, of an increasing global monopolization of power:

> Byzantium was a world and an *ecumene;* Russia (the third Rome), Europe, the Arab world, the Hindus and the Chinese were five coexistent ecumenes. On their parts, the Aztecs and Incas were likewise ecumenes. . . . Each one considered itself the sole ecumene and affirmed that outside the horizon lived the infidels and barbarians. But in the 16th century one ecumene will conquer the rest and the first to be oppressed is America. . . . From the 16th to the

> 20th century there is suddenly a new global structure: the seven ecumenes are reduced to *only one* and the "center" of this ecumene is Europe, later Russia and the United States (to which we could add Japan, Canada and Australia).[26]

A global center and periphery thus already becomes established at this early time, as the other six ecumenes are stripped of their autonomy by expansionist Europe. Within the peripheral ecumenes Latin America is destined to exercise a unique role (by the 20th century) as the only *Christian* culture in the periphery. As such, it initiates a new age of *Christian* history:

> Latin America comes to be situated as the *sole* dependent Christian global entity, since *Christianity* became constituted among us, but it was the only *colonial* Christianity (as neither the Byzantine nor the Latin were).[27]

In Dussel's eyes, therefore, Latin America occupies a unique place both in world history, inasmuch as Latin America is formed from the clash between East (the third cultural stage of universal history) and West (the second stage), and, more specifically, in the history of Christianity, inasmuch as Latin American Christianity represents a new kind of Christianity, i.e., colonial, or dependent Christianity. These two components of Latin American uniqueness are, however, inextricably intertwined since the Western powers which subjugated Latin America and, in the beginning, established themselves at the center were precisely *Latin* and *Christian* Spain and Portugal. Consequently, the peripheralization of Latin America is, in general, concomitant with its peripheralization *within Christianity*, first at the hands of the Spanish and Portuguese, then at the hands of the British and North Americans—all Christian nations.

Dussel divides the development of dependent Christianity in Latin America into major periods, which he denominates "the Christendom of the West Indies (1492–1808)" and "the Agony of Colonial Christendom (1808–1962)," with a third era (1962–present) being characterized by the growing struggle for Latin American liberation. While chronologically sequential, these periods comprise a cultural dialectic. In each period, Latin American Christianity is, even in the midst of foreign domination, becoming increasingly conscious of its dependency—first, in the wake of national independence, and then in the wake of Vatican II—yet each succeeding historical era continues to bear the imprints of its past, though now in new, hybrid forms. So, while the Church in the independent nation-states of the second period had liberated itself from the direct tutelage of the Spanish state, the attendant pluralization of society necessitated the development of new *Christian* institutions which would help recover the Church's old social effectiveness in the context of a new, secular society where the Church could no longer depend on state patronage. Likewise, the *popular* liberation essayed in the third period—and prefigured in the Mexican Revolution of 1910—seeks to form institutions which will both incorporate national independence goals and go beyond these to include anti-oligarchical goals in a new, more comprehensive movement of liberation.[28]

As the supersession of both colonial theology and the neo-colonial theology of independence, liberation theology, then, represents an attempt to articulate a theology which will be both genuinely Latin American and genuinely liberative. It will seek autonomy from its dependent predecessor theologies and will both symbolize, on the theoretical level, Latin American Christianity's post-Vatican II struggle for ecclesial identity and give theological voice to that struggle. As bearer of its past, however, liberation theology, like Latin American culture in general, cannot simply reject that past, but must transform it by continuing the dialectical retrieval of the liberative elements of its past. So, for instance, just as the present-day liberation movement cannot afford to overlook the necessity of national liberation, a necessity first realized—though admittedly only in partial form—in the transition from colonial to neo-colonial Christianity, neither can liberation theology afford to overlook its own theological roots in the prophetic theology of the Conquest (e.g., the theology of Bartolomé de las Casas).[29] Figures like las Casas and Tupac Amaru, who took inspiration from the Catholic religion in his struggle to liberate the Amerindians, are incarnations of the theme of liberation in Latin American history.[30] Only after a reappropriation of that history as an *a priori* will liberation theology be able to advance an *ana*dialectic of liberation, i.e., one that truly expresses Latin America's "otherness."

The Anadialectical Method

Having grounded his project in the present-day experience of Latin America, from which perspective he essays a reinterpretation and retrieval of Latin American pre-history and history in their dialectical relation to the present, Dussel now proceeds to develop a hermeneutical framework for understanding that project. This framework is what he calls the anadialectical method, which, in turn, is premised upon an anadialectical metaphysics-ethics (the meaning of these terms as Dussel uses them will become clearer in the course of our discussion). The anadialectical method, as well as its Latin American metaphysics-ethics, is not, therefore, "abstract" in a conceptualist sense, but, on the contrary, is "abstract" only insofar as it "abstracts" from a very concrete, lived history. As such, it represents both a dialectical retrieval of the Western dialectical tradition and an authentically "new" ontology which, because grounded in Latin American historical praxis, goes beyond the old ontology of the European Totality to express and articulate a Latin American metaphysics of the Other.

The Totality

The first key category in Dussel's anadialectical method is "the Totality." According to Dussel, objects always confront us, not as isolated atoms, but as differentiated *parts,* or *moments,* of an interconnected Whole which orders them and in relation to which they derive meaning. There exist, therefore, two levels of meaning: 1) the ontic level (that of the individual entities), and 2) the ontological level (that of the ordered Whole, the ultimate horizon of meaning, or world view, against which the entities are interpreted). The individual entities, then, are defined *deductively,* in their relation to the Whole, or the "Totality," and in the context of their assigned role, or position, within that all-embracing Totality. Without the *a priori* Totality it is impossible to attach meaning to any object. This Totality, the ultimate horizon of meaning, is always moving and expanding as our world of meaning expands. It is this fact that distinguishes us from mere animals, whose ultimate horizon is fixed biologically.

The term "Totality," then, is not, in itself, a static notion for Dussel, but represents the whole of the dialectical relationship (between the two levels of meaning) as understood within the Western tradition. Dussel contends that that relationship has an inherent tendency to become closed to novelty precisely inasmuch as each moment of the dialectic is defined in relation to the others and to the dialectical relationship as a whole. If what is considered reality, or being, is thus limited to the scope of the totality of the dialectical relationship, the possibility of existence beyond (*ana-*) that "Totality" is excluded. The dialectic then sets itself up as a Totality in that it excludes the unforeseen, the unexpected from its own logically-deduced boundaries. (If even the negation of the negation is defined by its role within the Totality, then there is no possibility of an irruption from the outside, from mystery.) Consequently, the only possibilities within the dialectic are those foreseeable within the dominant Totality, or ontological horizon—in this case, Europe and North America. The Hegelian identification of being and thinking is, conversely, an identification of non-being and the unthinkable. Meaning is ascribed to individual entities only in reference to the dialectical Totality, only as they relate to the system as a whole: what has no meaning for me within my world of meaning is, in fact, meaning*less*. Entities are simply the differentiation, or mediation, of the totality and, as such, are dependent on the Totality. The Totality is complete, and the individual entities within the Totality either succumb to its logic or are destroyed as unreal and meaningless.[31]

What this implies in temporal terms is that there is no truly unforeseeable future, since the future is simply the playing out of what is already given in the present, simply the realization of what already exists "in potency." The closed, European dialectic's emphasis on the future masks, therefore, a reification of the present as the Totality in which the future already resides, even if only in potency.[32]

Consequently, Dussel begins his project, not with the future, but with the past, advancing its dialectical retrieval from the perspective of the present. Through such a retrieval, he explains, Latin America experiences itself as dependent upon and exterior to the European Totality. On the other hand, such a retrieval grounds a Latin American liberation in a new ontological horizon of comprehension, but now one which is pre-conceptual inasmuch as it extends beyond the totalizing identification of being and thinking (consciousness-praxis always exceeds the grasp of the Concept). The possibility of an exteriority thus becomes thinkable; hence, a Latin American liberation ontology becomes thinkable—but only because its thinkability is already premised upon a prior pre-conceptual apprehension of the ultimate horizon as always beyond the limits of my Totality, i.e., beyond the limits of my conceptual grasp.[33]

The Other

Counterposed to the Totality, and the category which, in Dussel's own estimation, is the key to a Latin American liberative methodology, is "the Other." This category makes possible the rethinking of the Totality, this time from outside its boundaries. Also, it is this category which, building on the work of Levinas, represents the major breakthrough of the anadialectical method as properly Latin American. This breakthrough records, articulates, and gives impetus to the "new historical reality" which is Latin America.[34]

Among the many entities which comprise our everyday world there is one that stands out as unique: the human person. When we lead a vulgar existence, inattentive to an everyday world which presents itself to us as a given, as "reality," and thus as a reified status quo, that unique entity, the human person, confronts us as not unique at all, but as simply one more "thing" among others within this "reality," or Totality:

> The taxi driver appears as a mechanical extension of the car; the housewife as one more instance of cleanliness and the culinary art; the teacher as an ornament of the school; the soldier as a member of the army . . . It would seem that it is difficult to extract another person from the system into which he or she finds him or herself inserted. The person is then an entity, a part of systems.[35]

There are times, however, when the human person, otherwise seen as merely a part of the system, presents him or herself to us as an exteriority, as a free subject who "resists instrumental totalization," as not some*thing*, but some*one:*

> Such as when, all of a sudden, the taxi driver turns out to be a friend and tells us, catching us unawares: "How are you?" The unexpected question arising out of a horizon of entities makes an impact: someone appears in the world! Much more so when we are told: "Help me please!," or "I am hungry; give me food!"[36]

What we affirm at such moments, and what Latin America affirms at the moment when it recognizes itself as dependent and seeks in-dependence, is that "reality also exists beyond being" (if being is identified with the Totality-as-horizon of comprehension).[37] This ontological shift is accompanied, furthermore, by an epistemological shift as the logic of the Totality is inverted, with the starting point now located in the *exterior:*

> The logic of the Totality establishes its discourse from identity, or the fundament, towards differentiation. . . . It is the

> logic of the alienation of exteriority or the objectification of otherness, of the other human person. The logic of exteriority or of otherness, on the other hand, establishes its discourse from the abyss of the Other's freedom.[38]

The dialectic as such is not rejected, but exteriority now becomes the locus of the judgment of the Totality (rather than vice-versa) as the Other affirms his or her rights, undetermined by the Totality, which rights are *absolute* since they are grounded in the human person's very personhood, that is, in his or her "proper exteriority, in the real constitution of his or her human dignity."[39] While the dialectical critique of the everyday within the ontological horizon of meaning is necessary in order to move beyond the "vulgar" everyday, that dialectic must be sublated in an *ana*lectic which recognizes the *exteriority* of that unique entity, the person, to any dialectical Totality. The person reveals him or herself as a free subject whose history is irreducible to the history of the Totality. The person resists comprehension within my horizon of meaning, within my Totality. He or she speaks to me from *outside* my Totality, from *outside* my horizon of comprehension. As "exterior" to my ontological horizon, the person is thus always "the Other." The Other is not given meaning by *my* Totality, but must reveal his or her meaning *to* my totality, from *outside* that Totality. Beyond the *ontological* horizon of the Totality is the *trans*-ontological, or *meta*-physical (beyond *physis;* beyond my "world") Other.[40]

The revelation of the Other in his or her dignity as a human person is, moreover, always at the same time a revelation of Other*s*, of an oppressed *group*. To limit the face-to-face encounter between the Totality and the Other to the exclusivity of an encounter between two individuals is to "forget that the personal mystery always plays itself out in the exteriority of popular history."[41] The Other always bears on his or her shoulders the history of a people:

> Every countenance, unique, unfathomable mystery of decisions not yet made, is the countenance of a sex, a generation, a social class, a nation, a cultural group, an age of history.[42]

Openness to the oppressed groups' revelation in their human dignity involves an act of both faith and liberation. As the "speculative human capacity by which one sees or discovers what the entities are and of what the world, the system or Totality, consists," reason can only comprehend *that* system, even if the Totality is understood as an ontological horizon, and its multiple differentiations.[43] This is so because reason, as understood within the Totality, is simply the "reason" of the Totality, beyond which there exists only "irrationality." The irruption of the Other into the system, however, reveals the irrationality of this "reason," which is incapable of acknowledging the existence of the Other. Consequently, Dussel maintains, the basis of our acceptance—from the Totality—of the Other's self-revelation cannot be the "reason" of the Totality, but *faith:*

> To accept the word of the Other because the Other reveals it, for no other reason than because he or she pronounces it, is faith. What is revealed to me has no other criterion of certainty than the very reality of the Other as Other. What he or she reveals to me is accepted neither for the evidence of its contents nor for its certitude. It is accepted because behind the Other's word one finds the very reality of someone, immediately, open and exposed in a metaphysical openness in relation to which the ontological openness to the world is a distant imitation.[44]

"Reason," as comprehending only what is embraced by the ontological horizon of my being, cannot account for the real existence of someone beyond *(meta-)* the limits *(-physis)* of being; only a metaphysics of the Other can do that. Reason cannot "explain" the Other; only the Other can reveal him or herself to us.[45]

More than an act of faith, the metaphysical openness to the revelation of the Other is also, in itself, an act of liberation. The Other is accepted as *free*, not in the sense of the Totality's "freedom" to choose between different mediations of the same system, but insofar as the Other is undetermined by my world and is the center of his or her world. As such, the Other is free to think the unthinkable and speak the unspeakable. Metaphysical exteriority alone makes possible human freedom, since, as merely a part of a Totality, or a system, the human being cannot be a "person" but remains a functional cog in the totalized machine. Only in his or her otherness is the human individual free to be a human *person*.[46]

The Five Moments of the Anadialectical Method

The anadialectical method is, essentially, a hermeneutical framework for interpreting the encounter between the Totality and the Other, and the implications of this encounter. It incorporates dialectics, but, in order to ensure the openness of the dialectic to the Other outside the Totality of the dialectical relationship, sublates the dialectic within an analectic, thus extending the dialogical movement beyond the systemic boundaries of the dialectical relationship itself. The anadialectical method, as described by Dussel, contains five moments: 1) an origin in the everyday, 2) the ontological demonstration of the entities, 3) the analectic as such, 4) the ethical self-revelation of the Other, and 5) service in justice.[47]

Origin in the Everyday

The anadialectical method, as we have seen, grounds itself in concrete experience, in the everyday. The historical *a priori* comprises the first moment of the anadialectical method. Yet, already within this first moment, there must be a distanciation, through critical judgment, from the everyday, more precisely, from acritical everyday existence. Otherwise, the Totality's everyday will continue to reign undisturbed as the unquestioned status quo and there will be no possibility of openness either to the ontological horizon of comprehension (a particular people's, or age's, horizon of meaning) or to the metaphysical Other. Critical distanciation is needed in order to discover the distortions promulgated by the "reason" of the Totality.

Consequently, this first moment already involves a dialectical critique of the everyday-as-given and, hence, a movement towards the ontological horizon. This distanciation from the everyday represents an existential crisis in which one "dies to the obvious and ingenuous manner of living in the world." So, for example, Latin America experiences that crisis when, through the appropriation of the dialectical progress of liberation in her history, she experiences herself no longer as simply a dependent (because merely a differentiated mediation of the Totality) appendage in the Totality's everyday, but as separate from that everyday and, because the center of her own world, grounded in her distinct everyday.[48]

The Ontological Demonstration of the Entities

Having begun with the everyday, which we first experience existentially as "everyday existence," as "common sense," and having initiated a dialectical critique and movement away from that everyday understanding of reality, we move, through intermediate horizons, towards the ontological horizon, from which the entities presenting themselves to us in the everyday can be systematically interpreted in relation to one another and to the ontological horizon of meaning. This moment is expressly philosophical in that it involves an ontological interpretation of the everyday, that is, a critical explicitation—by placing the everyday against the backdrop of the horizon of meaning—of what was first accepted and interpreted acritically, as the status quo.[49]

The Analectic as Such

If we fail to move beyond the second moment, we remain trapped within the Totality of the dialectical relationship between the ontological horizon and the entities. Among the ontic entities interpreted from the ontological horizon of meaning, however, there is one which escapes such interpretation: the human person. While the movement from horizon to horizon until reaching the ontological horizon is dialectical, the passage beyond that horizon to the mystery of the Other who cannot be comprehended within that horizon is properly *ana*lectical. This passage contains a negative moment insofar as "one thinks of the impossibility of thinking of the Other positively from the same Totality," and a positive moment insofar as "one thinks of the possibility of interpreting the revelation of the Other from the Other's perspective."[50]

In this third moment of the anadialectical method, then, the ontology of being is sublated within a metaphysics of exteriority. What ontology is to the dialectic, metaphysics (in Dussel's sense) is to the analectic:

> I will call the meta-physical method "ana-lectic," which is different from the "dia-lectical" method. This latter goes from one horizon to another until reaching the first [i.e., the ontological], where its thinking is clarified; the dia-lectic is a "through which." On the other hand, ana-lectic implies that the *logos* "comes from beyond . . ."[51]

Unlike the strictly dialectical process, which is dependent upon my initiative alone, the *ana*dialectical process is dependent, first, on the initiative of the other, for I can only advance towards the Other "to the extent that the Other receives me, or pleads for my aid." As such, the anadialectical method is metaphysical, since it locates the source of the crisis which disrupts my everyday existence outside my horizon of comprehension, outside my *physis*. The everyday, which was ontologically interpreted in the second moment, is now metaphysically interpreted, from "outside" the Totality.[52]

The Ethical Self-Revelation of the Other

The metaphysical revelation of the Other is, according to Dussel, "already a fourth moment, because the primary negativity of the Other has placed into question the ontological level, which is now created from a new ambit."[53] It is here that the anadialectical method is revealed as *intrinsically* ethical in that, since the primacy of the ontological is called into question by the trans-ontological, or metaphysical reality of the Other, one discovers oneself as *not* bound by one's horizon of meaning, but as open to other horizons of meaning, whose loci are outside oneself as subject, outside one's world; that is, one discovers that empathy *is* possible. This openness to the other already reflects an ethical option and commitment, a negation of one's world as a Totality:

> In this case, the philosopher, before being an intelligent person, is an ethically just person; a good person; a disciple [of the Other].[54]

The theoretical material of the philosopher is thus grounded in a fundamental ethical option, a commitment to the Other. Since by its very nature, then, philosophy (or any other "academic discipline") is ethical, it must be entered into in the midst of, not apart from, historical praxis:

> The conversion to ontological thinking is a death to the everyday. The conversion to meta-physical thinking is a death to the Totality. The ontological conversion is an ascent to an aristocratic way of thinking. . . . The conversion to analectical or meta-physical thinking is an exposure to a popular way of thinking . . . that of the oppressed.[55]

What is more, as fundamentally ethical the anadialectical method differs significantly, argues Dussel, from the Western dialectical tradition. For both the Greeks and the moderns the ontological (as opposed to metaphysical) foundation of the dialectic is intrinsically *non*-ethical, since that foundation is "natural," or, in other words, simply "is." Without an Other with whom we can enter into a relationship there can be no ethics; therefore, "if there is only the Totality, the ultimate horizon of the Totality is not ethical or moral, but is 'as it is.'" The only possible morality within the Totality is that of carrying out, at the ontic or intramundane level, what is already posited at the ontological level (i.e., the only choices are those between the alternatives provided for within the system). A certain sense of tragedy, or even fatalism, thus pervades both the Hellenistic and the modern ontologies.[56]

In locating good and evil at the metaphysical rather than at the ontological level, the anadialectical method, on the other hand, affirms the radical nature of human freedom: our horizon of comprehension is not an ontologically-given limitation of our freedom to a choosing between "possibilities-of-being," but is established by a prior, metaphysical, and ethical option for either closure or openness. The oppression of the Other, whom the Totality considers a mere mediation of itself, can no longer be deemed "ontologically justified" as an ontic necessity in the face of the one ontological Totality which unifies all (even those who refuse), but must be seen for what it is, namely, the most radical, fundamental sin:

> The a-version to the Other is the trans-ontological or metaphysical evil which constitutes the ethicity of the ontological itself.[57]

The primary evil is the objectification of the Other *(el otro)* by denying his or her exteriority and making him or her into simply one more thing *(lo otro)* within my world.[58]

Service in Justice

The metaphysical revelation of the Other as Other and the ethical commitment which this revelation suggests make possible the fifth and final moment of the anadialectical method: analectical *praxis*, or "service in justice." Human *perfectio* does not consist, therefore, in a realization of *my* "potential-being," but in "a love that first loves the Other: love-in-justice." The one who embodies such love is the *prophet*, who then constitutes him or herself as an Other vis-a-vis the Totality, and who will, therefore, inevitably be attacked by the Totality as he or she becomes the voice of the voiceless in the courts of the system (though not by a simple reiteration of the Other's words, but by a critically-reflected-upon articulation).[59]

The emergence of the prophet, as the one who loves and serves the Other in justice, marks the concomitant emergence of the anadialectical method as a *pedagogy* of liberation. This pedagogy is premised, first, on the *analogous* nature of the Other. Communication between being-as-beyond-the-Totality and being-as-the-fundament-of-the-Totality is possible because these are not absolutely different, but rather analogous terms. The Other is neither absolutely other nor the same: he or she is *similar*. This similarity precludes either absolute separation and the impossibility of communication or complete comprehension. As implying distinction, it precludes complete comprehension and thus, the closure of the Totality, but as implying analogy it is the condition of the possibility of service through "con*fide*nce, faith, in the Other: 'because he or she says so.'"[60]

In this anadialectical pedagogy, the prophet, before being teacher, is a disciple of the Other: the future teacher must begin by being disciple to the future disciple! Before giving articulation to the voice of the Other in the face of the Totality, the prophet must listen to and serve the Other. This pedagogical process involving listening, service, and through the accession to the Other attained by means of service, interpretation of the Other's word, is always ongoing. The interpretation, though adequate to the degree that the prophet is committed to serve the Other, thus arriving at a greater *degree* of identity with the Other, is never complete.[61]

From Domination to Liberation: Toward a New Sexual, Pedagogical, and Political Totality

The trans-ontological process of liberation is not anarchic, in the sense that it is not simply a rejection of the system, with no concomitant affirmation, but is the reconstitution of a Totality *outside* the closed, dominant Totality. This new Totality, reconstituted *from the Other,* is not, however, a closed Totality; it is what Dussel calls an analogical, or analectical Totality.[62]

The newly constructed trans-ontological order is, first, a Totality in that it is characterized by its own ethos, or horizon of comprehension, and is itself a locus of being, of *esse* (though not *esse* as understood within the dominant Totality). However, it is also an *open* Totality in that it remains open to the Other, to the new. Consequently, as an open Totality it is an analogical Totality vis-a-vis the closed, dominant Totality.[63]

Thus far, "the Other" and "the new Totality" are terms fairly devoid of content. In the following paragraphs we will see how Dussel concretizes these categorizes within the context of what he considers the three paradigmatic human relationships: 1) the sexual, or erotic, 2) the pedagogical, and 3) the political. The first relationship, between male and female, involves the greatest initial distinction and yet is capable of embodying a unity that "resembles 'the Same.'"[64] The second form of human encounter, the parent-child, or teacher-student relationship, is a cultural extension of the domestic, matrimonial relationship. The third form is the brother-brother, or sister-sister relationship. The extension from one form to another is dialectical. The most intimate of human relationships thus reaches dialectically to the national, regional and international levels.[65] In all the forms of human encounter there exist the

> possibilities of the relation of *service* between two free persons, of *pedagogy* between the elder and the younger, of *domination* between the oppressor and oppressed.[66]

Domination and liberation thus play themselves out in these central human relationships.

Sexual Domination and Liberation

Both the cosmology of the Greeks and the egophanic subjectivism of the moderns function, opines Dussel, to oppress the woman within the dominant male Totality. For the Greeks, "homosexual [here, *male* homosexual] *eros* is valued (*eros* of "the same" for "the Same") and heterosexual *eros* is accepted only as an instrumental mediation for the generation of the son." Through such generation, "the Same" is preserved from mortality. Eros is thus simply a stopgap measure meant to remedy an originary fall—a fall "from the a-sexual soul into a sexual body." The logic of the Greek cosmological Totality yields, therefore, an ineluctable conclusion: "if being is 'the Same,' the supreme *eros* is consummated between those who are 'the same' (males)."[67]

A similar logic results in the objectification of the woman in modernity. The male Totality cannot but treat the woman, Other by nature, as simply its tool, as one more "object of the man and person at his disposition, a domestic instrument of the male."[68] The history of women in modernity is a history of progressive forms of oppression, in which the woman is seen as merely a mediation of the male horizon of comprehension:

> The woman, as Sombart has shown, enters into modern society in the 16th century, first as lover of the princes or grand bourgeoisie; later, as the rich woman of the noble, impoverished man; lastly, as the bourgeois woman of the common bourgeois man. The whole culture of comfort is based on the home and in it the woman has dependent dominion (oppressed, oppressor of the child). Nevertheless, the male-female relation continues to be one of the *domin-*

> *ion* of the male (who is simply "man") and the *alienation* of the female.[69]

Domestic domination is, therefore, one manifestation of the logic of the closed Totality.

The objectification of the woman in modernity results in the same love of self, albeit in a more roundabout way, characteristic of the Greek Totality. Man's objectification of the woman, besides oppressing the woman, fosters a narcissistic kind of male impotence since it prevents the possibility of sexual relations with some*one*, thus resulting in "a solipsistic masturbation with an object that fulfills his auto-eroticism." This autoeroticism symbolizes the death of eros and, as an assassination of the woman-Other, is uxoricide.[70]

For Dussel, Sigmund Freud's thought represents a clear articulation of this alienation of the woman in the European Totality. Freud sees sexuality as masculine by nature, with penile *activity* being counterposed by vaginal *passivity*. As Dussel points out, therefore, the female is, in Freud's thought, a sexual object for the male subject (hence "penis envy"):

> "Being is, non-being is not," in the erotic ontology should be expressed: "The phallus is, castration is not."[71]

The encounter with the woman-object will, furthermore, necessarily be incestuous, since, because non-being knows no differentiation, such an encounter takes place, indifferently, with both wife and mother ("the woman is, without difference, mother-wife.")[72]

In the analectic of eros, on the other hand, the woman is respected as the Other. The primarily *visual*, hence reductionist, "eroticism" of the phallocratic Totality is replaced by the primarily *tactile*, hence corporeal, existential, and other-directed eroticism of the new sexual order.[73] In this latter, new sexual order, the sexual encounter is truly metaphysical. It is the realization, through the erotic desire, of a reality beyond my world. The sexual organs, as symbols, are then not related as dominant to dominated, but as mutually-implicit significations of the absence of the Other. They are biological reminders of the existence of the Other.[74]

Respect for woman as the Other, i.e., as a human person, must extend, however, to all the forms of human encounter. Wherever one finds oppression, there one will find women who are *doubly* oppressed—as Amerindians, poor, etc. *and* as women:

> The common woman, the woman of the peripheral culture, suffers in this way a double attack, a double violation: vio-

> lated as an oppressed culture and nation, as a member of a dominated class, as a woman.[75]

Sexual domination is present at all levels of domination as an added instrument of oppression. The liberation of women, not as a simple negation of sexual diversity (which negation would be nothing more than a return to the Totality of the Same), but as an affirmation of sexual otherness-through-distinction, is thus a prerequisite to a genuine, comprehensive liberation.[76] The poor woman needs to experience liberation not only *qua* poor, but also *qua* woman.

Pedagogical Domination and Liberation

The new Totality that is "the couple" remains ambiguous, however, in that it can either revert to closing in upon itself, becoming totalized by refusing to open itself to the Other, now in the form of "the child," or it can remain open to the mystery of new life through the procreation and education of an Other. In the open Totality, the child is born as truly Other, distinct from his or her parents; not, like the Platonic child, as one who is "the Same" as the parents.[77]

This new human person, from the time spent in the mother's womb to the time of death, will undergo an educational process. Unlike the closed Totality, where oppression of the child-Other takes either the form of abortion or of cultural repression, the open Totality undertakes a pedagogical analectic in which, as noted previously, the "teacher" becomes a disciple of the Other, in this case, of the child.[78] In the ontology of the closed Totality, "education" takes place through a process of "depositing" received knowledge into the receptacle which is the child's mind (note the similarities between sexual and pedagogical objectification). The child then "remembers," or memorizes what, though "forgotten," is already given, be that remembrance in the Platonic sense, the Heideggerian sense of *Wiederholung*, the Hegelian sense of *Erinnerung*, or the Rousseauian sense of "bringing to light what is already given in *le bon sauvage*."[79] In the new pedagogical analectic the child's otherness demands respect from the parents, who must then be open to the word of the child. The parents learn as well as teach. Parents and teachers give the child only the "form," in the sense that "they do not give *being* to the Other, but rather the ability to think about what already is."[80] Being is not given the child by the parents but is revealed to the parents by the child. Only the child can say what he or she is. The role of the parent and educator, as the "creative nothing," is to encourage this self-revelation, that is, to encourage creativity and novelty.[81] In fact, the educator's own creativity, hence historical progress, is only possible through this analectic, in which teacher learns from student and student from teacher. The teacher, however, does not "deposit" knowledge, but transmits knowledge *from the existential position of the student* ("the teacher should teach in a critical manner . . .; he or she does not transmit the traditional as traditional, but rather . . . revives the conditions that made it possible as *new*, as unique, as creation"), so that the teacher's creativity becomes progressively identified with the student's creative self-revelation.[82] Such a pedagogical analectic would thus tend to unify parents and children, teachers and students, in a collaborative effort rather than separate them as subject from object: "No disciple is only a disciple; no teacher is only a teacher."[83]

This analectic is a necessary prerequisite for the cultural liberation of the Latin American people, not only inasmuch as Europe and North America need to respect the particular historical project of Latin America (by desisting from playing the role of dominative "father" to Latin America's "child," or *bon sauvage*) and the Latin American people need to affirm the particular values of their culture, or their history, against the cultural imperialism that equates "civilization" with "Europeanization" (or "North Americanization"), but also inasmuch as those Latin Americans who assume the roles of teachers need to do so as "organic intellectuals" in the Gramscian sense.[84] In other words, the intellectual should enter into the pedagogical analectic with the people, thereby increasingly becoming identified with their historical project. Through such participation, moreover, the organic intellectual will not only identify with the Other in the people but will, in the process of articulating their concerns, place him or herself in a "critical position." The intellectual's critique will be directed at the Totality, but, as such, will also impact popular culture insofar as that culture has accepted its role as "*mass* culture" within the dominant Totality. (As "the multitude"—*ochlos, rabim*—or that inorganic segment of the Totality lacking its own history, the poor are not constituted as "a people" to the extent that they continue to internalize the values of the Totality.) Liberation must be initiated by the people, but needs the critique proffered by the organic intellectual in his or her systematization of the popular project:

> The people alone cannot liberate themselves. The system has imbued them with mass culture, or what is worst in the

> system. Therefore the critical consciousness of the organic intellectual, of the critical groups, of the critical communities or parties, is indispensable in order for a people to acquire such a critical consciousness and discern what is worst in them (the vulgarized imperialist culture . . .), and what already is best from of old (the cultural exteriority . . .).[85]

The necessary critical consciousness is possible, however, only if the intellectual exercises it *among* the people; otherwise, "all education will be elitist, dominant."[86] The analectical task of the intellectual is, in short, one of affirming the exteriority, i.e., the authenticity, of the popular culture while attacking, through antiideological critique, the absorbed deceitful values of the system, thereby aiding in a "construction of the cultural exteriority."[87]

Political Domination and Liberation

Like the sexual relationship, the pedagogical relationship can become closed. This happens when the teacher and the student isolate themselves from the voice of the oppressed by closing their own Totality to that voice, or when a family becomes its own Totality, with the house taking on the role of a fortress. On the other hand, the pedagogical analectic can open up to a political analectic. In this case, the family would leave its home, not to dominate others, but to serve them. This political analectic would extend, moreover, to all levels of society, including the international, lest a people become closed to their brothers and sisters in other lands in the name of nationalism.[88]

The political (which, as Dussel uses the term, includes economic)[89] analectic always plays itself out in the context of historical institutions, and, beyond those institutions, the people:

> Beyond the functionally structured political Totality . . . one finds the people. . . . We define "the people" as those oppressed by a political Totality, but who yet retain cultural exteriority: the political peripheral Other.[90]

The people form a dysfunctional part of the political Totality in that they are alienated by a system "which prevents them from satisfying the needs that the system itself produces in them." Yet they retain a political and cultural exteriority insofar as they maintain "a distinct way of living, manipulating, understanding, interpreting the technological instruments, the mediations." This distinctiveness comprises the "social formations of the periphery,"[91]

The *deepest* roots of this exteriority are not found in the nation as such, but in its oppressed classes. National liberation will be authentic, not when it issues from a vague, "classless" populism, but when it is rooted in the exteriority of a nation's oppressed classes, defined primarily as the rural and urban working poor. Since these retain the highest degree of exteriority vis-a-vis the dominant Totality, "they alone can present a real and new alternative for future humankind. . . ."[92]

The political analectic, therefore, sublates two dialectics: that between political and economic domination (insofar as these reinforce each other), and that between national and international domination. The first reveals the comprehensiveness of imperialist domination; the second the internationalization of the dominant classes through control of local elites and the concomitant enmiseration of peripheral oppressed classes vis-a-vis the working classes of the metropoli. In both cases, the system functions to establish a global division of labor favoring the extraction of profits from the periphery and their absorption by the metropoli—which system is replicated at the national and regional levels. Political economic liberation, therefore, should attack all these interrelated forms of domination.

A Comprehensive Anadialectical Liberation

A metaphysical liberation must, then, be affirmative of the Other *in his or her different concrete manifestations:* woman, wife, mother, child, student, dependent nation, oppressed class. However, while tactical flexibility should be maintained, so that, at different historical junctures, one particular manifestation may be emphasized over others, the strategic objective is the liberation of the oppressed classes, for their economic domination grounds the other forms of domination:

> As economic alienation is the source of all alienation (since it enslaves human beings, forcing them to work upon nature for the master; emptying their very being), economic liberation is the concrete realization of human liberation.[93]

It is because economics is the poietic mediation—*qua* "production"—of erotic, pedagogic, and political praxis, thus concretizing those relationships, that economic liberation is a necessary concomitant of sexual, pedagogical, and political liberation.[94] In other words, unless those "modes of production" through which we make our relationships to one another concrete are altered, the "liberation" of persons in those relationships will remain abstract and unrealized in social structures. (The paradigmatic relationships make the anadialectical method concrete; and economics makes the paradigmatic relationships concrete.)

On the other hand, economic liberation, as indicated above, must be worked out in all its practical contexts. By acknowledging the interdependence of the relationships of domination/liberation, Dussel proposes a liberation which will not sacrifice one form of liberation for another, but will rather, foster a concrete and comprehensive liberation.

That comprehensiveness extends, moreover, to the oppressor. Anadialectical liberation "does not include the death of the oppressors but rather admits their conversion, because in turning to the more authentic self they can become reintegrated without having to disappear."[95] Such a possibility is ontologically precluded within the exclusively *dia*lectical Totality. Dialectical liberation is liberation "from below," where a person "rises" only if another "falls." *Ana*dialectical liberation, on the other hand, aims at a liberation which, because *always* open to the Other beyond one's Totality, is never complete but is, rather, an ongoing *process*.

Theological Implications

The *anthro*pology proposed by the anadialectical method yields an anadialectical *theo*logy as well. For Dussel, theology is defined as

> theoretical thinking that emerges from praxis grounded in existential, supernatural comprehension, that is, in faith. . . . The practical function of theology is the systematization and elucidation of what is already validated in existential, day-to-day faith.[96]

Theology is grounded, then, in faith—but not faith understood "*essentially* [as] a belief or blind trust," but primarily as a "*supernatural* and *existential comprehension*."[97] As such, faith is concrete and practical. It is concretized *in history*, in the relationship with the Other. The *factum* of faith and theology is history. When concrete history is overlooked in theology, as when Europeans overlook Latin American history, a Totalization—in this case, a Europeanization—occurs in which what is but an analogical Totality is taken for an enclosed Totality (as when Latin American theology is studied as "*liberation* theology," i.e., a particular *kind* of theology, but European theology is studied as "Theology" pure and simple).[98]

The theological horizon opened to us in history is non-objectifiable. Because God is revealed to us precisely in and as the Other (pedagogical = Father; political = Son; erotic = Spirit), that revelation can never be fully comprehended by my Totality:

> The Hebrew-Christian understanding of being is not theoretical comprehension; the Greeks thought of being as something permanent or eternal. Rather, being in the biblical sense is the hearing of the word spoken from the mystery of the Other as freedom.[99]

Since, like Moses, we cannot *see* God, we can only discern God's signs in history; for, as human economy is what makes human relationships concrete, so divine economy is what makes God's self-revelation concrete and, therefore, existentially "visible" through the eyes of faith. Faith provides a practical—not scientific or theoretical—hermeneutic for interpreting the signs of the times. God is revealed to us in the revelation of the meaning of history. Faith provides us with "prophetic insight" into that meaning. By means of this insight we are able to discern the Word of the divine Other as it is mediated through the word of the human Other. (Human exteriority is the locus of the revelation of divine exteriority.) The task of evangelization, then, is, on the basis of such a discernment, to help reconstitute the "masses" into a "people" who are free human subjects in history.[100]

Christian faith implies, therefore, an atheism of the Totality, since only a non-believer of the system can be a believer in the Other. Only one who believes in the word of the human Other can genuinely believe in the Word of the divine Other. The ultimate sin for anadialectical Christian theology, then, is the killing of the Other, for, in killing the Other, we kill God's own epiphany. Cain and Adam are both example of this desire to kill the Other in order to become "God," in order to become the Totality. This original sin—the killing of the Other—has become embedded as part of every individual's ontological horizon of comprehension, for every person is born into a world which has for centuries been denying and killing the Other in every conceivable way.[101]

Grounded in the historical praxis of the Other, therefore, a Latin American liberation theology raises its voice against this fratricide. By recovering the meaning of Latin American history and reappropriating its symbols, liberation theology interprets the voice of the oppressed Other (the epiphany of the divine Other) so that, in discovering him or herself as Other, he or she may struggle for liberation.[102] This theology is not a mere "differentiation" of the European/North American theological Totality but is, rather, a distinct, analogically similar theology. Consequently, while liberation theology maintains the "appearance" of theology-as-discipline, it is nevertheless unique, new:

> When the "appearance" becomes univocal, the history of theology can only be European. When the "distinct" in a theology is absolutized, it becomes equivocal. It is not Hegelian identity nor Jasperian equivocity. It is analogy.[103]

Having examined the dialectical method, the dialectics of dependency, the dialectics of Latin American history, and having followed their dialectical evolution into a Latin American anadialectical method, we can thus see how liberation theology appears as the theology of the Other, an anadialectical theology. It is the theology of a God who has become one with the Other in his or her exteriority as woman, child, oppressed class, etc. It is the theology of a Latin America now emerging out of its history of dependence and struggling to retrieve and build upon its history of liberation.

NOTES

/1/ Dussel, *La cristiandad colonial,* p. 92.
/2/ Ibid., p. 100.
/3/ Dussel, *The Church in Latin America,* p. xvi.
/4/ Dussel, *La cristiandad colonial,* pp. 99–100.
/5/ Ibid., p. 100.
/6/ Ibid., pp. 100–01.
/7/ Ibid., p. 101.
/8/ Ibid., p. 102.
/9/ Ibid.
/10/ Ibid., p. 103. See chapter 6 *infra* for an explanation of how this view represents, not a form of reductionism, but on the contrary, a *safeguard against* reductionism.
/11/ Ibid.
/12/ Ibid., p. 15.
/13/ See Dussel, *The Church in Latin America,* p. xvi.
/14/ Ibid., p. xvi.
/15/ Ibid., p. 38.
/16/ Dussel, *La cristiandad colonial,* pp. 32–33; Dussel, *Filosofía ética,* 5:60–75.

/17/ Dussel, *La cristiandad colonial,* pp. 33–37; Dussel, *Filosofía ética,* 3:29–37.
/18/ Dussel, *La cristiandad colonial,* p. 34.
/19/ Ibid.
/20/ Ibid., p. 37.
/21/ Ibid.
/22/ Ibid., p. 39.
/23/ Ibid., pp. 41–43.
/24/ Ibid., pp. 43–46. Dussel, "Crisis de la Iglesia latino-americana y situación del pensador cristiano en Argentina," *Stromata* 26 (1970) 287–309.
/25/ Dussel, *La cristiandad colonial,* p. 94.
/26/ Ibid., pp. 94–95.
/27/ Ibid., p. 95.
/28/ Dussel, *The Church in Latin America,* pp. 73ff., 125ff.
/29/ Dussel, *La cristiandad colonial,* pp. 115ff.; Dussel, "Modern Christianity in Face of the 'Other:" From the 'Rude' Indian to the 'Noble Savage,'" in *The Dignity of the Despised of the Earth,* eds. Jacques Pohier and Dietmar Mieth (New York: Seabury, 1979) pp. 54–56.
/30/ Dussel, "Supuestos histórico-filosóficos," in *La nueva frontera,* ed. Gibellini, p. 175.
/31/ Dussel, *Método,* pp. 259–75; Dussel, *Etica de la liberación,* 1:103–28, 2:22–34; Dussel, "Para una fundamentación dialéctica de la liberación latinoamericana," *Stromata* 28 (1972) 54–57, 60–72. See also chapter 2, *supra;* Dussel, *Filosofía de la liberación,* pp. 41–42, 48, 164–65.
/32/ Dussel, *Filosofía de la liberación,* p. 44. See also chapter 2, *supra;* Dussel, *Etica de la liberación,* 1:52–56.
/33/ Dussel, *Filosofía de la liberación,* pp. 47, 55–56.
/34/ Ibid., pp. 49–50; Dussel, *Etica de la liberación,* 1:97–156, 2:13–64; Dussel, *Método,* pp. 170–97; Dussel, "Fundamentación dialéctica," pp. 54–72.
/35/ Dussel, *Filosofía de la liberación,* p. 50.
/36/ Ibid.
/37/ Ibid., pp. 50–51.
/38/ Ibid., pp. 51–52.
/39/ Ibid., pp. 53, 68–70. See also Dussel, *Método,* pp. 173–74; Dussel, *Etica de la liberación,* 2:39, 53, 59–64, 89, 92–95.
/40/ See chapter 5 *infra* for an explanation of "exteriority" as a *metaphysical* category. Because "exteriority," as "internal transcendence," is *not* a *physical* category, it does not presuppose a dualistic ontology.
/41/ Dussell, *Filosofía de la liberación,* p. 54; see also Dussel, *Método,* p. 182.
/42/ Dussel, *Filosofía de la liberación,* p. 54.
/43/ Ibid., pp. 55–56.
/44/ Ibid., p. 56.
/45/ Ibid., pp. 55–56; Dussel, *Etica de la liberación,* 2:37–38, 52–61, 69–73.
/46/ Dussel, *Filosofía de la liberación,* p. 54; see also Dussel, *Método,* pp. 173–74; Dussel, *Etica de la liberación,* 2:39, 53, 59–64, 89, 92–95.

/47/ Dussel, *Método*, pp. 182–84.
/48/ Ibid., p. 183; Dussel, *Introducción a una filosofía de la liberación latinoamericana* (Mexico: Editorial Extemporáneos, 1977) p. 118.
/49/ Dussel, *Introducción*, pp. 123–24.
/50/ Dussel, *Método*, p. 183. See also Dussel, *Etica de la liberación*, 1:97–103.
/51/ Dussel, *Introducción*, p. 127. As mentioned earlier, Dussel will eventually refer to his method, not as analectical, but more specifically as anadialectical.
/52/ Ibid., pp. 128–29.
/53/ Enrique Dussel, "La religión en el joven Marx (1835–1849)," *Los Universitarios* 205 (Dec., 1982) 25–31.
/54/ Ibid.
/55/ Ibid., p. 184.
/56/ Dussel, *Etica de la liberación*, 2:20. Dussel, *Filosofía de la liberación*, p. 68: "For Heidegger, the ontological foundation of ontic morality is 'culpable being' *(Schuldigsein);* however, in this case the culpability is but a negative moment of the ontological structure of the person as such. The person as 'potential-being' includes its opposite: potential 'non-being. . .' This inclusion of non-being at the ontological level is the 'existential condition of the possibility' of ontic good or evil. But that ontological 'potential-*non-being*' is not moral, is non-ethical. In this sense, it is said that 'existential negativity *(Nichtigkeit)* has in no way the character of a privatio, of a deficiency relative to an exalted ideal not attained in the *Dasein;* rather, the being of this entity *is*, before anything which it may pro-ject and, normally, attains at times, and a pro-ject, *already* negative (*nichtig:* null). This *a priori* negativity is the tragic aspect of the ontology of the Totality, which appears in Heidegger in new clothing." (Dussel, *Etica de la liberación*, 2:20.)
/57/ Dussel, *Etica de la liberación*, 2:25–26.
/58/ Ibid., 2:34, 74–81.
/59/ Ibid., 2:37, 41, 177; Dussel, *Método*, pp. 194–95, 246–51. See also the discussion of pedagogical domination and liberation in this chapter *infra* and the discussion of the pedagogical economy in chapter 4 *infra*.
/60/ Dussel, *Método*, pp. 187–91; Dussel, *Etica de la liberación*, 2:122; Goizueta, p. 124.
/61/ Dussel, *Etica de la liberación*, 2:171; Dussel, *Método*, p. 192; Goizueta, p. 125; Dussel, *Filosofía de la liberación*, pp. 73–74.
/62/ Dussel, *Etica de la liberación*, 2:60–64; Dussel, *Filosofía de la liberación*, pp. 66–75; Dussel, *Introducción*, pp. 50–51.
/63/ Dussel, *Introducción*, p. 50; Dussel, *Etica de la liberación*, 2:60–64; Dussel, *Filosofía de la liberación*, pp. 73–74.
/64/ Dussel, *Etica de la liberación*, 1:128; Dussel, *Filosofía de la liberación*, pp. 91–92.
/65/ Dussel, *Etica de la liberación*, 1:128.
/66/ Ibid.
/67/ Ibid., 1:129; Dussel, *Filosofía de la liberación*, p. 90; Dussel, *Introducción*, pp. 88–89.

/68/ Dussel, *Etica de la liberación*, 1:131; see also Dussel, *Introducción*, pp. 90–91.
/69/ Dussel, *Etica de la liberación*, 1:131.
/70/ Dussel, *Filosofía de la liberación*, pp. 92–93; Dussel, *Filosofía ética*, 3:72.
/71/ Dussel, *Filosofía de la liberación*, p. 92.
/72/ Ibid., p. 93. See chapter 4 for a further elaboration of Freud's significance for the modern male Totality; see also Dussel, *Filosofía ética*, 3:60.
/73/ Dussel, *Filosofía de la liberación*, pp. 90–94.
/74/ Dussel, *Filosofía de la liberación*, pp. 91–93; Dussel, *Filosofía ética*, 3:68–84.
/75/ Dussel, *Filosofía de la liberación*, p. 94. See also Dussel, *Introducción*, p. 90.
/76/ Dussel, *Introducción*, p. 90; Dussel, *Filosofía de la liberación*, p. 95.
/77/ Dussel, *Filosofía de la liberación*, p. 96; Dussel, *Método*, p. 277; Dussel, *Filosofía ética*, 3:123–25; Dussel, *Introducción*, pp. 91–92.
/78/ Dussel, *Filosofía de la liberación*, p. 101; Dussel, *Filosofía ética*, 3:145–56; Dussel, *Introducción*, pp. 93–95.
/79/ Dussel, *Método*, pp. 277–78. See also Dussel, *Etica de la liberación*, 1:139.
/80/ Dussel, *Método*, p. 277; see also Goizueta, p. 128.
/81/ Dussel, *Método*, p. 277; Dussel, *Etica de la liberación*, 1:139; Dussel, *Filosofía ética*, 3:153.
/82/ Dussel, *Etica de la liberación*, 1:141–42.
/83/ Ibid.
/84/ Dussel, *Filosofía de la liberación*, p. 104; Dussel, *Introducción*, pp. 92–95. See also Gramsci, *Selections From Prison Notebooks*, pp. 5–23 for a discussion of "organic intellectuals;" Dussel, *Filosofía ética*, 3:172, 181–82; Dussel, "Modern Christianity in Face of the 'Other' " in Pohier and Mieth, eds., p. 57.
/85/ Dussel, *Filosofía de la liberación*, p. 105.
/86/ Ibid., p. 106.
/87/ Ibid., Dussel distinguishes "popular culture" from the "proletarian culture" which is still "defined within the industrial, capitalist, competitive system." Dussel, *Filosofía ética*, 3:179.
/88/ Dussel, *Método*, pp. 278–79; Goizueta, pp. 128–29; Dussel, *Etica de la liberación*, 1:144–45; Dussel, *Introducción*, pp. 99ff.
/89/ See chapter 4 *infra*.
/90/ Dussel, *Filosofía de la liberación*, p. 79.
/91/ Ibid., pp. 79–80; Dussel, *Filosofía ética*, 4:78–80.
/92/ Dussel, *Filosofía de la liberación*, p. 81; As "proletarian culture" is sublated within "popular culture," so is "class" sublated within "the people." See chapter 1 *supra* for a discussion of the dialectics of dependency.
/93/ Ibid., p. 147.
/94/ Dussel, "Analysis of the Final Document of Puebla: The Relationship Between Economics and Christian Ethics," in *Christian Ethics and Economics: The North-South Conflict*, eds. Dietmar Mieth and Jacques Pohier (New York: Seabury, 1980) pp. 101–9. Dussel draws upon Aristotle to posit

the notion of *poiesis* as the human being-nature relationship of *production* and the notion of *praxis* as the human being-human being relationship, or *interpersonal activity*. See chapter 4 *infra* for a more detailed analysis of Dussel's notion of *economic* liberation.

/95/ Dussel, *Método*, p. 286.

/96/ Dussel, *The Church in Latin America*, p. 16.

/97/ Ibid., p. 13.

/98/ Ibid., p. 18.

/99/ Ibid., p. 13. See also Dussel, "Supuestos histórico-filosóficos," in Gibellini, ed.

/100/ Dussel, *La cristiandad colonial*, pp. 13–17; Dussel, "The Kingdom of God and the Poor," *International Review of Mission* 220 (1979) 127.

/101/ Dussel, *Método*, pp. 271–74; Goizueta, p. 127.

/102/ See Dussel, *Filosofía de la liberación*, p. 137.

/103/ Dussel, *The Church in Latin America*, p. 20.

CHAPTER FOUR

THE LIBERATION OF POIESIS

In the first chapter we analyzed the emergence of dependency theory as both grounded in the dialectics of internal-external *economic* dependence *and* dialectically open to political, cultural, and ideological categories. This relationship between economic and social forms of domination arises from the fact of their inseparability in reality. The separation of the economic from the social results, on the one hand, in the materialistic reductionism of liberal capitalism or "orthodox" (i.e., Engelsian-Leninist-Stalinist) Marxism, and, on the other, in the abstract populism of a Perón. In incorporating dependency theory at the second, i.e., critical, methodological level, therefore, liberation theology is charged with safeguarding both the comprehensiveness of domination as both an economic and non-economic category *and* the specificity of dependency as a macroeconomic category. Further, this exigence must be firmly grounded methodologically so as to avoid the dangers alluded to above.[1]

This Dussel does in his understanding of economics as the poietic mediation of human praxis.[2] The political, pedagogical, sexual and religious analectics remain abstract unless they include the analectical liberation of productive forces, or poiesis; and the liberation of those forces is inconceivable without a concomitant liberation of socio-historical relations, or praxis, to allow the analectical irruption of the Other into the Totality.[3] The relationship between praxis (human being-human being) and poiesis (human being-nature) thus predicates liberation upon the exteriority of the erotic economy, the pedagogical economy, the political economy, and the theological economy. (This last economy arises out of the self-identification of the divine Other with the human Other, as noted in the previous chapter.) Furthermore, as we will see, that relationship grounds the specificity of poiesis in the dialectical retrieval of Latin American (the Other's) historical praxis, thereby providing historical conditions of possibility for the liberation of praxis-poiesis.

The Erotic Economy

If the male-female relationship is one of the utmost proximity in that, while the male and female are physically the most distinct, in the sexual act they effect the most immediate union, that proximity is mediated through the "remoteness," or distanciation, implied in the economic:

> The "economic" (from the Greek *oikia:* house, home) is the human being-nature relation which proposes to construct a totalization within which . . . one would be able to live in the security of the face-to-face.[4]

The mediation of proximity through distanciation is, moreover, universal in that it is intrinsic to all praxis:

> In the end, all economic work, that is to say, all labor which transforms the cosmos, from the natural reality of the elements, all culture (from agri-culture to the satellites) is a protection of proximity through the mediation of the surrounding remoteness.[5]

Hence, the face-to-face encounter with the Other in the proximity of *practical* immediacy is mediated *poietically* inasmuch as the sociohistorical concreteness, thus the real effectiveness, of that encounter depends upon a certain distanciation implicit in the production of the material of the new analectical relationship.[6]

According to Dussel, by failing to develop modes of production supportive of the exteriority of the woman, Latin American historical, erotic praxis (e.g., "*machismo*") has failed to develop an analectic, erotic economy. The colonial "*encomienda*" and "*mita*" are but two examples of the conquistador's subjugation of the Amerindian woman as a mere instrument, or moment, of his avaricious designs. This exploitation of the woman is continued under the commercial oligarchies of the 19th century. Economic *machismo* is, then, gradually integrated into the neo-colonial macroeconomy dominated first by England and later by the United States.[7]

In an *anadialectical* erotic economy human production becomes not a means of enslavement but a continuous renewal, or prolongation of the erotic relationship.[8] (The house is constructed not as a prison for the woman but as an extension of the sexual relationship and erotic service-in-justice.) Consequently, production itself is not impersonal, but is production "for" some*one* (not, as in the dominative relationship, *against* someone):

> Work is the creation in the Other of the mediations which make it real, human: it is work liberative of the Other who, as the sexual Other, in beauty and insinuation provokes what is owed him or her in justice.[9]

Hence, the anadialectical erotic economy is grounded in an understanding of production-for-someone not as the positive right of "private property" but as the metaphysical right of the Other—in this case, the sexual Other. The erotic economy, or the construction of structures supportive of "the couple" as an analectical Totality, is thus not merely, as in Hegel, the "depository of private property . . . of goods obtained in politico-civil society," or a moment of politico-civil society, nor is it merely a moment of the political economy, as in Engels; rather, it is the realization of sexual praxis as the trans-ontological service of the Other issuing from the felt absence of the Other. That absence is symbolized physiologically by the genital organs (in the female, not only the "passive" vagina but the "active" clitoris as well). By making the home the realization of the service of the Other, the anadialectical erotic economy thereby precludes the exploitation inherent in an economy which grounds rights exclusively in either politico-civil or political-economic society.[10]

In so doing, the anadialectical erotic economy goes beyond the Freudian bipolarity of the erotic pleasure and repressive reality principles—which are but different moments of *one*, initial Totality, i.e., Nature, and a *male* Totality at that—by revealing the priority of the "metaphysical desire of or impulse towards the Other . . ."[11] As "erotic" this desire is not of the Other-as-object (where the "Other" is merely an autoerotic mediation), but of the Other-as-person (not constituted by the ego's intention, but confronting the ego as an external person who, from outside the ego, *proposes* that the relationship be sexual). As "economy" the desire becomes the guarantee that this primal impulse will issue in genuine service and not in mere autoerotic narcissism. The distanciation of the economic guarantees the proximity of the couple as "a couple," i.e., as two equal persons. In working *for* the sexual Other, we ensure that our desire for the Other will not be merely egocentric. By constructing an economic order that will put nature at the service of woman, we ensure that the woman will not become but a moment of Nature ("to-be-worked-upon") for man. The desire for the other would then be directed not at the satisfaction of the ego's needs but, rather, at the satisfaction of the Other's needs.[12]

The Pedagogical Economy

In Dussel's framework, the pedagogical economy differs from the erotic economy in that, unlike the latter, it is not *first* established through distanciation but, rather, "the pedagogical *proximity* is already at the same time the 'economy.'" The first extension of nourishment to the child takes place in the proximity of the nursing relationship. Likewise, in the teacher-student relationship, nourishment (here in the form of knowledge) takes place in the immediacy of the face-to-face encounter. It is the uniqueness of the pedagogical economy-in-proximity that provides the strongest argument against the priority (i.e., economistic reductionism) of the human being-nature relation:

> The human being is born in a human being and his or her first relation is with a human being, not with nature. We are born in *someone's* uterus; we are nourished by *someone*. . . .[13]

This, however, does not obviate the human being-nature relation, but reveals its internalization in the pedagogical-practical relation. The pedagogical economy *then* develops as the process of moving away from the immediacy of the nourishing face-to-face (or mouth-to-breast), in which the nourishment is immediate as a "gift" rather than as something deserved, to "structure a *remoteness* which, through work, constructs the now-deserved proximity."[14] The paradigmatic proximity of the nursing relationship is thus reimplanted in the remoteness of the social structures, both those charged with properly educational functions and those charged with extending physical "nourishment," e.g., health services, retirement security.[15] This passage from the home to the social sphere is what Dussel calls "the passage from the domestic-erotic pedagogy of the child to the political pedagogy."[16] The passage from nourishment-as-proximity to nourishment-as-proximity-in-remoteness is, then, already the passage from the erotic economy to the political economy:

> The erotic pedagogy implies the relation to the father-mother; the political pedagogy opens, on the other hand, the realm of the State, social classes, enlightened and popular culture, science, technology, mass communication, etc.

> It is the passage from the psychic to the social; it is an opening up to the political space.[17]

It is here, in the *constructed* proximity of the social, that "the pedagogical economy attains its full meaning." The movement from the erotic pedagogy to the political pedagogy is an explicitly economic process in that it represents the construction of pedagogical systems (e.g., educational systems, health systems) all of which imply certain *costs* for society. Within the dominant Totality these systems become involutively self-propagating and end up exploiting those whom they purport to serve. The systems become the domain of "experts" who see themselves as beyond the scrutiny of those outside the systems. It is, then, the task of the pedagogical economy to divest these systems of their power to totalize.[18]

Because the system perceives itself to be the only pedagogical means to the desired end, it eliminates all existing subsystems and all those which arise to supply what the system itself lacks.[19] As an example of this presumptive totalization, the medical industry itself actually engenders new diseases:

> The antibiotic, a chemotherapic means so abusively present in the existing "health system," at times destroys the pathogenic bacteria, but it likewise eliminates other subsystems of bacteria extremely necessary for the vital equilibrium of the so-called sick person. With this, the "antibiotic system" arrogates to itself the exclusive right to cure disease, destroying a whole host of other "natural" systems which exist prior to the administration of the antibiotic dose. With this, the organism becomes predisposed to contract new diseases.[20]

The fundamental error at the source of the mal-administration of antibiotics is the failure to take into account the fact that, before any introduction of medicines, the human body is already a "health system."[21] (The violence of chemotherapy and surgery thus replaces popular health education and prevention as the focus of the health profession.)[22]

This same error pervades the totalized educational system. Like the human body in the totalized medical system, the child is here seen as defenseless, as a *tabula rasa,* as "un-cultured." The result is the elimination of the pre-existing subsystems of education: the family, the neighborhood, the religious leader, etc. As these subsystems are cheaper by far than the totalized educational system, education then becomes "extremely expensive, unique, exclusive, and the people become disengaged from the education of their own."[23]

The removal of the educational process from the domain of the people to the domain of the "experts" engenders a pedagogical distortion in that it alienates the student by "educating" him or her, not in his or her proper culture, but in that of the political, social, ideological vested interests. Education is instrumentalized and becomes the "production" of "good citizens" who are able to carry out their assigned tasks within the totalized system. When poiesis does not mediate praxis it becomes identified with praxis; when production does not serve the person, the person becomes but another product. The process then culminates in the university through the professionalization of an elite able to sustain and propagate the consumerist economy. A major part of the instrumentalization of the university is, in turn, the politicization of the sciences and technology (which, as Varsavsky, Chomsky, Marcuse, and others have demonstrated, are not "objective" or "universal" but are conditioned by sociopolitical options). Thus the very technological base of economic development is consigned to the control of an elite.[24]

The pedagogical analectic, on the other hand, demands a pedagogical economy which would supersede "the *exclusively academic* conception of the educational process."[25] The people must themselves be reintegrated into the educational process. This would involve not only the schools themselves but also the mass media, all of which are today controlled by local and foreign elites. Through radio, television, etc., these elites promote a communications "market" in which the people are the *tabula rasa* whose "needs" are created by the elites themselves.[26]

The demystification of the academy as the exclusive educational context must be accompanied then, by the demystification of the mass media, human services, and medicine. Dussel argues that only through such a demystification of the dominant pedagogical systems will we be able to "show their disproportionate costs and indicate a liberative path."[27]

The Political Economy

If the erotic economy tends toward the political as eros extends beyond the doors of the home in the movement from erotic pedagogy to political pedagogy, the political economy becomes, in turn, a mediation of the erotic economy:

> What are orgasm, the satisfaction of desires, the liberation of the woman, if not appropriate means of constructing the social community, of creating new institutions of justice and defending against the enemies of the people?[28]

And, on the other hand:

> What is the market (in the capitalist model) or the consumer (in the socialist model) if not a socio-"cultural" *desire* or *eros*?[29]

The erotic and political economies are thus co-implicit: if the movement from erotic to political economy is a movement out of the house, into the remoteness of work, politics, etc., that remoteness itself has erotic or appetitive ends. (This, however, is still ontologically-limited desire, and hence not Other-directed desire, or love-in-justice.) Consequently, the starting point of the capitalist economy is the production of desire, a theme more proper to social psychoanalysis than to economics as such.[30]

What grounds the capitalist economy, therefore, is "need." At the root of capitalism is greed, no longer a physical desire, but now a historically-determined desire, whose realization is, in Marx's words, "bourgeois society as the historical organization of production."[31] The economy is organized so as to provide for the satisfaction of the "needs" of the consumer, "needs" created by the system itself.[32]

According to Dussel, the self-perpetuating economic system then becomes ideological when it posits itself as "natural," when it posits as "eternal" what is in fact historically determined. The division of labor which arises to meet the needs created by the system is posited, for example, as rational, or natural, thereby obscuring "the new reality that is born beyond the dominant system (as socialism was born in the time of the formulation of the capitalist political economy)." Finally, the movement from ontological desire, through greed and the creation of need, to the division of labor necessary to meet those needs culminates in the alienation of labor which accompanies the capitalist division of labor.[33]

Dussel emphasizes, however, that to be able to speak to the Latin American historical reality (and this is where dependency theory will enter), the above archaeology of capitalism must continue on to an examination of *inter*national *monopoly* capitalism.[34] In monopoly capitalism the political production of needs finds expression, on a much grander scale, in the creation of international markets. This process involves the further politicization of economy as the civil authorities and military elites become partners and accomplices in the maintenance and expansion of the international markets.[35]

According to Dussel, the passage from national economics to international economics is what reveals the drive towards self-perpetuating totalization inherent in capitalism (see our previous discussion, in chapter 1, of the internal contradictions of global capitalism) and, concomitantly, the reality of a new epistemological realm beyond the capitalist Totality. Not a mere "theory of development," which, as still infra-systemic, would remain subject to the demands of the Totality, the new realm reveals the structural contradictions of capitalism, which contradictions are reflected in the inequality intrinsic to the international capitalist division of labor (center-periphery).[36]

Dussel points out, however, that the above argument, essentially that of dependency theory, is still incomplete in its analysis. Citing Ricaurte Soler and Anouar Abdel-Malek, he proffers a critique of dependency theory for its "imperialization" of Latin American history: in their haste to thematize the reality of Latin American dependency as the consequence of European and North American imperialism (even if also including the complicity of local elites), dependency theorists have, by and large, ignored the dialectically-functioning liberative moments latent in Latin American history. Without a truly dialectical retrieval of Latin American history as both fundamentally dependent *and* struggling to emerge as its own locus of meaning Latin American liberation will never succeed in grounding itself in its conditions of possibility, but rather will vainly attempt to be born out of a historical vacuum.[37] Unless dependency theory can account for *exteriority,* i.e., the lower classes as not merely forming dysfunctional *parts* of the system but as also embodying *already* and carrying on trans-ontological values which have surfaced at various points in the popular history,[38] liberation will never become truly analectical and, hence, genuinely Latin American:

> Because there is an analectic moment, liberation is not merely the dialectical negation of the negation (giving liberty to the oppressed as oppressed within the system), but rather the affirmation of exteriority, the origin of the negation of the negation. . . . The dialectical economy affirms, then, only the continuity (even if by revolutionary leaps) of

> immanence, of "the Same;" the economy that interprets with an analectical method also affirms novelty . . . by originating in Exteriority, in the Distinct, in "the Other."[39]

Within the Totality, this political economic exteriority is manifested in unemployment, underemployment, marginalization. As surplus labor, the unemployed are the appearance, within the Totality, of historical subjects whose praxis-poiesis, or productive role, cannot be defined solely within the wage-salary system.[40]

Hence, the properly analectical moment of the political economy occurs only after 1) the exteriority of the values embodied in the history of the people is 2) made concrete, inside the system, with the emergence of surplus labor as the expression of the inability of the capitalist Totality to define poiesis exclusively within the framework of wages and salaries, thereby providing the conditions of the possibility for 3) the self-consciousness of surplus labor as exteriority to foster the constitution of a historical agent, a "surplus class," capable of seeing beyond the capitalist Totality and struggling to install a new, analectical productive Totality. As "surplus productive force," the analectical historical subject is the "internal manifestation of exteriority or the transcendental anticipation of the new system."[41]

The Theological (Archaeological) Economy

Beyond the anthropological economies is the theological economy (or "archaeological" since it refers to the ground, or origin, of the anthropological):

> "The Other" . . . has an analogous meaning: it can be the anthropological Other . . ., or it can be the absolutely absolute Other: other not only than the world but than the very cosmos.[42]

Beyond the trans-ontological Other, whose reality is prior to the world of *meaning,* is the trans-ontological *and* trans-cosmological Other, whose reality is prior to the very matter (cosmos) which, when incorporated in our world of meaning, becomes a meaning-thing.[43] This latter is the divine Other who is revealed in our world of meaning both as Presence (God's "footprints" in history) and as Absence ("footprints imply the absence of the one who left them").[44] It is the divine Other, as Exteriority, revealed in the historical, human Other, as exteriority.

If culture (world) is "the totality of the entities which are the fruit of human work or production [vis-a-vis cosmological 'matter']," then, in the archaeology "the cultural question takes on the physiognomy of the cultic (not forgetting that culture and cult have the same etymology: to inhabit, to work, to worship the gods)."[45] What distinguishes the archaeological economy, or poiesis, from the other economies, however, is that archaeological, or theological service, because offered to the absolutely absolute Other, cannot be carnal or material.

> What could one offer to the absolutely absolute Other? What could He/She receive which would truly befit One who transcends all possible needs? What could one hand over to the One who has no consumption, use of instruments, or mediations for His/Her project?[46]

According to Dussel, these questions can be responded to in either of two basic ways: that of the Totality, or that of exteriority. In the first, worship is offered to "the Same."[47] Here, the system-as-Totality is divinized, or fetishized:

> The supreme act of worship is the supreme blindness honored in the name of certitude; the supreme irrationality in the name of perfect rationality.[48]

When the system is seen as "natural" and "eternal" it becomes a fetish to whom are sacrificed, in worship, the bodies (the "bread" of the anti-feast) of so many Third World peasants and before whom the masses (not "the people") are but passive spectators: "They devour my people like bread" (Psalm 14:4).[49]

In the analectical archaeological economy, on the other hand, where culture is placed at the disposal of the human Other, other than any fetishized system, worship takes the form of "liberative praxis with respect to and for the oppressed in whom one recognizes the epiphany of infinite Exteriority."[50] It is by putting culture at the disposal of the human Other in praxis, therefore, that we place it at the disposal of the divine Other and, thus, render worship to the divine Other. In both cases we are opened to exteriority. The bread offered to the poor is bread offered to God. This distinguishes analectic worship from ontological worship:

> The worship of the ontology and the empires is an act of vision; the meta-physical worship of the people who are liberating themselves is a practical act which offers material goods and justice. Ontological worship is passive; meta-physical worship is active. . . .[51]

In ontological worship the poor are the material of worship; in metaphysical worship the poor are the necessary (because of our inability to offer adequate material sacrifice directly to God, and, hence, because of the sacramental nature of God's self-revelation) mediation of our material—i.e., bread—offering. When bread, as the bodies of those sacrificed in the name of the Totality, is taken out of the Totality's involutive cycle of consumption, it becomes, as poietic material, or the material of work, the satisfaction of the human Other's hunger. (Again, either production is put at the service of persons, or persons will themselves become mere products.) That bread is at the same time service of the human Other and worship of the divine Other. The erotic, pedagogical, and political economies thus find their ultimate analectical grounding, their ultimate condition of possibility, in this identification of service and worship. (E.g., in the political economy, genuine worship depends upon giving to the worker the fruit of his or her labor.) Because no appropriate worship could ever be offered the absolutely absolute Other—"One would have to be outside history and be divine"—He/She becomes the ultimate criterion and condition of the possibility of historical praxis-in-justice.[52]

As that ultimate criterion, then, worship is dysfunctional in any system, impeding the installation of any system as itself "eternal," or outside history, and irrupting in the system as the sign of the finiteness of all systems:

> The absolutely absolute Other is the only radical and definitive guarantee that every historical economic system is only historical, that is, transitory, possible, contingent.[53]

Moreover, in revealing the finiteness of the system the divine Other concomitantly reveals, in and through our service to the human Other, the utopic opening beyond the system to trans-ontological reality.[54]

It is, finally, in the identification of worship and trans-ontological service that the meaning of the Christian eucharist (as cult, or theological economy) is made manifest. There is a link between "bread as the fruit of common human labor, exchanged among those who produce it" and "bread as the substance of the eucharistic offering."[55]

Dussel divides the eucharistic economy into three central elements: earth, bread, and work (cf. the Offertory prayer in the Roman Catholic mass—"this *bread* . . . which *earth* has given and human hands have *made*"). Bread is the fruit of the subject-nature relationship, in which the earth becomes the material (the "with which") of work.[56]

In the Bible, bread is "life to the destitute."[57] The term "destitute," or "poor," is a relational category. That is, for there to be poor people there must also be rich people:

> Robinson Crusoe would, alone, be neither poor nor rich, but simply "a man." To be poor means occupying a precise place in the person-to-person relationship.[58]

The two terms are mutually exclusive: "one cannot be both poor and rich in the same relationship *hic et nunc*."[59]

The poor are poor because they are unable to satisfy their own needs through their labor since the fruit of that labor is alienated, i.e., it is appropriated by the rich. The rich thus consume the fruit of both their own *and others'* labor:

> "Rich," as a biblical category, means not simply the sinner, but the structural, historical, economic sinner; that is, he who enjoys, consumes, utilizes the product of others' work as an instrument of domination over them.[60]

The sinful relationship is not only the relationship of praxis as such but also that of praxis-poiesis.[61] If "bread is life" (Prov. 3:16; Mac. 8:36; Ecc. 34:18–22) then the extraction of bread from the one who produces it is the extraction of that person's very life. It is murder. This is "mortal" sin in the most concrete sense of that term.[62]

Because eucharistic bread is, first, *real* bread, the product of someone's work, it has both a sacramental meaning *and* an economic meaning. The bread on the altar is "the objectivized life of the worker." Consequently, "those who offer God bread stolen from the poor give God the life of the poor as their offering." God, however, does not want His/Her children killed and offered up; on the contrary, God's children are to be free. That is to say, what God asks as worship is that bread be given to the hungry, that the worker be given back the fruit of his or her labor. If the bread offered at the altar is not life *to* the destitute but is, rather, the life *of* the destitute, it is offered not to God but to the fetish-system.[63]

The worship that God desires is service (the Hebrew word for worship—*habodah*—being the same as that for work, or service, which, in the Greek, is translated *diakonein*). True worship occurs in the praxis of service-in-justice. The poor are, thus, "a necessary mediation of worship of the Infinite."[64]

In its consumption, the bread of true worship gives life to the children of God: "The death of the bread is the beginning of life for those who receive it." When the bread offered on the altar is offered in fetishistic worship it is the death of the servant, as the bread of the poor, that then becomes "the beginning of life for those who receive it." The fetish kills those who, in service of the poor, interject themselves between the dominator and the dominated. Jesus was the "bread of life" who "did not come to be served, but to serve, and to give up his life as a ransom for many (Matt. 20:28)." The martyr-prophet offers up his or her body in the struggle to give to the poor the bread which is their life. This is the meaning of the "Lamb of God." This is the meaning of the assassination of Msgr. Oscar Romero during the celebration of the eucharist, where the bread *was* "economic bread in justice," thus directly challenging the fetish, i.e., the military and the junta.[65]

The ultimate sign of the connection between service and true worship, between fetishistic worship and martyrdom, and between personal and structural sin is thus the eucharist.

This fact, moreover, appears as a liberative moment in Latin American history itself. Dussel refers especially to the life of Fray Bartolomé de las Casas. On August 15, 1514, las Casas, finding that he was no longer able to celebrate the eucharist since "he as a priest was thinking of offering the bread stolen from the Indians," instead set his Indians free, thus beginning his own struggle for justice, which would continue for the remainder of his life.[66] It is to this historical moment, of the revelation of the identification between eucharist and liberation, that Dussel points as the origin of the Latin American struggle for liberation.

In conclusion, Dussel makes clear the necessity of mediating social scientific theory, e.g., dependency theory, to the liberation movement by means of a dialectical retrieval of both Western thought (Schelling, Marx, Marcuse, Hilferding, etc.) and, especially, Latin American history. He is thus able to specify his method at the economic level while nevertheless maintaining the openness implicit in Latin American history as the history of the Other. This accomplishment offers the twin advantages of safeguarding the organic praxis-poeisis relationship while also providing historical conditions of possibility for the liberation of that relationship beyond a simplistic, and hence ineffective, rejection of all previous Western thought and Latin American history.

The relative priority of economic liberation (see chapter 1 *su-*

pra) is affirmed as the *sine qua non* of liberation, though not as "mechanistically" leading to other forms of liberation; rather, as being the *concrete form* that *all* liberation takes and without which it would thus remain abstract. The relationship between economic liberation and other modes of liberation is not linear, or even circular, but organic.[67] Consequently, for Dussel, economic liberation is not *really* one more mode of liberation among others, but is intrinsic to all the modes of liberation specified in the praxis relationships.

Beyond his incorporation of economics as organically related to praxis, moreover, Dussel makes explicit the need to ground that organic relationship methodologically *in history.* The self-discovery of Latin America as dependent does not lead, then, to a blanket denunciation of her past but rather to a recovery and sublation of those moments in her past which have been expressive of emancipatory values. If the history of domination has been well-documented by dependency theorists and others, the same cannot be said for the history of liberation. Without a history of liberation, Latin America may discover the oppressive power of Europe and North America, but she will not discover the liberative power latent in her own history.

NOTES

/1/ See chapter 1, *supra.*
/2/ See chapter 3, *supra.*
/3/ Ibid.
/4/ Dussel, *Filosofía ética,* 3:85.
/5/ Ibid.
/6/ Ibid.; Dussel, *Filosofía de la liberación,* p. 144.
/7/ Dussel, *Filosofía ética,* 3:93.
/8/ Ibid., 3:94.
/9/ Ibid., 3:95.
/10/ Ibid., 3:96; Dussel, *Filosofía de la liberación,* pp. 94–95.
/11/ Dussel, *Filosofía ética,* 3:65, 72.
/12/ Ibid., 3:72–73, 96; 5:83–84.
/13/ Ibid., 3:156–57.
/14/ Ibid., 3:158.
/15/ Ibid., 3:160.
/16/ Ibid.
/17/ Ibid., 3:161.

/18/ Ibid.
/19/ Ibid., 3:162.
/20/ Ibid.
/21/ Ibid.
/22/ Ibid., 3:167–68.
/23/ Ibid., 3:162.
/24/ Ibid., 3:162–65.
/25/ Reforma de la educación peruana. Informe general. (Peruvian government's Decree no. 19,326 of 1972) quoted in ibid., 3:164.
/26/ Dussel, *Filosofía ética*, 3:167.
/27/ Ibid., 3:168.
/28/ Ibid., 4:82.
/29/ Ibid.
/30/ Ibid., 4:82–84.
/31/ Marx, quoted in ibid., 4:85.
/32/ Dussel, *Filosofía ética*, 4:85.
/33/ Ibid., 4:86–87.
/34/ Ibid., 4:87. Here Dussel refers to the work of Hobson, Hilferding, Bukharin, Lenin, Baran and Sweezy, and others whose analyses have concentrated on this latest stage of capitalist development.
/35/ Ibid., 4:87–89. See also chapter 1, *supra*.
/36/ Dussel, *Filosofía ética*, 4:89.
/37/ Ibid., 4:71ff., 90.
/38/ Ibid., 4:77ff. Here Dussel refers, for example, to Latin American utopian socialists.
/39/ Ibid., 4:90–91.
/40/ Ibid., 4:79.
/41/ Ibid., 4:79, 93.
/42/ Ibid., 5:51.
/43/ Ibid., 5:62–63.
/44/ Ibid., 5:55.
/45/ Ibid., 5:76.
/46/ Ibid.
/47/ Ibid., 5:77. Dussel cites Hegel's system as an example of such worship.
/48/ Ibid., 5:78.
/49/ Ibid., 5:78–83. Dussel draws upon Freud to argue that the origins of social repression in the repression of the *Urvaters* is reflected in the elites' betrayal of their heroic fathers (e.g., Lenin, Washington, San Martín, Hidalgo). Thus, the fetishized system's betrayal of its own ancestral liberators makes possible the bloody sacrifice of the Other.
In Marx, Dussel also finds an analogous critique of the fetish. Inasmuch as Marx offers a thoroughgoing critique of capitalist idolatry (see Dussel, "La religión en el joven Marx: 1835–1849"), he offers a "religious" critique of society. That is, his condemnation of the capitalist god, Money, and hence, of the instrumentalization of the person before that god is concomitantly an implicit affirmation of exteriority. While he did not take the explicit step to an affirmation of the creator God and instead remained at the level of an "atheism of the fetishized Totality," this atheism is the condition of the

possibility of genuine religious faith, i.e., faith in a transcendent God (see, again, Dussel, "La religión en el joven Marx: 1835–1849").
/50/ Dussel, *Filosofía ética*, 5:77.
/51/ Ibid., 5:79.
/52/ Ibid., 5:79, 84–85.
/53/ Ibid., 5:85.
/54/ Ibid.
/55/ Dussel, "The Bread of the Eucharistic Celebration as a Sign of Justice in the Community," in *Can We Always Celebrate the Eucharist?*, Mary Collins and David Power, eds. (New York: Seabury, 1982) pp. 56–65.
/56/ Ibid., p. 57.
/57/ Ibid., p. 58. Dussel emphasizes that, correctly translated, the Biblical text "does not say: 'Bread is life to man,' but 'to the destitute,' the poor."
/58/ Ibid., p. 59.
/59/ Ibid.
/60/ Ibid.
/61/ Ibid., p. 60.
/62/ Ibid. I am also indebted to Matthew Lamb for this insight.
/63/ Dussel, "The Bread of the Eucharistic Celebration," pp. 60–62.
/64/ Dussel, "The Kingdom of God and the Poor," *International Review of Mission* 220 (1979) 130.
/65/ Dussel, "The Bread of the Eucharistic Celebration," p. 62.
/66/ Ibid., pp. 63–64.
/67/ See Meiksins Wood, "The Separation of the Economic and the Political in Capitalism."

PART TWO

CHAPTER FIVE

NORTH AMERICA'S OPENING TO EXTERIORITY: TOWARD AN EPISTEMOLOGICAL MEDIATION OF CONVERSION TO THE OTHER AS OTHER

Dussel's project, as we have seen, consists of three major methodological steps: 1) a dialectics of Latin American history; 2) a dialectical retrieval of the Western intellectual tradition; and 3) the anadialectical method itself. By mediating the past to the present, the first two steps ground the anadialectical mediation of the present to the future. A hermeneutic is thus constructed for interpreting Latin American historical praxis as an analogically distinct locus of meaning irreducible to the Totality of European and North American historical praxis. Likewise, a methodology is proposed for promoting a human liberative praxis grounded in the consciousness—reflected in the new Latin American self-consciousness—of the irreducibility of any one locus of meaning to any other.

In the last methodological step, then, Dussel retrieves the first two steps but goes beyond them (hence, "sublates" them) to thematize methodologically the *conversion* from the domination represented by the closed Totality to the liberation represented by the analogical Totality, or the *response* from the heretofore-closed Totality to the Other's plea.

Our contention in this chapter will be that while as we have argued, Dussel's anadialectical method provides a sociohistorically (praxis) and economically (poiesis) grounded foundation for an openness to and service of the Other (liberative praxis-poiesis), the trans-ontological conversion itself needs further criteriological specification. While Dussel mediates praxis *externally*, or materially (i.e., in the human being-, or person-nature relation), through poiesis, he fails to provide an adequate *internal* (i.e., epistemological, or criteriological) mediation of conversion praxis. In other words, prior to the poietic question of the concreteness or abstractness of the encounter with the Other is the epistemological question of the *existence* or *non-existence* of an Other and the criteriological question of *how* one becomes converted to the Other. These, however, are *non*-questions for Dussel, since he sees their answer as being self-evident.

Dussel's well-founded aversion to any reductionist ontology or anthropology leads him to an understanding of metaphysical conversion as calling for existential faith alone, since all one need do is "give in" to the power of suffering in and of itself to bring about conversion. His answer to reductionism is thus, at this level at least, an existentialism, somewhat akin to naive realism, which, because based on the assertion of the self-evident nature of suffering as its own call to liberation, becomes a truly critical, or mediated realism only at a secondary, interpretative level (e.g., as theology or critical social theory). He thus immunizes the face-to-face encounter itself from any need for internal, epistemological, criteriological mediation.

We will argue that an analogically similar *North American* perspective, namely that of Bernard Lonergan, reveals such an "immunization" to be unwarranted. (By an *analogically similar* North American perspective here we mean one which, as we will see, is in fundamental agreement with the anadialectical method as *trans-ontological*.) Through an analogical extrapolation of Dussel's own dialectical retrieval of the Western intellectual tradition we find the possibility of the criteriological mediation of conversion, understood as precisely trans-ontological, and hence non-reductionist, in the work of the Canadian philosopher theologian Bernard Lonergan. As Dussel has critiqued and recovered elements of European philosophy to formulate intellectually the tasks and orientations of a Latin American liberative intelligence, so Lonergan has critiqued and recovered European philosophy to formulate intellectually the tasks and orientations of a North American liberative intelligence.[1] In short, Dussel's anadialectical method and Lonergan's transcendental method, or meta-method, while arising out of distinct cultural and historical perspectives, share the same methodological foundation, i.e., trans-ontological (or "anadialectical") praxis.

The Epistemology of Trans-Ontological Praxis

While Dussel locates the starting point of the analectic in Latin American historical praxis, or the historical praxis of the Other, and then predicates conversion upon openness to and trust in the voice of the Other encountered in the face-to-face, the conversion experience itself is seen as somehow "automatically" following upon that encounter. Although this view of the encounter and conversion as existential, or epistemologically unmediated, is understandable given Dussel's theological context as one who is daily in the midst of the victims of history and who, therefore, might interpret attempts to epistemologically mediate that encounter as evasive, North American historical praxis, if it has taught us anything, has taught us how manifold and powerful are the ideological obstacles which the closed Totality raises to shield itself—not only at the level of reflection, but also at the foundational level of sight-blindness or hearing-deafness—from the evocative countenance of the suffering Other. These obstacles distort not only our interpretation of the Other at the level of critical social science and theology, but, more importantly, they distort the fundamental pre-thematic experience itself. Consequently, the *praxis* of conversion itself needs mediation through criteria which would promote the authenticity of conversion as conversion *to the Other.*[2] The power of suffering in and of itself to bring about conversion is itself to some extent conditioned by ideological forces.

An analogical Lonerganian, North American perspective suggests the possibility of incorporating the needed mediation within the context of a trans-ontologically grounded method. By turning to the internal structures of human praxis Lonergan furnishes—in the *practical* self-appropriation of those structures, in the *practical* movement toward heightened consciousness—criteria for critically mediating the encounter with the Other, while still affirming the trans-ontological and ongoing nature of that encounter. In short, our contention is that an appreciation of Lonergan's meta-method as itself, qua *meta*-method, *anadialectical* would suggest possibilities of a further explication of analectical conversion—hence, an explicitation of Dussel's third key methodological step.

Meta-Method and Conversion

Our attempt to correlate Lonergan's meta-method and Dussel's anadialectical method speaks to what is an ongoing dialogue between those liberation theologians who take a certain amount of inspiration from Lonergan's work and those who are suspect of his project.[3] In attempting such a correlation, therefore, we argue that some of the suspicions of the latter are based on a serious misunderstanding of Lonergan's project. That is, Lonergan's meta-method can in some significant ways be correlated with Dussel's anadialectical method precisely because, contrary to the assertions of liberation theologians like José Comblín, it is *not* characterized by a deductivist, conceptualist, logical formalism unconcerned with "the struggle between truth and falsehood."[4] In point of fact, meta-method involves a praxis-grounded, *in*ductive, self-appropriation inherently concerned with the struggles between truth and falsehood, value and disvalue, good and evil. Meta-method is not the "extinction of novelty" through the instrumental application of an already-devised set of methodological categories.[5] On the contrary, it involves a fundamental *openness* to novelty through the appropriation of human practical activity, through an attentiveness not to a set of methodological "rules" but to the inductively *lived* structures of human praxis—and the transcendental precepts implicit *in* those structures—which structures are not "proposed" but, in Dussel's own terms, "dis-covered." (And, as we will see, for both Lonergan and Dussel "dis-covery" implies not only disclosure but also transformation, i.e., conversion.) It is precisely the inductive nature of Lonergan's method that distinguishes it as *meta*-method.

By way of further explanation it will now be necessary to examine the relationship between the abovementioned structures of human praxis and Lonergan's understanding of conversion in order to then posit both the complementary correspondence between Lonergan and Dussel and, further, the usefulness of the former's meta-method in the formulation of a criteriological and epistemological mediation of the latter's "conversion to the Other."

The Subject-as-Subject and the Internal Structures of Human Praxis: Meta-Method as Grounded in Human Praxis

Lonergan's meta-method is grounded in the "subject-as subject." The discovery of the subject-as-subject as "the prior reality that both grounds horizons and the determination of the field [of all human activity],"[6] i.e., as, in Matthew Lamb's words, "consciousness as living self-presence in the world,"[7] (consciousness being characteristic of all human activity, unless one is in a "deep and dreamless sleep"), reveals meta-method's explicit incompatibility with any subjectivist identification of being and thinking. Prior to any reflection upon or affirmation of the subject is our concrete, lived, conscious, pre-thematic experience of love, hate, joy, suffering, etc.[8]

Unlike an object, the subject-as-subject is irreducible to any horizon of comprehension (or, in Dussel's words, the human person is a unique entity because, unlike mere objects, he or she cannot be fully comprehended within any horizon of meaning):

> It is not any object known objectively and it is not the subject known objectively, for all objects are known within some stream of consciousness and so within a horizon.[9]

At the point where one adverts to the subject, one is already "comprehending" the subject within a particular horizon and is thus now in the realm of the subject-as-*object:*

> There is the presence of the object to the subject, of the spectacle to the spectator; there is also the presence of the subject to himself . . .; it is presence in, as it were, another dimension, presence concomitant and correlative and opposite to the presence of the object. Objects are present by being attended to; but subjects are present as subjects, not by being attended to, but by attending. . . .
>
> I have been attempting to describe the subject's presence to himself. But the reader, if he tries to find himself as subject, to reach back and, as it were, uncover his subjectivity, cannot succeed. Any such effort is introspecting, attending to the subject; and what is found is not the subject as subject, but only the subject as object; it is the subject as subject that does the finding.[10]

The subject-as-object is involutively deduced; the subject-as-subject is ex-volutively auto-determined. The *praxis* of the subject-as-subject is the condition of the possibility of the *knowledge* of the subject-as-object. Any affirmation of the freedom intrinsic to the human person as always to some extent beyond any horizon of meaning must, therefore, be grounded in the foundational praxis of the subject-as-subject. This, in turn, carries with it the implication that human liberation demands, not a subjective introspection (contemplation), which would remain trapped within the subject-as-object, but a raising of the subject-as-subject's level (qualitatively, not necessarily quantitatively) of activity, a heightening of consciousness in praxis. It is to this conscious praxis, then, that we must look to find the norms of human liberation as the affirmation of the unobjectifiable nature of the person.[11]

Those norms are what Lonergan refers to as the basic structures of human consciousness, or, what we will call the internal structures of human praxis. It is, thus, through the self-appropriation of these trans-ontologically oriented structures in the praxis of the subject-as-subject that the person affirms his or her trans-ontological freedom. It is also in this process of self-appropriation that one encounters ideological bias and alienation.[12]

The basic structures, or levels, of praxis are the empirical (perception, imagination, feeling, sensing), the intellectual (inquiry, understanding), the rational (marshaling of evidence, judgment), and the responsible (deliberation, decision, action.)[13] The experiencing, understanding, judging, deciding, and acting of the subject-as-subject (the subject-as-subject being *defined* as his or her experiencing, understanding, etc.), as a dynamically related "normative pattern of recurrent and related operations yielding cumulative and progressive results," is not a set of deductively prescribed rules which, if followed, would yield some infinitely repeatable result, but is rather the discoverable structure of human conscious activity, which, inasmuch as it yields "cumulative and progressive results," is both synthetic and open to unprescribed and unprescribable novelty.[14]

As universally valid and invariant, these levels of human praxis implicitly contain, as internal to praxis, corresponding "transcendental imperatives:" Be attentive, Be intelligent, Be critical, Be responsible.[15] Human freedom and alienation are then defined in reference to these fundamental normative precepts, the former as their realization and the latter as their obstruction.[16] The process of self-appropriation is thus at the same time a struggle between authenticity and inauthenticity, i.e., between attentiveness and inattentiveness, intelligence and stupidity, rationality and irrationality, responsibility and irresponsibility.[17]

This struggle, moreover, is not merely individual but intrinsically social as well, for the individual is always and everywhere a member of sociohistorical groups. Consequently, the subject-as-subject and the structures of conscious activity are not limited to any one social reality, but include them all insofar as they contribute to or frustrate the realization of the transcendental imperatives.[18] Insofar as they contribute to the realization of the imperatives they promote the trans-ontological freedom of the subject-as-subject. Insofar as they impede that realization they remain trapped within the involutive subject-as-*exlusively* object, whose ideologically buttressed inability to appropriate his or her practical foundations prevents him or her from entering into that process of liberation which finds its source only in the trans-ontological, social-personal subject-as-subject, whose continuous openness to further possibilities of experiencing, understanding, judging, deciding, and acting (i.e., trans-ontological freedom) is not possible for the ontologically-bounded subject-as-object, who, by definition, is objectively comprehended within his or her horizon of meaning. In the former, consciousness always outstrips knowledge; in the latter, if, as in Hegel, not grounded in the pre-thematic praxis of the subject-as-subject, consciousness and knowledge are identified.

Conversion as Normative Trans-Ontological Praxis

As "cumulative and progressive," the process of self-appropriation involves a movement to higher levels of consciousness, or self-presence:

> What promotes the subject from experiential to intellectual consciousness is the desire to understand, the intention of intelligibility. What next promotes him or her from intellectual to rational consciousness, is a fuller unfolding of the same intention: for the desire to understand, once understanding is reached, becomes the intention of the right intelligible, of the true, and through truth, of reality. Finally, the intention of the intelligible, the true, the real, becomes also the intention of the good, the question of value, of what is worthwhile, when the already acting subject confronts his or her world and adverts to his or her own acting in it.[19]

It is at this fourth level that you make a "decision about whom and what you are for and . . . whom and what you are against, . . . a fully conscious decision about one's horizon, one's outlook, one's worldview."[20] If that foundational, because not ontologically-bounded, decision is not arbitrary, but rather involves a "total surrender to the demands of the human spirit: be attentive, be intelligent, be reasonable, be responsible, be in love," then it is an authentic *conversion*.[21] An authentic conversion is the concrete, personal and social realization of the trans-ontological orientation of human praxis. Only in the experience of conversion is that praxis *made* trans-ontological. And it can be "made" trans-ontological only because it is already intrinsically oriented beyond *any* horizon of meaning.

If, in Lonergan's vocabulary, a horizontal exercise of freedom is "a decision or choice that occurs within an established horizon" ("dialectical," in Dussel's sense of the word), then conversion involves a vertical ("*ana*lectical") exercise of freedom.[22] Conversion thus reveals our radically trans-ontological nature. It makes explicit the implicit trans-ontological orientation of the internal structures of human praxis by revealing the existence of external loci of meaning. In conversion-praxis, in the practical commitment to another horizon of meaning more conducive to the transcendental principles, we discover that we are not bound by our present horizon of meaning (nor, since conversion has social ramifications, by our membership in any particular group). The horizonal shift which occurs in conversion is—though Lonergan does not use the term—*analectical* in that it involves an "about face" which "begins a new sequence."[23] Conversion, then, is defined not by the mere (dialectical) development of what is already "given," but by the acceptance of a new locus of meaning which is outside of (*ana*lectic) and discordant—even contradictory—with the old. Moreover, in choosing the new, external locus of meaning we make manifest the fact that human conscious activity, i.e., the praxis of the subject-as-subject, is not bound by "horizons of meaning" in a *generic* sense. By putting into question the old horizon of meaning as the exclusive starting point of praxis, by choosing a new starting point, or beginning a "new sequence," we put into question the claims of *any* horizon to be foundational. As distinct from the merely dialectical movement (i.e., "sequence") of horizons, the analectical movement of conversion involves a practical questioning of the very category "horizon" as foundational. If conversion is an "about face," then it is anything but a merely dialectical development of the old horizon; rather, it is the properly analectical moment of human praxis, wherein we choose a new, discordant locus of meaning and, in so doing, assert and make most concrete our radical freedom as persons through the affirmation of the radical freedom of other persons as external loci of meaning. Because it is the explicit realization of the trans-ontological nature of human praxis, therefore, conversion reveals itself as *normative*, foundational praxis; only in conversion is the reality of external loci of meaning made manifest.

According to Lonergan, this conversion may be intellectual, moral, or religious. To these we can add a fourth, psychic conversion, which, while not explicitly developed by Lonergan himself is, as he acknowledges, implicit in his work.[24]

Intellectual conversion involves the recognition that beyond the immediate world of the senses there is the world mediated by meaning:

> For the world mediated by meaning is a world known not by the sense experience of an individual but by the external and internal experience of a cultural community, and by the continuously checked and rechecked judgments of the community. Knowing, accordingly, is not just seeing; it is experiencing, understanding, judging, and believing.[25]

The criteria of objectivity are thus given not simply in the immediacy of ocular vision, but in the mediated praxis of experiencing, understanding, judging, deciding, acting, and believing. Naive realism and empiricism give way to critical realism. The world of the infant gives way to a world which, because meaning is always "on the move," is caught in the precarious struggle between progress and decline.[26]

The second form of conversion, moral conversion, "changes the criterion of one's decisions and choices from satisfaction to values."[27] Moral conversion consists, then, in an exercise of vertical freedom wherein the individual opts "for the truly good, even for value against satisfaction when value and satisfaction conflict."[28] As an exercise of vertical freedom, moral conversion—qua conversion—places us in an "open and dynamic orientation" which resists closure and "keeps us restless, in this life, pursuing an absolute goodness which lies beyond our powers of criticism."[29]

The third form of conversion, religious conversion, is a surrender to unrestricted love. It is an initiation into the dynamic state of other-worldly love which satisfies our desire for self-transcendence (as reflected in the internal structures of praxis and the correspondencing transcendental imperatives) and grounds our acts. For the Christian, religious conversion is "God's love flooding our hearts through the Holy Spirit given to us."[30]

While Lonergan's own explicit articulation of the conversion process does not extend beyond these three forms of conversion, the work of Vernon Gregson and Robert Doran has pointed to a fourth form of conversion, psychic conversion, which Lonergan understands as a valid enrichment of his own explicitation of the conversion process in that psychic conversion thematizes the "sensitive undertow," or feelings, as the archaeological matrix out of which both values and knowledge emerge and integrates that matrix into the conversion process.[31] To the conversion to intelligence, value and love is now added the conversion to beauty.[32] Doran describes psychic conversion as

> the acquisition of the capacity to disengage and interpret correctly the elemental symbols of one's being and to form or transform one's existential and cognitive praxis on the basis of such a recovery of the story of one's search for direction in the movement of life.[33]

By effecting a mediated return to the immediacy (cf. Ricouer's notion of "second immediacy") of those primal, or "elemental symbols of one's being," psychic conversion assists in the appropriation of the "aesthetic component that permeates the normative order of inquiry," thereby revealing the mytho-poetic matrix underlying that order and the integrity, or lack thereof, of limitation and transcendence in the development of human authenticity. Transcendence is grounded in limitation.[34]

The recovery of mythos in mediated immediacy forestalls the alienation of intelligence and rationality from sensitivity reflected in the Greek and modern option for logos over psyche. By exposing the disproportion between transcendence and limitation, psychic conversion also exposes the fundamental scotosis, or *sin* at the root of the Western "egophanic desire for the practical [i.e., technological] mastery and domination of nature and even of humanity." The irony, of course, is that human activity proves itself *most* self-limiting and shortsighted precisely when it "severs its own capacities for transcendence from the counterbalance imposed upon human ambition by the countervailing dimension of limitation that makes itself known in our spontaneous sensitivity." Put simply, "to deny limitation is to be destroyed by limitation; to affirm and respect limitation is to achieve transcendence." Through psychic conversion we appropriate our aesthetic consciousness and, in the symbology of the sensitive psyche, integrate transcendence and limitation in creative tension, thereby avoiding the temptation to dissolve the tension in either of the two directions.[35]

Toward a Lonerganian Understanding of Analectical Conversion to the Other as Other

Our aim in the above paragraphs has not been to make an exhaustive presentation of Lonergan's meta-method and his notion of conversion (which presentation is beyond the scope of this work and could readily be found in any of a number of published works on the thought of Lonergan),[36] but rather to highlight some salient points which reflect a compatibility between Dussel's notion of conversion and Lonergan's and which suggest possibilities—to be developed further in the remainder of this chapter—for enriching our understanding of the analectical encounter with the Other in the ways indicated above. Our argument for offering Lonergan's meta-method as an analogue to Dussel's notion of analectical conversion (as articulated in the context of his anadialectical method) proceeds, then, from 1) an acknowledgment of the complementarity between certain key features of Lonergan's understanding of the praxis of the subject-as-subject as foundational and Dussel's own understanding of trans-ontological praxis as foundational, to 2) the differences in their *perspectives* on foundational praxis, to 3) the discovery of the internal structures of human praxis as providing an epistemological, criteriological mediation of trans-ontological praxis as foundational, to, finally, 4) the recognition that the complementarity in (1) precludes a mechanistic or conceptualist rendering of (3), thereby yielding two notions of conversion which, while reflecting the differences in (2), are nevertheless complementary.

Turning to the first step in our Lonerganian, or North American, perspective on trans-ontological praxis, we uncover a fundamental agreement as to the foundational role of trans-ontology. The subject-as-subject in Lonergan and the Other in Dussel perform quite similar methodological functions in that both safeguard the radical freedom of the person as unique among all entities, as unable to be fully comprehended within any horizon of meaning. To say, as Lonergan does, that the subject-as-subject is the "prior reality that grounds horizons" is to restate, in different terminology, Dussel's discovery of the Other as some*one*, not some*thing*. If, for Dussel, liberation begins with the Other, this is precisely because the Other, as other, is the normative sociohistorical incarnation of the radical freedom intrinsic to the trans-ontological subject-as-subject. Likewise, a neglect of the subject-as-subject as prior to and grounding the subject-as-object can only issue in a corresponding neglect of the metaphysical, or trans-ontological Other as not simply an object within the dominant Totality but as a locus of meaning independent of that Totality. Neglect of the subject-as-subject results, therefore, in the same totalizing, infra-ontological dialectic as does neglect of the Other.

For both Dussel and Lonergan, moreover, trans-ontological praxis is intrinsically *ethical*. In Dussel, trans-ontological praxis reveals the fundamental ethicity of the analectic over against the non-ethicity of the exclusively infra-ontological dialectic, where "the only possible morality . . . is that of carrying out, at the ontic or intramundane level, what is already posited at the ontological level."[37] Always prior to the "morality" of particular infra-ontological choices (praxis as such) is the radical ethicity of one's stance (*foundational* praxis) as either open or closed to trans-ontological possibilities of being. This fundamental ethicity may be neglected, but it cannot be avoided. That is, either we live in openness to and service of the other (i.e., either we appropriate our trans-ontological nature as acting subjects) or, by refusing to do so, we live in service of the dominant Totality, which denies the Other's existence both *meta*physically and physically, through every conceivable form of fratricide, homicide, and genocide.

Despite the asseverations of several Latin American liberation theologians to the contrary,[38] Lonergan's meta-method—qua *meta*-method—like Dussel's anadialectical method, is grounded in human praxis. Prior to the encountered subject-as-object is the subject-as-subject who does the encountering. Hence, the *praxis* of the subject-as-subject (again, somewhat redundant terminology since the subject-as-subject is, by definition, the *acting* subject) always precedes the *knowledge* of the subject-as-object.[39] The trans-ontological freedom of the subject-as-subject is, thus, neither an abstract freedom on the one hand nor the "freedom" of the dominant Totality on the other, but is precisely the existential choice, revealed in praxis, between openness to unconceptualizable, trans-ontological reality and closure within the false security of the "given" world and world view. As grounded in foundational praxis, meta-method, Matthew Lamb points out, "seeks to explicate the value commitments, or value conflicts operative in decisions and actions."[40] Our response to, or stance vis-a-vis other persons always precedes and grounds our thematic knowledge of that response or stance.[41]

Exteriority and Internal Transcendence: Different Perspectives on Internal Transcendence

Beyond their common notion of human foundational praxis as trans-ontologically oriented, one encounters, in Lonergan and Dussel, a seemingly irreconcilable difference: Dussel's notion of that praxis is of the praxis *of the Other,* whereas Lonergan's is of *my* or *our* praxis. The starting point for Lonergan is defined in terms of the "subject," even if the *acting* subject.[42] For Dussel, the starting point must be defined as outside my horizon; only then can I act—in response to the Other.

Upon closer examination, however, one finds that this difference is not so much one of substance as one of perspective. By positing "exteriority" as the starting point of praxis, Dussel does not mean to say that the Other exists *really* outside the world—that would be a natural impossibility, unless one were God. For Dussel, the notion of "exteriority" is a *meta*physical category; hence, it is only *metaphorically* spatial.[43] As a term denoting spatial location, or a spatial "starting point," outside a given "area," it can—and should—be construed only metaphorically. To construe it otherwise would be to mistake metaphysical exteriority for physical exteriority.[44]

Given this distinction, Dussel himself suggests the compatibility between "exteriority" and the "internal" subject-as-subject:

> The concept of exteriority should be complemented with that of transcendence internal to the system as Totality. Exteriority manifests itself in the system as a transcendence which is not entirely defined by the Totality.[45]

Metaphysical exteriority *manifests* itself, i.e., is visible or audible as a concrete reality, only as the "surplus meaning" *in* but not *of* my world, that is, only as "internal transcendence." It could not be otherwise, since the notion of "encounter" presupposes some common point of convergence. If the Other were absolutely exterior in every sense of the word, then I could never encounter him or her.

As exteriority manifesting itself as surplus meaning within the Totality, the starting point of foundational praxis is correlative to Lonergan's notion of the subject-as-subject in that this latter, as itself trans-ontologically oriented praxis, is the infra-ontological presence (spatially) of the trans-ontological praxis (metaphysically) of the subject-as-subject, which is, by definition, the "surplus meaning" in but not of the Totality. The subject-as-subject is Lonergan's term for describing the presence of internal transcendence, the metaphysical term for which is "exteriority."

The difference, therefore, is one of the perspective from which one views the reality of internal transcendence, or surplus of meaning. These perspectival differences are, as we will see below in greater detail, quite complementary. For both Dussel and Lonergan, conversion as trans-ontological is conversion to internal transcendence as a locus of meaning in but not of my world. As a North American, Lonergan views this metanoia from the perspective of the acting subject, caught within the dominant Totality, but seeking to extricate him or herself from its grasp; as a Latin American, Dussel views metanoia from the perspective of the exteriority to which the acting subject converts.

Yet both perspectives meet *in reality* inasmuch as the subject-as-subject *is* internal transcendence and exteriority *is* internal transcendence. Moreover, because this meeting point is internal *transcendence,* the self-liberation of the oppressed Other "puts the Totality into crisis"[46] and is thus concomitantly (hence the complementarity of perspectives) the incipient deliverance of the oppressor from the dehumanization of his own oppression—even if he resists with all his might.[47] Once the oppressed Other proclaims "I am a person" the oppressor is stripped of his *meta*physical power over the oppressed Other, even if his *physical* assaults on the Other increase, through repression.[48] In conversion, this deliverance from the most fundamentally, or radically oppressive power, namely, that of denying the Other's metaphysical being itself, becomes effectively realized as the oppressor acquiesces in the Other's, and hence in his own, liberation. Since the oppressor could continue to resist conversion, however, that conversion is not "automatic" (an interpretation towards which Dussel's method tends) but needs epistemological, or criteriological mediation.

Conversion Praxis as Criteriologically Mediated

Dussel's perspective leads him understandably, though not inevitably, to a notion of conversion, i.e., the affirmation of internal transcendence, as unmediated. His own history as a Latin American leads him to posit openness and commitment to the Other as themselves requiring no epistemological mediation. For Dussel, the only mediation occurs at the second, thematic level of *interpretation*.

From the perspective of the dominant Totality of North America, on the other hand, Lonergan articulates the need for mediating the pre-thematic orientation to, or the trans-ontological reality of, conversion using criteria inherent in the very structures of foundational human praxis. The need arises as a result of not only the socio-ideological structures attacked at the interpretative level by critical social science (e.g., dependency theories), but also the ideological distortion, or bias, of the structures of foundational human praxis ("conversion" if that praxis is effectively appropriated) itself. While Dussel sees the need for *socio*-ideological critique, his confidence in the power of the Other's suffering as trans-ontological prevents him from taking the need for criteriological mediation one step further, to the level of the trans-ontological conversion itself. Consequently, though the dialectic between faith in the Other and critique, e.g., of the Other's internalization of the dominant Totality's values, follows upon the conversion to the Other, that conversion is itself untouched by the faith-reason dialectic inasmuch as faith in the Other is not internally mediated (i.e., Lonergan's second and third basic levels of foundational human praxis are sidestepped). At this key point, then, Dussel's method retains a certain dualism—fideism is not the answer to rationalism.

Lonergan, on the other hand, provides an epistemological, criteriological mediation of conversion in the form of the basic structures of consciousness intrinsic to the subject-as-subject. Moreover, by extending the domination-liberation, or alienation-freedom dialectic to the foundational trans-ontological stance (as attentiveness-inattentiveness, intelligence-stupidity, rationality-irrationality, responsibility-irresponsibility), Lonergan maintains the openness of the stance without sacrificing its critical nature. Openness to trans-ontological reality is maintained insofar as we are willing and able to realize the basic transcendental imperatives of foundational praxis as trans-ontologically oriented. Those imperatives function dialectically to critique ontological closure as the result of fundamental inattentiveness, stupidity, irrationality, and irresponsibility, thereby providing—or, more specifically, dis-covering—criteria for *critically* mediating the foundational encounter with the Other. (One does not "leap" from experience to decision, or, if one does, he or she may find that leap is only from "the Same" into "the Same.")

Dussel makes openness to the Other its own criterion. The immediacy of the conversion to the trans-ontological Other can only posit itself as its own criterion in a circular fashion: we become open to the Other by becoming open to the Other. This might seem a valid approach from the perspective of the oppressed person, who experiences his or her suffering directly, as constituting its own call for justice. It is less effective from the perspective of one seeking to *become* open to the oppressed but having to engage in an intense struggle against both personal and social inattentiveness, stupidity, irrationality, and irresponsibility to do so. It is not sufficient to say, as Dussel does, that the reality of oppression is self-evident and that mediation is only necessary in order to "better detect *who* the poor are" (my emphasis).[49] Prior to the question "Who is the Other?" is the question "Is there any Other?" Certainly our North American experience has demonstrated that the answer to this latter question is anything but self-evident to most people of the dominant Totality.

The Forms of Conversion

Lonergan's criteria as inherent in foundational praxis do not impose a conceptual framework on the process of conversion from the dominant Totality to the Other. The dialectical operation of the criteria is thus not closed but inherently open because grounded in praxis as open, dynamic, and trans-ontologically oriented. That what he speaks of here is indeed an *open* dialectic is reflected, above all, in Lonergan's notion of conversion as a vertical exercise of freedom resulting in the acceptance of a new horizon that is not merely a (dialectical) development of the old, but is in fact discordant with the old and represents an about-face (hence, in Dussel's terms, an "analectic"). Lonergan's dialectic, because open, is thus quite compatible with Dussel's *ana*dialectical understanding of conversion.

This compatibility is evident, further, in the striking similarities between their non-reductionist notions of conversion as four-fold. Both allow for four forms of conversion which, though reflecting their two different perspectives, reveal these perspectives as mutually implicit, with Dussel's providing the socioeconomic and political specificity it lacks epistemologically.

	Dussel	*Lonergan*
CONVERSION	*Pedagogical*	*Intellectual*
	Political . . .	*Moral*
	Religious . .	*Religious*
	Erotic	*Psychic*

Intellectual and Pedagogical Conversion

The first of Lonergan's forms of conversion, already adumbrated above, is intellectual conversion. In the appropriation of the basic levels of consciousness we come to understand that knowing is more than just seeing. Beyond the empirical world of the senses, the "objectified" world, is the world mediated by meaning, the world reflecting the historical praxis of the community. And, because meaning is always on the move, the world mediated by meaning is always to some extent beyond our grasp.

This conversion from the ontologically-determined "body," or "object," to trans-ontological meaning is paralleled in Dussel by the notion of pedagogical conversion. Here the conversion is from *knowledge* as the dominant Totality's "remembering" of what is already "given" to *meaning* as an analectical, or trans-ontological, praxis-transformative event. The instrumental empiricism of knowledge as "already out there—or in here—now real" (in Lonergan's words) or as a "deposit" (in Dussel's words) is replaced, in both Lonergan and Dussel, by meaning as trans-ontological. For Lonergan, the reality of trans-ontological meaning is revealed in praxis-transformative self-appropriation and, hence, in the foundationally transformative, as well as disclosive, nature of education.[50] For Dussel, it is revealed in the teacher-student analectic, where the student's word as Other becomes transformative of the teacher's praxis, enabling the latter to ground his or her *later* critical stance in the student's exteriority.[51] Both Lonergan and Dussel, then, acknowledge the irreducibility of meaning-as-praxis-transformative to knowledge-as-disclosive.

Nevertheless, Dussel's notion of the conversion to trans-ontological meaning as fundamentally unmediated shows up again here. In this case, it is manifested in a sharp separation between faith in the word of the child or student and the critical stance later required of the teacher in order to discover the dominant Totality's values as internalized in the Other. This results in a separation of the analectical conversion *event*, or the "analectical moment," from the preceding and subsequent dialectical conversion *process*. (The dialectical process occurs, first, within the ontological horizon and, subsequent to what Dussel calls the "analectic as such," or the "analectical moment," in the empathic, but *critical* stance of the teacher vis-a-vis the student.) As noted earlier, conversion itself is thus divorced from, on the one hand, the dialectical struggle, within the dominant Totality, to become open to exteriority, and, on the other hand, the dialectical struggle, subsequent to the conversion "event," to become *increasingly* though *critically* (cf. Antonio Gramsci's "organic intellectual" referred to above) identified with the Other's historical project. The analectical moment, then, does not truly sublate dialectics at this point; rather, the two are divorced from each other.

In Lonergan's meta-method, however, conversion is grounded not only in praxis-as-self-appropriation, or in trans-ontological reality, but in that praxis as *both* the result of experience and decision, *and* of judgment, deliberation, etc. Trans-ontological conversion to the Other, as an existential commitment, is *at the same time* an act of attentiveness, intelligence, rationality, and responsibility.

Moral and Political Conversion

If intellectual conversion is, for Lonergan, the conversion to trans-ontological value, moral conversion also involves a vertical exercise of freedom, the commitment to a new ontological horizon in conflict with the old, yet one which, unlike the givenness of the old, is always open to further value in the pursuit of the good, in the pursuit of moral judgments proceeding more and more from trans-ontological praxis. This is the conversion from satisfaction to value.[52]

Much as Lonergan's notion of moral conversion involves, thus, a conversion from the objectification of the person implicit in the option for satisfaction, or gratification, over value to the personalization of the person implicit in the option for value, Dussel's notion of political conversion involves a turning from the objectification of the person in the reductionist political Totality, where money and greed are the supreme "values," to the personalization of the person implicit in his or her radical freedom as exterior to the dominant Totality. This involves the recovery and liberation of that in the dominated Other which, as *dis*value to the dominant Totality, represents trans-ontological value over against the dominant Totality's reductionist identification of value with "market value."[53]

Like Lonergan, then, Dussel understands value, not as defined by its relationship to or function within the dominant Totality, i.e., as that which serves and buttresses the system, but rather as an end in itself. Therefore, moral or political conversion is a conversion away from "value" as defined solely by its relation to the closed Totality to value as incarnated in the trans-ontological reality of the person. In the former, "value" is purely instrumental, inasmuch as it exists for the maintenance, or satisfaction of the system. In the latter, value, because embodied in the trans-ontological character of the person, challenges, and even contradicts the dominant Totality by unmasking its "values" and identifying these as, in reality, *dis*-values.[54]

Religious Conversion

Lonergan's third form of conversion, religious conversion, involves a surrender to the unrestricted, dynamic love of God revealed in the praxis of the self-transcending subject-as-subject. By subverting the facticity, or absolute significance of death, religious conversion gives meaning to the human struggle for authenticity. By revealing to us our innate dignity as children of God, God's love poured out in our hearts obviates "the need to establish our value by diminishing others." The value of the person is now grounded in God as the ultimate source of value. In opening our eyes to the mystery of God's love, religious conversion opens our eyes to the incarnation of that love in the person: "consequently, we can actually do the good with ease because we are in love." Religious conversion thus empowers us to discover and serve Ultimate Meaning-Value in its dynamic self-revelation in history. This process, in turn, unfolds in trans-ontological praxis, where the person as the locus of God's self-revelation as Absolute Love is, at the same time, revealed as innately free, i.e., as trans-ontological.[55]

In Dussel, the notion of religious conversion as the discovery of the mystery of God's love revealed in the extra-systemic mystery of the person is expressed in terms of the self-revelation of the divine Other in the human Other.[56] If, for Lonergan, religious conversion empowers us to perceive the "true and mysterious value of other persons," thereby making *agape* the ground of the personalization begun in moral conversion, for Dussel, it empowers us to perceive the "true and mysterious" exteriority of the Other (especially as that exteriority finds its most concrete sociohistorical manifestations in the woman, the poor, etc.), thereby revealing divine exteriority as the ground of human exteriority. In both cases, religious conversion implies a theological grounding of human exteriority, or of political and moral conversion. It also implies a concomitant atheism of the subject-as-object, or of the ontological horizon, or closed Totality, as foundational.

Psychic and Erotic (Sexual) Conversion

Gregson and Doran's major contribution to meta-method in the notion of psychic conversion has the result of thematizing the affective underside of conversion, thus adverting to the foundational import of feelings and the heuristic import of archeological symbols ("surplus of meaning") as trans-ontological. Through the recovery of the sensitive psyche and, hence, the integrity of transcendence and limitation we can escape the univocal objectivization, or objectivizing univocity, inherent in the option for logos over psyche. The appropriation, in the second immediacy, of the aesthetic consciousness (the elemental symbols of the psyche) undergirds the plurivocity of the normative order, or the trans-ontological praxis of the self-transcending subject-as-subject. The integrity of psyche-logos, and of anima-animus, militates against the male-oriented domination of nature and other human beings inherent in the totalizing univocity of logos.[57]

Dussel understands the Hellenistic and modern option for logos in much the same way as Lonergan does: as inherently totalitarian. In the erotic analectic, the Argentine posits the need for a recovery of the plurivocity of the tactile and aural *(dabar)* as a means of safeguarding the exteriority of the woman to the male Totality.[58] The logic of the Greek and modern logos is the reductionist, univocal logic of "the Same," where the woman is a non-person, objectified as an instrument of the male. Erotic, or sexual conversion involves, then, a recovery of the integrity of the visual and the aural, the logical and the aesthetic, logos and psyche. The liberation of woman is concomitantly the liberation of psyche (for Dussel, through *dabar*) from the domination of logos.

Conversion as Revealing the Mutual Implicitness of the Lonerganian and Dusselian Perspectives

The common underpinning provided by trans-ontological praxis, or internal transcendence, yields, therefore, quite similar views of conversion as a four-fold about-face in which one accepts a new horizon of meaning and value, which horizon is exterior to and conflicts with the old. Because internal transcendence is here perceived from different perspectives, however, conversion is also perceived from the different sociohistorical perspectives of the Latin American struggle to emerge as a free historical subject, on the one hand, and the North American struggle to discover itself as an obstacle to human liberation and to act upon that practical discovery on the other.

Precisely because they are both grounded in the internal transcendence of foundational praxis as trans-ontological, however, these different perspectives are not mutually exclusive, but, on the contrary, mutually implicit since the self-liberation of the oppressed is at the same time the beginning—at least—of the liberation of the oppressor from his (we use the pronoun quite consciously) self-dehumanization. Conversion, as normative trans-ontological praxis is, by definition, a conflict between *two* horizons. That praxis, then, can be *viewed* from the *perspective* of either horizon and, in fact, must be so viewed if there is to be any communication between loci of meaning, even if as "analogous" Totalities (analogy implying similarity as well as distinction). Conversion is always conversion to *internal transcendence*. And that conversion is always *between* two loci of meaning.[59]

Each perspective makes its own contribution to an explicitation of the conversion process: Lonergan's thematizes the internal structures, or levels, of the dominant Totality's conversion to the Other and thus uncovers epistemological criteria for mediating that conversion; Dussel's translates the internal structures of conversion into their socioeconomic and political manifestations as woman, child, student, poor class, dependent nation, incarnated divine Other, within the context of *Latin American* history as reflective of those manifestations. What makes possible the complementarity between Lonergan and Dussel is their common insistence on grounding conversion in trans-ontological praxis.

NOTES

/1/ See chapter 2 *supra* for an examination of Dussel's dialectical recovery of European philosophy.
/2/ See Dussel's discussion with Comblín, et al., in Dussel et al., *Liberación y cautiverio,* pp. 516–17.
/3/ See especially Dussel, et al., *Liberación y cautiverio,* pp. 515–90.
/4/ José Comblín, quoted in ibid., p. 518.
/5/ Cf. Comblín's argumentation in ibid., p. 526.
/6/ Bernard Lonergan, quoted in Matthew Lamb, *History, Method and Theology: A Dialectical Comparison of Wilhelm Dilthey's Critique of Historical Reason and Bernard Lonergan's Meta-Methodology* (Missoula, Montana: Scholars Press, 1978) p. 358.
/7/ Lamb, *History, Method and Theology,* p. 360.
/8/ Ibid., p. 359. Bernard Lonergan, *Method in Theology* (New York: Seabury, 1972) pp. 8, 14–15.
/9/ Lonergan, quoted in Lamb, p. 359.
/10/ Bernard Lonergan, "Cognitional Structure," in *Collection: Papers by*

Bernard Lonergan, ed. Frederick E. Crowe (New York: Herder and Herder, 1967) pp. 221–39.
/11/ Lamb, pp. 360, 364; Lonergan, *Method in Theology* pp. 8, 14–15.
/12/ Bernard Lonergan, *Insight: A Study of Human Understanding,* rev. ed. (New York: Longmans, 1958) pp. 217–44.
/13/ Lonergan, *Method in Theology,* p. 9.
/14/ Ibid., p. 6.
/15/ Ibid., p. 55.
/16/ Ibid.
/17/ Lamb, p. 368; Lonergan, *Method in Theology,* pp. 55, 359.
/18/ Lamb, p. 68; Lonergan, *Method in Theology,* pp. 231, 358–68; Lonergan, *Insight,* pp. 217–44.
/19/ Bernard Lonergan, *The Subject* (Milwaukee: Marquette University Press, 1968) pp. 22–23.
/20/ Lonergan, *Method in Theology,* p. 268.
/21/ Ibid.
/22/ Ibid., p. 237.
/23/ Ibid., pp. 237–38.
/24/ See and compare Doran's comments on Lonergan's reactions to the notion of psychic conversion as these comments appear in *Dialogues in Celebration,* ed. Cathleen M. Going (Montreal: Thomas Moore Institute, 1980) p. 147, and Lonergan's own analysis of the role of symbols as affective ciphers of reality in *Method in Theology,* pp. 64–69, 237–44, 267–71.
/25/ Lonergan, *Method in Theology,* p. 238.
/26/ Ibid., pp. 52–55, 76–81; Michael Rende, "The Development of the Notion of Conversion in the Works of Bernard Lonergan" (Ph.D. dissertation, Marquette University, 1983) chapter 3, p. 119.
/27/ Lonergan, *Method in Theology,* p. 240.
/28/ Ibid. Like the other forms of conversion, this is an ongoing process, for "deciding is one thing, doing is another." One still has to discover and root out those individual and social ideological biases—including those of so-called "common sense"—which militate against conversion (see Lonergan, *Insight,* pp. 217–44).
/29/ Rende, chapter 3, pp. 132–33.
/30/ Ibid., chapter 3, p. 39; Lonergan, *Method in Theology,* p. 241.
/31/ See Robert M. Doran, *Subject and Psyche: Ricoeur, Jung, and the Search for Foundations* (Washington, D.C.: University Press of America, 1977) p. iii; Lonergan, *Method in Theology,* pp. 31ff.; and Going, ed., *Dialogues in Celebration,* p. 147.
/32/ Robert M. Doran, "Theological Grounds for a World-Cultural Humanity," in *Creativity and Method: Essays in Honor of Bernard Lonergan, SJ,* ed. Matthew Lamb (Milwaukee: Marquette University Press, 1981) p. 112.
/33/ Robert M. Doran, *Psychic Conversion and Theological Foundations: Toward a Reorientation of the Human Sciences* (Chico, CA: Scholar Press, 1981) p. 142.
/34/ Ibid., pp. 139–41; Doran, *Subject and Psyche,* p. 118.
/35/ Doran, *Psychic Conversion,* pp. 128–31, 140, 152.
/36/ See, e.g., David Tracy, *The Achievement of Bernard Lonergan* (New

York: Herder and Herder, 1970) and Frederick Crowe, *The Lonergan Enterprise* (Cambridge, Mass.: Cowley Publications, 1980), as well as the abovementioned books by Matthew Lamb and Michael Rende.

/37/ See chapter 3 *supra*.

/38/ See Dussel, et al., *Liberación y cautiverio*, pp. 515–90.

/39/ See Lonergan, *Insight*, pp. 390–91.

/40/ Matthew Lamb, *Solidarity with Victims: Toward a Theology of Social Transformation* (New York: Crossroad, 1982) p. 129.

/41/ Ibid.

/42/ In my own discussions with Dussel, he raised this particular point to suggest a difference between his own method and Lonergan's. Nevertheless, Dussel was open to the possibility that the notion of "internal transcendence" might provide some common ground between Lonergan and himself. What we attempt to do in this chapter is to show how such a common ground does in fact exist.

/43/ Personal conversations with Dussel. Accordingly, Dussel's understanding of exteriority as "transcendence," "trans-ontological," or "metaphysical" should not be confused with Lonergan's notion of the "already-out-there-now-real" of naive realism.

/44/ Personal conversations with Dussel.

/45/ Dussel, *Filosofía ética*, 4:92; see also Dussel, *Filosofía de la liberación*, 1:81.

/46/ Dussel, *Método*, p. 274.

/47/ Ibid.

/48/ Ibid.

/49/ Dussel, quoted in Dussel, et al., *Liberación y cautiverio*, p. 517.

/50/ See Walter Conn, "Moral Development: Is Conversion Necessary?" in *Creativity and Method*, ed. Matthew Lamb, pp. 307–24.

/51/ See chapter 3 *supra*; Lamb, *Solidarity with Victims*, p. 106.

/52/ See chapter 3 *supra*.

/53/ See chapter 3 *supra*, pp. 33ff.; Lonergan, *Method in Theology*, pp. 36ff.

/54/ See chapter 3 *supra*.

/55/ Rende, chapter 4, pp. 7–9; Lonergan, *Method in Theology*, pp. 240–44.

/56/ See chapter 3 *supra*.

/57/ Lonergan, *Method in Theology*, pp. 31ff.; Doran, *Psychic Conversion*, pp. 139–43; Doran, "Theological Grounds for a World-Cultural Humanity," in *Creativity and Method*, ed. Matthew Lamb, pp. 111–12.

/58/ See chapter 3 *supra*, pp. 27ff.

/59/ Dussel, *Filosofía ética*, 2:37, 51.

CHAPTER SIX

THE ANADIALECTICAL METHOD AND "EXTERNAL" CRITIQUES OF LIBERATION THEOLOGY

In the previous chapter we suggested the possibility of complementing Dussel's anadialectical method with an analogously trans-ontological North American method. Consequently, the critique offered was "internal" inasmuch as it accepted the fundamental structures of Dussel's method while nevertheless suggesting that a different perspective on those structures might "fill them out" in a manner still consistent with the structures themselves.

In this chapter we will examine three major "external" critiques, i.e., critiques of the very methodological foundation of liberation theology as "reductionist." We will argue, in turn, that 1) all three suffer from a distorted interpretation of that foundation and 2) an appreciation of Dussel's work as a major contribution to Latin American liberation thought, and an in-depth reading of Dussel, could function as correctives to such an interpretation.

While all three are misinterpretations, there are, however, differences. The two critiques originating in the United States, those of Michael Novak and Dennis McCann, are doubly distorted in that they take "liberation theology" as a monolithic system the interpretation of which is—at best—an extrapolation from superficial analyses of a few "representative" theologians (and in some cases a sheer abstraction, unsupported by any analysis), which theologians are themselves misinterpreted. The method is thus one of inferring certain points from these theologians (which inferences are themselves suspect) and, from those inferences, hastily erecting a generalized conceptual framework within which "liberation theology" as a "whole" is judged—and found wanting.

The third critique, originating out of the Latin American Centro de Estudios para el Desarrollo e Integración de América Latina (CEDIAL) in Bogotá and represented principally by the work of CEDIAL's founder and director Roger Vekemans, S.J., is distorted in a more subtle sense. While the North American critiques' distortion of liberation theology results from the superficiality of their understanding of that theology, which superficiality then yields misinterpretations, the distortion represented by Vekemans' critique does not result so much from superficiality as from a simple misinterpretation of the foundations of liberation theology. The difference here is that Vekemans, as we will see, is always conscious of the difficulties implicit in any attempt to critique a "movement" which, by definition, is "in motion." He thus admits that his understanding of liberation theology is *necessarily* incomplete (this, despite the fact that, as is evident from the breadth of the works he refers to and footnotes, his understanding is far more complete than either Novak's or McCann's).[1] Vekemans' critique of liberation theology, therefore, while still not fully appreciating the complexity and import of the notion of foundational praxis, is itself—ironically perhaps—an implicit critique of Novak and McCann insofar as these represent liberation theology, not as a movement, but as a "system" by failing to be more conscious of their methodological limitations in attempting to move uncritically from inference to generalization (i.e., conceptualization) and then to judgment based on that generalization.

The differences among these critiques, however, do not obscure the fact that all these criticize liberation theology's understanding of foundational praxis for failing to safeguard the transcendental dimension of human praxis. Our response to this critique will include an explication of what has been implicit in our preceding chapters, namely, that an understanding and appreciation of Dussel's scholarship as itself already a refutation of the critique would preclude an interpretation of liberation theology as reductionist. Consequently, our intention will be both to respond directly to the specific critique as articulated by the above theologians and to argue that the ignorance and/or misunderstanding of the scope of Dussel's thought specifically—the most prolific Latin American liberation theologian and a major figure in the movement—can only lead to a distortion of one's understanding of liberation theology "as a whole." A broader knowledge and appreciation of Dussel's work would thus go a long way toward answering such critiques.

Michael Novak

Before addressing Michael Novak's specific critique of liberation theology's notion of foundational praxis, it will be necessary to examine the very notion of "liberation theology" as this is employed by Novak. In the course of that examination we will see how the methodological weaknesses of his critique lead to an incomplete and superficial understanding of liberation theology and, particularly, of the notion of foundational praxis.

In his book *The Spirit of Democratic Capitalism* Novak puts forth a critique of "liberation theology" and "liberation theologians." The only problem is that one is never sure—nor, it seems, is Novak—of what he means by those terms. According to Novak, liberation theology adopts a "Marxist perspective, analysis, and future."[2] That is as precise as he gets. The question of who the "liberation theologians" are receives an even more vague answer. Rather than refer to specific works of specific theologians he prefers to use the generic "liberation theologians"—notwithstanding the fact that, excepting a footnoted laundry list of translated works, almost none of which is ever referred to again, his primary source references are limited to Segundo (once), Míguez Bonino (once), Freire (once), and Gutiérrez.[3] What is more, almost all the references to Gutiérrez are either to Michael Dodson's *interpretation* of Gutiérrez (this interpretation being taken as definitive) in a secondary source, Dodson's article "Prophetic Politics and Political Theory in Latin America," or to Joseph Ramos' interpretation of Gutiérrez in a series of published essays.[4] Novak cites Dodson's and Ramos' interpretative essays far more often (28 times) than he cites the actual works of all liberation theologians combined.

A further example of such generalization can be found in Novak's manipulation of the term "pedagogy of the oppressed." While, in a footnote, he locates the origin of the term in the work of Paulo Freire, Novak's text baldly proclaims that "liberation theologian*s* speak of 'the pedagogy of the oppressed.'" (my emphasis).[5] He thus implicitly identifies Freire with liberation theology *per se*—a highly questionable proposition, particularly given Gutiérrez' own explicit acknowledgment of the need for a further development and modification of Freire's method.[6]

Even more astounding than the vagueness of Novak's category of "liberation theologians," and his assertion that because Paulo

Freire's method is the "pedagogy of the oppressed" that is then the method of all liberation theologians—even more astounding than Novak's later identification of Gutiérrez with liberation theology *per se*, is his inclusion of *Fidel Castro* as a liberation theologian:

> Latin American liberation theologians seem to be ambivalent with respect to multinational corporations. Even if in theory they loathe them, in practice they often seem to think they may be useful. Fidel Castro is said to have advised Nicaragua in 1980 to keep lines open to an internal private sector and to Western financial markets, in order to avoid excessive dependence upon the Soviet Union.[7]

Novak thus accuses "liberation theologians" of inconsistency as regards multinational corporations by citing, as an example of their inconsistency, the noted liberation theologian Fidel Castro!

One can hardly offer a valid critique if one does not know what the object of the critique is. Not only does Novak not specify the object of his critique, but he then proceeds to make generalizations out of this foundational ambiguity. One ultimately gets the impression that the reason Novak characterizes liberation theology as adopting a "Marxist perspective, analysis, and future" is that, for him, *anyone*—at least any Latin American—who adopts such a perspective, analysis, and future is *ipso facto* a liberation theologian.

It is, therfore, this methodological proclivity toward generalizations based on incomplete analyses that leads to Novak's confused reading of liberation theology. Thus, on the one hand, he points out that "liberation theologians" base their analyses of domination on the findings of "empirical studies" of dependency and, on the other, accuses these same "liberation theologians" of failing to provide "minimal concrete descriptions" of the political and economic realities of Latin America.[8] The only possible conclusion is either that Novak has contradicted himself or that the "liberation theologians" are different in each case—but here again he fails to specify and, in fact, in the first instance, again refers to Freire in a footnote as representative of "liberation theologians."[9] It seems that it is not the "liberation theologians" who are guilty of abstraction, but Novak himself.

In reference to the incorporation of dependency theory, Novak reads "liberation theologians," i.e., Gutiérrez, through the eyes of Joseph Ramos, who criticizes Gutiérrez for assimilating the weaknesses of dependency theory, among which are, according to Ramos, 1) its inability to account for the universality of dependency;

2) its ignorance of the internal, or national causes of underdevelopment; and 3) its reduction of social relations to economic relations.[10] Had Novak at this point gone directly to the writings of dependency theorists, Gutiérrez, Segundo, Dussel, and others he might have discovered, as we discussed in the first chapter above, 1) that, while all nations are to some extent "dependent" on others, Cardoso, Falletto, Frank, and all the liberation theologians referred to above identify "dependency" with that dependence which subordinates one nation to another so that the development of the former is determined by the development of the latter; 2) that external dependence is always viewed as dialectically articulated with internal dependence (Gutiérrez explicitly refers to and quotes Cardoso's elaboration of this relationship);[11] and 3) that, as we have already seen, dependency theory, specifically as drawn upon by Dussel, posits a *non*-reductionist dialectic between economic and social forms of domination.[12]

Novak fails to see this because, among other things, he fails, at the outset, to go directly to the primary sources. And, because he fails to go directly to the primary sources here, he cannot identify the object of his critique. That is, he does not specify the theologian(s) to which he refers at each point in his critique precisely because he *cannot* do so. He has nothing to refer to since his critique is not of particular liberation theologians but of some ethereal *concept*, "liberation theologians." Consequently, when he does refer to a Gutierrez or a Freire he immediately identifies them with "liberation theologians" and, therefore, seriously misinterprets the *historical movement* which is liberation theology. (Abstract concepts are notoriously impatient with the plurivocity of history.) Novak thus dissolves the complexity of the historical liberation movement within the monolithic, because abstract, concept of "liberation theology *per se*," or, more specifically, the generic concept of "liberation theologians."

This abstractness, or premature universalization of the particular, is, finally, nowhere more evident than in Novak's critique of the notion of foundational praxis. Here again, incomplete analysis leading to premature universalization yields misinterpretation as Novak makes evident his confusion regarding the notion of praxis used by different liberation theologians:

> Many commentators ascribe to liberation theology not only a superior interest in theory (and "prophecy") but also a superior emphasis on praxis. They understand the concept

> in the Marxist sense, not in the Anglo-American sense of *practice*, the experimental method, pragmatism, and self-reform.[13]

Novak's reference in the first sentence is to "commentators," hence not to any liberation theologian but to critics who ascribe these views to "liberation theology."

Next, Novak points to "two elements in the Marxist meaning [of praxis which] appeal to liberation theologians:"

> It [i.e., praxis] claims to take shape out of the "revolutionary consciousness" of the oppressed, and to be in touch with the people. It also claims to be in touch with the "real" reality of daily revolutionary struggle.[14]

From there it is but a short step to the proclamation that

> in this sense, Marxism is a form of illuminism familiar enough in mystical and religious writings. Instead of being applied to the other world, it is now applied to this world. Indeed, liberation theologians sometimes identify religious liberation with the this-worldly struggle for revolution against tyranny and poverty.[15]

Unsupported by *any* reference to liberation theology texts, the "logic" of Novak's analysis goes as follows: 1) "liberation theologians" employ the notion of praxis; 2) they "sometimes (Novak does not specify) identify" that notion with the "this-worldly struggle for revolution against tyranny and poverty;" 3) such an identification finds a parallel in "two elements" of the Marxist meaning of praxis; 4) therefore, "liberation theologians" are Marxists.

As the third premise and the conclusion stand or fall on the validity of the second premise, it is to the refutation of this latter that we will now turn, for it is here, in the allegations of an *identification* of praxis with political revolution, that the distortion of Novak's interpretation of the nature of liberation theology is rooted. We will therefore prescind from what would necessarily be a lengthy analysis of the Marxist understandings of praxis (and they are numerous, since Marx's understanding of the term developed and became more complex in the course of his career, to which understanding others were later added by the so-called "hyphenated" Marxists),[16] and proceed to show how neither Gutiérrez (the liberation theologian most alluded to by Novak) nor Dussel reduces the notion of praxis to *revolutionary* praxis understood in a strictly political sense.

In *La fuerza histórica de los pobres*, Gutiérrez explicitly responds to the critique of those who allege such a reductionist understanding of praxis on the part of liberation theologians. He argues, as he did earlier in *A Theology of Liberation* (though too few seem to have noticed), that praxis involves a *number* of dialectically-related dimensions:

> In effect, one of the oldest themes of liberation theology is the totality and the complexity of the process of liberation. A total liberation which is presented as one process, within which one must distinguish dimensions or levels: economic, social, political liberation, the liberation of the human being from all types of servitude, liberation from sin and communion with God as the ultimate foundation of human fraternity.[17]

All the levels, or dimensions, are mutually implicit. Hence, Gutiérrez avers, far before those who today argue for "*integral* liberation" liberation theologians were proposing a *real* integral liberation, not one which serves as a smoke screen for a spiritualizing intent:

> The synthetic and complete perspective . . . quickly gave rise to lively polemics. It was affirmed at the outset that one ran the risk of reducing Christ's liberation to its historical and social implications; from there, without blinking and without taking the trouble to read the relevant texts, [the critics] went on to say that those consequences were the only ones of interest to Christians committed to the process of liberation. Given the former argument as a self-evident presupposition, there then emerged the use of the expression "integral liberation" as an answer to that supposed reductionism. The curious thing was that liberation thus understood did not seem to be too faithful to the adjective "integral" which was used extensively, because its defenders insisted on *reducing it*, in turn, to a liberation exclusively situated on a so-called religious or spiritual plane.[18]

Praxis, in other words, *cannot* be reduced to any one dimension. Another North American critic, Schubert Ogden, understands this well, pointing to Gutiérrez' distinction between *historical* praxis (human interpersonal activity) and *liberating* praxis (a form of historical praxis) to argue that, even though the latter should, in our historical situation, be the form the former takes, nevertheless liberating praxis is always grounded in historical praxis and, therefore, contingent upon it.[19] *Foundational* praxis is not *revolutionary* praxis. To interpret Gutiérrez in any other way is to *mis*interpret him.

Because more systematically attentive to methodological questions, Enrique Dussel presents an even more comprehensively-articulated case against any reductionist understanding of foundational praxis. We have already seen how, for Dussel, 1) praxis is a much more foundational reality than is specifically revolutionary praxis, and 2) human trans-ontological praxis is grounded in the exteriority of the Other and, ultimately, in the exteriority of the absolutely absolute Other, God. (The human Other is the sacrament of the divine Other, hence the latter is in no way reduced to the former.)

We need only review Dussel's understanding of praxis to see that he, as one more "instance" of "liberation theologians," by no means reduces praxis to political revolution. If, for Dussel, praxis is "revolutionary," it is so not primarily in a political sense but primarily in its more fundamental, metaphysical sense as the manifestation of the trans-ontological nature of the person. Political revolution may at times be one form which foundational praxis takes, but, if that revolution is not grounded in the trans-ontological nature of the person, that is, if it becomes dialectically closed (as in Stalinist Marxism), it becomes a *distorted* form of praxis.[20] "Political revolution" is but a secondary level of praxis, and an ambiguous one at that.

Consequently, for Dussel, praxis is not a *particular kind* of human interpersonal activity, but is that activity itself as the concrete sign of the irreducibility of the person—or God—to any Totality.[21] Dussel does not arbitrarily choose a particular kind of human praxis as methodologically foundational, but rather discovers human praxis as inherently trans-ontologically oriented (which orientation becomes realized in the self-liberation of and conversion to the Other) and, hence, as both open to liberation and susceptible to distortion, or domination. Foundational praxis so understood is, therefore, the only possible *foundational* praxis, since it is what defines human existence as *personal* existence, vis-a-vis both God and other persons. It is neither a "particular kind of praxis" nor an ambiguous "praxis," but trans-ontologically oriented praxis, which *is* human praxis. One may be, however, "more" or "less" open to the realization of the internal demands of praxis.

Trans-ontological praxis is the historical sign—either as realized or unrealized trans-ontology—of the radical freedom of the person. In foundational praxis, the irreducibility of the person is made manifest, whether by affirmation in liberation or by negation in domination (hence Dussel can speak of Latin American historical praxis as involving a dialectic of domination and liberation). By revealing itself as the negation of exteriority, therefore, even distorted praxis reveals exteriority, or the trans-ontological foundation, even if only as its negation.[22]

To deny the import of foundational praxis—as Dussel uses the term—is thus to deny the trans-ontological nature of the person; it is to deny human freedom as foundational and, hence, to reduce the person to one more object among others (whether through a conceptualist subjectivism, instrumental rationalism, or technocratic empiricism). In other words, the only way to safeguard the transcendence of God *qua* God and of the person *qua* God's image, i.e., the only way to safeguard transcendence *at all*, is precisely to discover human praxis as foundational.

In addition to many others not mentioned here (some of which we discuss below) neither Gutiérrez nor Dussel have any intention of reducing praxis to revolutionary praxis. Quite on the contrary, both are explicitly conscious of the need to affirm the irreducibility of human freedom. All they ask is that "integral liberation" be truly *integral* liberation. As Arthur McGovern correctly observes, if their *emphasis* is in one direction, it is only because, for centuries, the predominant emphasis has been in the other.[23]

Dennis McCann

Another major "external" critique of Latin American liberation theology is that set forth by Dennis McCann in his book *Christian Realism and Liberation Theology: Practical Theologies in Creative Conflict*. Like Novak's, this critique challenges the methodological foundations of liberation theology from "outside," that is, through the imposition of an abstract interpretative framework within which "liberation theology" is then judged to be reductionist. (Though some generalizations are inevitable, one ought at least to be conscious of when one is making them.) Consequently, McCann's work exhibits some of the same shortcomings as does Novak's. McCann's major objection to liberation theology is also that its method is reductionist inasmuch as it "tries to synthesize [an epiphanic religious perspective] with the dialectical vision, which is incompatible with it." He argues that the method of liberation theology is inconsistent with its content in that the method inevitably politicizes the content so that any properly "religious" perspective is lost. There are, therefore, two key elements in McCann's criticism: the notion of dialectical *method,* and the notion of religious *content*. These are deemed incompatible.[24]

In his book, McCann engages in a lengthy exposition and analysis of Reinhold Niebuhr's Christian realism as a paradigmatic example of what he means by a "religious vision" or religious content:

> Its theological categories are formulated in relation to a religious vision of the Hidden God whose meaning for humanity is paradoxically revealed in the general content and structure of human experience as confirmed through a pious reading of the Bible. Its insights are spelled out in a "Christian interpretation" of "the nature and destiny of man," which functions to provide a religious perspective on the ultimate limits of human thinking and acting.[25]

The vision of liberation theology, as described by McCann, differs markedly from that of Christian realism:

> By contrast, liberation theology begins with a religious vision not of a hidden God, but of one who emphatically stands revealed in the struggles of oppressed peoples.[26]

The historical emphasis of liberation theology implies the emergence of a liberation *methodology* which would be true to the historical *locus theologicus*. According to McCann, "it is clear that Paulo Freire's theory of conscientization provides the distinctive methodological principle." It is this methodological principle, concludes McCann, that, because of its "subversive" rather than "constructive" intent, "promises . . . to eliminate theological reflection entirely." The contradiction lies in the inability of the *subversive* method to carry through a "constructive theological intention," i.e., that of an epiphanically revealed God.[27]

What, then, are the characteristics of this "subversive method?" First, it is subversive of "academic" theology in that it proposes a theology defined in terms of a "critical reflection on praxis," which would be in marked contrast to a theology claiming to be "above" historical vicissitudes. Secondly, the method proposes a "political hermeneutics of the Gospel," a term which, according to McCann, liberation theologians (i.e., *not* e.g., Gutiérrez) have taken over from Metz and attempted to "adapt to the Latin American reality."[28]

Finally, argues McCann, the political hermeneutics of the Gospel, as adapted by liberation theologians in their insistence upon "utopia" as a necessary corrective to Metz' "eschatological proviso," implies a method which would satisfy the requirements of this transformative, or subversive, way of doing theology. Enter Paulo Freire. As a preface to his discussion of Freire, however, McCann refers to what he considers the "confusion" between the Medellín notion of evangelization and Freire's. That confusion arises, maintains McCann, from the inconsistency between the bishops' call to evangelize *both* the "popular sectors" and "key men" and Freire's "vision of a world divided between oppressors and the oppressed." By inserting these prefatory comments, McCann hopes to show that Freire, and the other liberation theologians, go "beyond the bishops' more cautious endorsement."[29]

Next, McCann presents an analysis of Freire's method. According to McCann, that method is characterized by what Lucien Goldmann calls the "dialectical vision," i.e., "a global perspective on history as a whole . . . which grounds the substantive values that inspire both the practice and the theory." It is this *subversive* dialectic which, McCann maintains, is incompatible with the other two, *constructive* intentions of Freire's pedagogy: literacy training leading to a "social awakening," and "a revolutionary theory of education derived from this practice."[30]

Consequently, the focus of McCann's critique of Freire is this subversive dialectical method:

> The dialectical vision that grounds this theory pictures the whole of history as a struggle for liberation. Freire clearly envisions a historic struggle in which human freedom as an "untested feasibility" is to be realized by overcoming alienation both in consciousness and in action.[31]

The key to the dialectic, then, is the "conflict over limit situation:" that is, "just as 'liberation' means overcoming limit-situations, so 'oppression' means being overcome by them."[32] McCann's critique is that Freire's dialectic "sees history as a struggle for freedom without defining the content of that freedom, save as overcoming all possible limit-situations."[33]

In addition to implying the necessity of deideologizing the "popular sector," therefore, Freire's method "implies that the liberating God of the Bible is identified with the struggle of the oppressed." According to McCann, this latter proposition both "transgresses the 'eschatological proviso' recognized by Metz" and "raises a question whether it is possible to speak of a liberating God and still remain faithful to the dialectical vision presupposed in the method of conscientization."[34]

McCann's negative answer to this question is based on his

assertion that "conscientization in principle recognizes no genuine limit-situations." The logical implication of the absence of any insurmountable limit-situations, he continues, is a Feuerbachian humanism which restores to "man" the powers projected onto "God." Ultimately, liberation implies the dissolution of religion, since religion posits certain limit-situations as insurmountable and, therefore, represents an obstacle to full human liberation. Consequently, "humanization no longer involves recognizing the limits of human knowing and acting, but adopting a strategy committed to overcoming them."[35]

McCann's critique of liberation theology's method as inconsistent with that theology's epiphanic vision of a God who "stands revealed in the struggles of oppressed peoples" is thus essentially a critique of that method as ultimately secularist and reductionist. His argument proceeds as follows: 1) Paulo Freire's theory of conscientization is reductionist; 2) "it is clear that Paulo Freire's theory of conscientization provides the distinctive methodological principle" of liberation theology; 3) therefore, liberation theology, if it remains true to its method, is reductionist. What is more, at this last step in the argument, liberation theology reveals itself as *Marxist* in that it incorporates the Feuerbachian humanism of the young Marx, thereby importing "Marxism's dialectical vision" into the very foundation of a liberation methodology. The key to McCann's critique of liberation theology, therefore, is his identification, first, of Freire's notion of liberation with the overcoming of *all possible* limit-situations, and, secondly, of that alleged notion of liberation with liberation theology *per se*. He can then claim that liberation theology's method, if consistently adhered to, recognizes no geniune limit-situations and that, consequently, liberation theology is no "theology" at all, since, for theology, God is the ultimate Limit-Situation.[36]

In response to McCann's critique we will now turn, first, to Freire himself, secondly to Gutiérrez and Segundo, and then, notwithstanding McCann's charge that a significant feature of liberation theology is "its neglect of theological ethics," to Enrique Dussel, a liberation theologian who has devoted a good twenty five years to the development of an ethics of liberation.[37]

If McCann's assertion that Freire's method implies a denial of any genuine limit-situations can be shown to be invalid, then the remainder of McCann's critique, constructed as it is upon this premise, must fall. A review of Freire's work provides ample evidence to contradict McCann's premise. Freire introduces the notion of limit-situation to describe those situations in which humans are reduced to mere objects: "In order to achieve humanization, which presupposes the elimination of dehumanizing oppression, it is absolutely necessary to surmount the limit-situations in which persons are reduced to things."[38] From Freire's quite tame acknowledgment of the existence of dehumanizing situations which must be overcome, McCann draws the inference—completely unsupported by any textual evidence—that Freire foresees the historical and anthropological possibility of "overcoming all possible limit-situations."[39]

Not only does Freire never argue—either explicitly or implicitly—for such as possibility, but he expressly *denies* the possibility of overcoming all limit-situations in history:

> The revolution . . . does not extinguish the dramatic tension of our existence. It resolves the antagonistic contradictions which make the tension *more* dramatic. But, precisely because the revolution forms part of the tension, the former is as *permanent* as the latter. Historically it is *impossible* to conceive of the installation of an imperturbable reign of peace. History is a "becoming," a human event. (My emphases)[40]

According to Freire, therefore, the overcoming of "all possible limit-situations" is a historical *im*possibility, for these very limit-situations *define* human beings as *historical* creatures. Liberative praxis may *reduce* the *degree* of tension between limit-situations and limit-acts, but the tension itself is *permanent*. Furthermore, it is precisely Freire's historical emphasis that leads him to make such an observation, for, if "history is a 'becoming'," then the overcoming of "all possible limit-situations" could only be a possibility in some transhistorical realm. The struggle against limit-situations *defines* our historical existence as human beings; therefore, were all limit-situations to be overcome, we would no longer be *human* beings. The struggle is permanent because the tension between limit-acts and limit-situations is permanent.

Building upon this misinterpretation of Freire, McCann goes on to posit that "it is clear that Paulo Freire's theory of conscientization provides the distinctive methodological principle" for liberation theology.[41] The major examples he gives of liberation theologians who succumb to the reductionist logic of Freire's method are Gutiérrez and Segundo.[42]

In attempting to force Gutiérrez into his framework, McCann

completely distorts the Peruvian theologian's intent, which is not that of replacing God by human beings as the "primary agent or 'Subject' in human history."[43] Gutiérrez argues instead for the *cooperation* of human beings in the liberative process, with *total* liberation, or salvation, including not only a "transformation of concrete historical and political conditions" but also a fulfillment "above and beyond" history, a fulfillment "not within the reach of human foresight or any human effort."[44] Repeatedly, as if in expectation of the reductionist critique, Gutiérrez warns against an oversimplified interpretation of "the complex relationship which exists between the Kingdom and historical events, between eschatology and politics."[45] He distinguishes between utopia as "historical projection" and the Kingdom as "the *gift* of the future promised by God."[46] These realities, however, are "profoundly linked:"

> The Gospel does not provide a utopia for us; this is a human work. The Word is a free gift of the Lord. But the Gospel is not alien to the historical plan; on the contrary, the human plan and the gift of God imply each other. The Word is the foundation and the meaning of all human existence; this foundation is attested to and this meaning is concretized through human actions.[47]

The promise of the Kingdom as gift is the condition of the possibility of our liberative praxis; and, in turn, that praxis is the historical concretization of the promise. Whereas the "Kingdom *come*" is *definitive* liberation, or salvation, the utopic vision, because historical, is always "dynamic" and "must be revised and concretized constantly."[48] In basic concurrence with Gutiérrez, Hugo Assmann explains the relationship as follows:

> The Kingdom of God is not a new historical order which could be planned in detail. It is a *process* . . . [and] as process . . . it is always within and always beyond. Liberation is also above all a process. But in its concretization it becomes a historical project and a plausible alternative. Every revolutionary process suffers from the necessity of institutionalization and runs the risk of attempting to institutionalize itself in such a way that its ulterior processual mobility is stopped. It then becomes a kind of "religion. . . ."[49]

Consequently, it is precisely the self-correcting nature of the utopic vision that *precludes* any absolute politicization of faith.[50] The Kingdom is a proleptic reality in that it is both "already" and "not yet" present: "already" insofar as the utopic vision is concretized, and "not yet" insofar as all such concretizations await their definitive fulfillment in "the" arrival of the Kingdom as gift. In Gutiérrez' words:

> Without liberating historical events there would be no growth of the Kingdom. But the process of liberation will not have conquered the very roots of oppression and the exploitation of human beings by other human beings without the coming of the Kingdom, which is above all a gift.[51]

What Gutierrez describes here as "gift" Dussel describes as "trans-cosmological," and Assman as "trans-processual."[52]

Through his eisegesis of Gutiérrez, therefore, McCann distorts the Peruvian's decidedly *non*-reductionist thought. He misconstrues Gutiérrez' categories of "Kingdom" and "utopia," since, for Gutiérrez, the Kingdom does *not*, as McCann maintains, "represent . . . a 'utopia.'"[53] Consequently, he misconstrues Gutiérrez' method and misrepresents it as reductionist.

Like Novak, McCann insists on reading Freire's method into Gutiérrez, thereby distorting Gutiérrez on two counts: by misinterpreting Freire, and then by attempting to read this misin terpretation into Gutiérrez, thus yielding a doubly distorted interpretation.[54] And McCann does this despite the aforementioned acknowledgment by Gutiérrez of the need for further modifications of Freire's method.[55]

McCann, however, does not stop with Gutiérrez, but extends his critique of "liberation theology" to Juan Luis Segundo, by averring that the Uruguayan Jesuit completes the secularization of theology begun by Gutierrez and that Segundo thus carries the logic of Freire's method to its own logical conclusion. Like Gutiérrez', then, Segundo's method is criticized for being—even more explicitly than Gutiérrez'—reductionist.[56]

McCann's misreading of Freire is now imposed on a concomitant misreading of Segundo. For instance, McCann contends that Segundo's method is elitist. Segundo is supposed to conceive of the basic communities as elitist, sectarian cadres who "manipulate" the masses.[57] This, however, is far from Segundo's understanding of the relationship between masses and minorities. The Uruguayan theologian understands "minorities" not as "elites" but more as "organic intellectuals" in the Gramscian sense. That is, the minorities, who become agents of social change, arise out of the masses and eventually return to and are dissolved within the newly-empowered masses (now, in Dussel's vocabulary, "the people"). Minorities are inevitably a feature of any society; the question is whether they will, as "elites," oppress the masses or whether they will serve the masses:

> Whether we label these minorities with the pejorative term "elites" will depend on whether or not they place the newly acquired and difficult skill at the service of the masses. Medical doctors, for example, will always be a minority. Whether the medical profession will be "elitist" or not will depend on whether it develops as a privilege for those who possess the skill in question or is placed *at the service of all*, though of course medical skill and knowledge will never be a capacity shared by all.[58]

Far from being a positive term for Segundo, therefore, "elite" is a pejorative term. Segundo's notion of "minorities" is more one of a "leaven in the mass" than one of "elites" *over* the mass:

> This minority effort among the masses is not meant to impose elitist demands on the latter, nor is it meant to construct a society based on minority exigencies.[59]

Next, McCann criticizes Segundo's "hermeneutic circle" and understanding of faith as "deutero-learning" (i.e., "learning how to learn") for evacuating faith of any content:

> In order to clarify the meaning of this shift from the content to the process of Jesus' teaching, Segundo makes a distinction between the faith and the ideology of Jesus. The substantive content of Jesus' teaching is understood as ideology, and is authoritative only for its immediate historical context. . . . [C]onscientization is no longer just a method for correlating the themes of liberation and salvation, but is itself the actual message of salvation.[60]

If, by saying that "Segundo makes a distinction between the faith and the ideology of Jesus," McCann means that Segundo understands faith as in*separable* from its historical manifestation in ideologies, then McCann is most assuredly correct in his assessment. For Segundo, and for anyone who takes history, and hence human beings, seriously, normative truths are not ahistorical concepts floating around in space, but are relational realities which, if they are to be at all meaningful, can *only* be apprehended contextually.

This is not to say, however, that faith *is* an ideology. Segundo explicitly denies such an identification: "faith certainly is not an ideology."[61] McCann refers to Segundo's characterization of the Nicaean formula as a "methodological symbol" to support his thesis that Segundo reduces faith to ideology. In so doing, however, McCann focuses on the adjective "methodological" to the exclusion of the noun "symbol." In quoting the following passage from Segundo,

> On the one hand they [i.e., methodological symbols] have no direct ideological translation; on the other hand they have no other function but to be translated into ideologies,[62]

McCann focuses on the second clause and ignores the first. The result is that his interpretation of Segundo's notion of faith is only half true, and hence false. It is indeed true that, for Segundo, the symbols of faith "have no other *function* but to be translated into ideologies," i.e., that the norms of faith have no *efficacy* apart from their historical meaning. It is *also* true, however, (and herein lies the dialectic which McCann fails to perceive), that those norms are symbols with "no direct ideological translation." Hence, while the norms of faith perform a methodological *function*, that function does not, in itself, *define* the norms.

McCann's distortion of Segundo here is further evidenced in the conclusion that, for Segundo, liberative method "is no longer just a method for correlating the themes of liberation and salvation, but is itself the actual message of salvation."[63] Again, the charge is that Segundo reduces salvation to political liberation.

This charge does little justice to Segundo's seminal attempt, in *Grace and the Human Condition*, to perform just such a correlation. In an attempt to contrast the Thomistic notion of the correlation with liberation theology's notion of the same correlation, McCann makes the following statement:

> While Thomism affirms that "grace builds on nature," grace represents an ontological change in human nature that prepares us for a heavenly fulfillment with God beyond history in the "beatific vision."[64]

However, if one understands "heaven" not as some pre-existing, ethereal realm to which we "go," Segundo would be in accord with the Thomistic view. As one educated in Thomist categories, Segundo sees his task precisely as that of demonstrating that grace builds—and is not superimposed—on nature.[65]

In chapter two of *Grace and the Human Condition* Segundo presents a lengthy refutation of the Pelagian attempt to reduce salvation to human works alone. First, in an exegesis of the Nicodemus pericope ("unless a man has been born again . . ."), he emphasizes the gratuitous nature of grace:

> [T]he aim of Christianity is not obtained by any sort of human means but by a "new birth," a "new creation."[66]

This "new creation" is ultimately "the gift of God."[67] Moreover, it is precisely the gratuity of grace that is the "subversive" message of the Gospel, for salvation is a gift revealed to children, to the poor and weak, and hidden from the wise, the rich, the powerful. Nicodemus was a "wise, powerful, and just man," but no amount of wisdom, power or virtue could gain him salvation.[68]

Segundo quotes with approval Vatican I's articulation of the notion of grace: "It also transforms us, above and beyond the bounds of nature. . . ."[69] While agreeing that the tendency has often been to interpret this statement in a Platonic context, Segundo interprets it not as identifying grace with "an elevation vis-a-vis the human," but as seeing in the movement of grace "an elevation *of* the human."[70] Such an assertion, however, by no means vitiates the character of grace as *both* "new" and "gift."[71]

In his discussion of Vatican II, Segundo becomes even more explicit on the question:

> Now what about the approach of arguing against the *separation* of the natural and the supernatural? Is that equivalent to denying the *distinction* between them? Or to suppressing the natural in the concrete? Certainly not, for that would be replacing one over-simplification with another.[72]

Like Gutiérrez, Segundo opts for a *genuine* "*integral* liberation:" "Work and gift are two facets of the same reality, like day and night."[73] Salvation would then be, not a "reward" for a good life, but the culmination of a life "graced" from the very beginning, which grace is the gift that makes the culmination possible.[74]

That culmination, moreover, is indeed "ontologically" new:

> Now what does this adjective "new" mean precisely? It is worth pointing out that while there are two Greek words to designate "new" (*neos* and *kainos*), the term used almost invariably to designate the new reality to which we are elevated by grace is *kainos*, not *neos*. And exegetical studies indicate that while *neos* signifies that which is new in time and hence *another* of something (e.g., a new year), *kainos*

> designates that which is new in quality and hence that which is renewed or transformed. . . . *Kainos* is also the term used to signify the results of transformations effected by God: i.e., renovations which come from above. . . . Hence the use of one single term joins the two meanings with the Greek word *anothen* which can also mean one of two things: anew or from on high. . . .[75]

This double meaning is the same one found in *Guadium et Spes*.[76]

At the risk of beating a dead horse—or, rather, one that by all rights *should* have been dead long ago—we turn to Segundo's "Clarification," at the end of *Grace and the Human Condition*, of the notion of "salvation." Basing himself in an exegesis of the development of the notion of salvation from the Old Testament, through the Synoptics, to Paul, Segundo concludes (citing especially not only the Romans texts but also Mk. 16:16 and Lk. 8:12) that salvation comes by grace through faith. In faith, gift (grace, salvation) and work (liberation) are united:

> Faith is the surrender of one's whole being to the person, community, and teaching of God *who*, strictly speaking, saves human beings with his grace *from the evils* which, here and now in this life, point toward absolute paralysis, absolute enslavement, absolute death.
>
> Thus the absolute, eschatological dimension of salvation is present, not as something opposed to the present "age" but as its gratuitous and actual, even though still invisible, absolutization.[77]

Citing Romans 8:14–24, Segundo shows how salvation, as salvation *from* "inner slavery and fear, the corruption of the surrounding universe (destined for vanity otherwise), and the subjection of our body . . . leads into the reality *par excellence: our liberty*. If we look closely, we will see that the evils from which we 'are saved' are nothing more nor less than the fetters on a creative existence." Hence, salvation implies liberation. The absolutization of salvation, on the other hand, does *not* imply an "other-worldliness." As further corroboration of this latter point, Segundo refers to Paul's use of past, present and future tenses in Romans 8:14–24. *All* of these tenses are used to describe salvation (" 'The Spirit you have received . . . we are God's children . . . while we wait for God to make up his sons.' "). "In reality," Segundo continues, "the Christian stands between two forms of knowledge, according to the first Epistle to the

Corinthians: that which comes from the *witness* of Christ, and that which will come from his *manifestation* (or apocalypse)."[78]

At this point, we will leave it to the reader to decide for him or herself whether, as McCann alleges, Segundo's method does not correlate the themes of liberation and salvation, having reduced salvation to political liberation.[79] Let it simply be noted that nowhere in either the text, the footnotes, or the bibliography of McCann's *Christian Realism and Liberation Theology* is *Grace and the Human Condition* (or *any* of Segundo's five volume *Theology for Artisans of a New Humanity*) cited, referred to, or otherwise mentioned.

One can attain further clarification of the non-reductionist character of liberation theology by turning to the writings of Enrique Dussel, none of which are referred to in McCann's book. More systematically than other liberation theologians Dussel explicitly challenges and disavows any reductionism, including that of the closed, negative dialectic.[80]

We have seen how the *ana*dialectical method is characterized both by an opening to transcendence—human and divine—and by a practical-poietic liberation *grounded in* that transcendence, or exteriority.[81] Moreover, as we have seen, the exteriority of the person is grounded in the exteriority, or transcendence, of God as its condition of possibility.[82] And the exteriority of God is defined as *the* "limit-situation:"

> When human beings reach the "limit" they confront the "beyond;" when finiteness discovers itself as such the question of the infinite can be proposed; when time enters into crisis the possibility of opening oneself to eternity is born.[83]

As against McCann, Dussel would aver that it is precisely *because* God is a *transcendent* God that God's self-revelation as "internal transcendence" in the world is most visible there where the greatest degree of exteriority exists, i.e., in the poor, the woman, the child, etc. If God is exteriority to our Totality, then God is most visible "*in*" exteriority. Consequently, the assertion that the countenance of the human Other is the epiphany of God in no way implies an "immanentization" of God; on the contrary, it *safeguards*—and is the *only* way to safeguard—God's transcendence against those who would wish to divinize the System.

If the Totality were the epiphany of God, then God *would* be completely immanentized. One would then be confronted with some version of pantheism, or its secularized form, ontological materialism (cosmological immanentization), classism, nationalism, or practical materialism (political immanentization), or patriarchy/phallocracy (sexual immanentization).[84] Precisely because these are not grounded in the absolute (trans-cosmological) exteriority of God, their worship is not religious but, as we have already seen, fetishistic:

> Our thesis, then, is the following: *The European ego, and later that of the entire "center," constitutes a divinized, fetishized Totality, which divinity demands that the oppressed of the periphery* (and those who are found within the divinized "order:" the child, the woman, and the worker) *render obligatory worship to it.*[85]

Consequently, the condition of the possibility of genuine religious worship is an atheism of the divinized Totality.[86]

The atheism of the divinized Totality is, as well, the condition of the possibility of human practical-poietic liberation, for, as long as the Totality remains closed, or divinized, the person will not be defined as an end in him or herself but rather will be defined by his or her function in the Totality.[87] Human liberation, however, is also the condition of the possibility of genuine religious worship, i.e., of the acknowledgment of a transcendent God:

> When the "center" becomes conscious of its offense and permits the liberation of the dominated peoples there will be an Other and, when the Other is acknowledged, only then will the possibility of the revelation of the Absolute Other emerge.[88]

Therefore, human liberation and divine transcendence are coimplicit in their mutual exteriority.[89]

Far from immanentizing God, Dussel "exteriorizes" God. Again, God is, for Dussel, the ultimate Limit-Situation:

> God is the one who "by his goodness and mercy saw fit to choose me"—Bartolomé tells us still. The anthropological Other is absolved from continuity with the system; therefore that Other is absolute, and also holy, worthy. But that which we are dealing with now is the "absolutely" absolute, the one absolved from continuity even with human history and humanity itself. Concerning the nameless, because situated beyond not only the entity and being but the distinctly human exteriority, concerning the absolutely absolute Other, there are only footprints, signs which give signals, vestiges. Paradoxically, a mystic finds him or herself

> newly united with a revolutionary, or with a logician who is apparently skeptical of meta-physics. They all coincide in that, concerning the unspeakable, one must maintain sacred silence, because concerning that which is not an entity, nor world, nor finite exteriority, there are only "footprints" of its Absence.[90]

We quote this passage at length because here we find beautifully expressed the intrinsic unity between the epiphanic vision, hence liberation, and worship, hence transcendence. Epiphany is not reduction, but internal transcendence (the divine Limit-Situation being revealed in the limit-situation that is the person).[91] This passage capsulizes the intent of Dussel's entire project and, in so doing, shows McCann's paradoxical dichotomy of historical praxis/contemplation to be a false one.[92] It shows how in McCann's notion of contemplation the only thing contemplated and worshipped is the divinized system; for if the divine Other is not to be found in the human Other, in the person insofar as he or she is exteriority, and thus, especially in those persons *most* exterior to the system, then what is worshipped is not a transcendent God but the system itself.[93] The human Other is the mediation of the divine Other:

> The infinity of the meta-physical liberty of the Other glows as the sign that points to the Infinite itself. Consequently, the access to the Infinite is the *real* affirmation of the one who reveals it and in whose epiphany it is bared: the oppressed as Other.[94]

Liberative praxis is, at the same time, worship of the divine Other.[95]

Dussel thus furnishes a liberation methodology that overcomes the transcendence/immanence dichotomy without thereby dissolving it in either direction. Moreover, his method is fundamentally both ethical and theological in that it is grounded in trans-ontological human praxis as open to human and divine exteriority. The anadialectical method thus relates ethics and theology as the co-implicit correlates to a metaphysics of exteriority. Despite McCann's criticism of liberation theology for not concerning itself with theological ethics, it is precisely in theological ethics that Dussel relates transcendence and immanence in a non-reductionist manner, through the epiphanic analogy between human and divine exteriority. Far from reducing transcendence to immanence, far from politicizing transcendence, the anadialectical method—like Freire's pedagogical method, *a* method of liberation theology—points to the transcendent ground of all existence.

Roger Vekemans, S.J.

Another variation of the critique of liberation theology as reductionist is that presented over the course of the last several years by the Belgian-born Jesuit Roger Vekemans. This critique, the most significant one issuing from Latin America itself, has taken shape in a series of articles appearing in the CEDIAL journal, *Tierra Nueva*. What primarily distinguishes Vekemans' *method* of critique from that of the North American critiques discussed above is 1) his broader knowledge of the material and, hence 2) greater sensitivity to the partiality, or incompleteness, of his observations:

> The theology of liberation is still a current in the proper sense of the word, and its very fluidity makes practically impossible the utilization of the technique of representative demonstration, which presupposes the existence of a universe to some degree already constituted, delimited, and stable.[96]

Unlike Novak and McCann, therefore, Vekemans is conscious of the difficulties and dangers inherent in his enterprise. He knows that "the theology of liberation, even if one confines it to Latin America, is almost as diverse as are the authors who invoke a relationship to it."[97]

What Vekemans focuses on, then, is not the "nature" of liberation theology, but its "tendencies." Moreover, he admits that these tendencies could be "ordered from the most positive to the most negative." He proposes to interpret the tendencies in their most negative light and explains, as his reason for doing so, that the acceptance of liberation theology by many Latin American theologians has often been so enthusiastic as to be acritical. "Nevertheless," he readily admits, "the adoption of a more positive projection would be equally legitimate."[98]

Such a critique, however, soon begins to lose its force, since *any* theology, philosophy, etc., has negative *tendencies*. The past hundred years have witnessed the untold suffering brought about by the "tendencies" of conceptualist, abstract philosophical systems.[99] To criticize liberation theology because it has negative tendencies is to criticize it for being a *human* movement. The question one must ask is not, "Are there negative tendencies?"—an inevitability in any case—but, "What internal, methodological safeguards are provided against the *realization* of those tendencies?"

The most sinister tendency which Vekemans and his colleagues detect in liberation theology is that of reducing faith to political, revolutionary, Marxist praxis. The methodological foundation of liberation theology would then be, not faith, but a particular social scientific paradigm (be that paradigm "class struggle" or "dependency theory") which calls for a particular type of praxis, i.e., revolution. However, despite the fact that Vekemans is well aware of the work of Dussel, he fails to appreciate the import of Dussel's project as providing a safeguard against the realization of this "negative tendency" of liberation theology. For whatever reason, the works of Dussel referred to by Vekemans and his colleagues are primarily his historical works. His methodological works are rarely if ever cited. Our argument will be that, vis-a-vis Vekemans' critique, these methodological works provide a good starting point for adopting a "more positive projection" of the "tendencies" of liberation theology.

Vekemans' critique of liberation theology for its "reductionist" understanding of foundational praxis finds its most cogent and systematic expression in a lengthy, two part article entitled "Panorámica actual de la teología de la liberación en América Latina—Evaluación Crítica." In that article he defines as "praxeological obscurantism" the tendency to make revolutionary praxis foundational, thereby reducing theory, e.g., theology, to a "legitimizing rationalization" of praxis.[100] (Like Novak and McCann, Vekemans interprets liberation theology as understanding *revolutionary* praxis to be identical with *foundational* praxis.)[101]

Consequently, Vekemans contends, Scripture loses its critical function and becomes an instrument for rationalizing a political position already taken.[102] Faith becomes dependent on politics—not vice versa.[103] And the politics which are the methodological starting point are not ambiguously historical, but are uncritically Marxist.[104] Foundational praxis, therefore, is not *really* prethematic, but is, at the very outset, already interpreted through the lenses of Marxist and dependency theory. Moreover, argues Vekemans, not only does liberation theology invert the faith-politics relationship, but it reduces politics to a particular *kind* of politics; faith is reduced to praxis, praxis is reduced to politics, and politics is reduced to Marxism and dependency theory. (As we will see, the major problem with this critique is that, whereas the move from the second to the third step is explicit, the move from the first step to the second is *implicitly assumed;* in other words, the "reduction" of faith to praxis *need not* mean its reduction to *political* praxis—or so we have argued and will argue.)

To refute this critique we will again refer to our analysis of the work of Enrique Dussel, with which Vekemans is well acquainted. In Dussel's work one discovers—even more systematically articulated than in Gutiérrez—an understanding of foundational praxis as 1) prior to and grounding political praxis, 2) faith in the divine Other and, therefore, in the human Other, and 3) irreducible to any interpretative social scientific theory.

First, as we have already seen relative to the North American critiques discussed above, it is precisely because trans-ontological praxis is the only kind commensurate with a transcendent, creator God that this starting point is not "arbitrary." Revolutionary praxis, in a political sense, is not foundational but is secondary to the more fundamental praxis-as-openness-to-exteriority (whether the exteriority be viewed from the perspective of the oppressed person's self-liberation or that of the oppressor's deliverance from the dehumanization of his own oppression). Revolutionary praxis, as Vekemans uses the term, is not foundational *ethical* praxis, but is already the *moral*—i.e., post-ethical—praxis of *carrying out* the demands "heard" *(dabar)* in foundational trans-ontological praxis (the difference here being similar to that between the "fundamental option"—if this is understood as both constitutive of and constituted by moral acts and not merely as some initial "decision" divorced from those acts—and individual moral acts themselves). What makes revolutionary praxis *possible* is the more fundamental "openness to exteriority" of the acting person. If a revolutionary act is not grounded in this foundational openness then it can only turn in upon itself as an oppressive, closed Totality.[105] In short, prior to *dialectical* revolutionary praxis there is *analectical*, trans-ontological praxis, which, as prior to any ontological *a priori*, grounds and judges dialectics. As we have seen, if Dussel is acritical it is not in the understanding of the praxis-politics relation, i.e., "*Who* are the oppressed and *how* are they liberated,?" but rather in the epistemology of trans-ontological praxis itself, i.e., "*Are* there any oppressed?"—a question which any of the critics discussed in this chapter would unhesitatingly answer in the affirmative. Vekemans misses this point because he identifies the praxis-politics relation with foundational praxis itself.

If Dussel does not reduce praxis to political, revolutionary praxis, neither does he reduce faith to politics. Faith is, indeed, "practical," but only if this term is understood to refer to *trans-ontological* praxis. In other words, faith is *not* primarily a rationalization of political praxis, *but* faith *is* primarily a lived openness and response to internal transcendence. Thus, faith is essentially trans-ontological praxis and not a set of dogmatic "beliefs:"

> Faith is not *essentially* a belief or blind trust. A psychological belief, opinion, or submission to the will of something or somebody, a lack of clarity or an uncertainty about something are all secondary elements of the intellectual-practical act of faith.[106]

Faith *does* judge political praxis: is political praxis genuinely analectical? Is it affirmative of the creator God and God's epiphany in the human Other? Consequently, while Yves Congar is quoted by Vekemans as accusing liberation theology of not letting "God be God,"[107] Dussel's concern is precisely that of articulating the conditions of the possibility of letting God be God, of letting the Other be truly Other.[108]

Faith is a response, though not to Scripture *per se*, since "Scripture" can be many things to many people (there being no "Scripture *per se*"), but rather to the exteriority inherent in the human Other and to the coimplicit, cosmological exteriority of the divine Other revealed epiphanically in the human Other. Revelation is not the fundamental reality, since for there to be revelation there must first be an Other (revelation implies non-identity between the subject and object of revelation).[109] Thus, before the "what" of revelation there is the actual *act* of revelation, which presupposes exteriority.[110] And the constitutive element of that revelation, the revelation *itself* is Jesus Christ. Christ is the foundational reality of the absolutely absolute Other incarnated as the human-divine Other: "Thus we have to distinguish between the Christic reality . . . and the *revelation* of that reality." According to Dussel, Scripture gives the "guidelines or the interpretative categories of that reality;" the function of the theologian is "knowing what they are." The doctrinal element of faith, then, is comprised of these "guidelines or interpretative categories" which the ecclesial community has come to accept as being disclosive of exteriority in its manifestation as internal transcendence in history.[111]

So, revelation, for Dussel, *is* prior to politics, *but* it is also prior to Scripture. Scripture gives the guidelines for interpreting exteriority, but our fundamental openness to exteriority is the norm by which that interpretation is judged.[112] We cannot dis-cover revelation if we are not open to the Other. And we are open to the Other through faith:

> Hence, "he who has ears to hear, let him hear" is about the anthropological structure of hearing and also about revelation.[113]

Finally, if Dussel provides safeguards against the reduction of faith to political praxis, he also provides methodological safeguards against the reduction of praxis to any interpretative social scientific theory.[114] We have already seen how Dussel's anadialectical method functions to critique any ontologically closed form of Marxism.[115] His appropriation of the dependency paradigm is also *critical* in that it is *contingent* upon that paradigm's openness to practical-poietic exteriority in all its forms. The same would apply to any other social scientific theory or paradigm.

Such a critical appropriation is inherent in Dussel's method inasmuch as that method sublates (and does not "negate") dialectics. The "prophet," for instance, adopts a stance in *critical* solidarity with the oppressed. The significance of this dialectic is, in turn, expressed in Dussel's own criticism of the dependency paradigm for its *un*-dialectical historical perspective (see chapter four above). Given Dussel's emphasis on the historical conditions of the possibility of liberation, therefore, one could hardly accuse him, as Karl Lehmann accuses liberation theology, of arrogantly dismissing the past in the face of a "pathos of transformation oriented towards the future," or of presenting a "total critique of the present . . . which makes of the present a tabula rasa and constructs a new society from the ground up . . ." (quoted with approval in Vekemans' article).[116]

If the full import of his method is appreciated, then, Dussel can be seen to offer a series of safeguards against that reductionism which Novak, McCann, and Vekemans so fear. Furthermore, within the context of an analysis of Dussel's method, the gross misinterpretations of the work of Gutiérrez, Segundo, and other liberation theologians come more clearly to light, for Dussel is able to explicitate methodologically what, while present in these other theologians, is not usually made so systematically explicit. Therefore, aside from the need—particularly among North American critics like Novak and McCann—to read all liberation theologians on their own terms, without imposing an external framework on them, there is the additional need to take more seriously the work of Dussel as not only the premier historian among liberation theologians but also a major *methodologist*. Before criticizing liberation theology for being naive we must make the effort to understand and appreciate those liberation theologians who, precisely because their work is complex, demand the most effort from us.

NOTES

/1/ Roger Vekemans, SJ, "Panorámica actual de la teología de la liberación: Evaluación crítica," *Tierra Nueva* 17 (April, 1976) 5–7.
/2/ Michael Novak, *The Spirit of Democratic Capitalism* (New York: Simon and Schuster/American Enterprise Institute, 1982) p. 287.
/3/ Ibid., pp. 402–04.
/4/ Ibid.
/5/ Ibid., p. 291.
/6/ Gutiérrez, *A Theology of Liberation*, p. 92.
/7/ Novak, p. 293.
/8/ Ibid., pp. 292–93.
/9/ Ibid., pp. 292, 403.
/10/ Ibid., pp. 303–07.
/11/ Gutiérrez, *A Theology of Liberation*, p. 85.
/12/ See chapters 1 and 4 *supra*.
/13/ Novak, p. 290.
/14/ Ibid.
/15/ Ibid. Here, Novak ignores the role of "praxis" in Marx's critique of Feuerbach. That critique, e.g., in the eleventh thesis on Feuerbach, is precisely a critique of Feuerbach's "illuminism." See Sidney Hook, *From Hegel to Marx: Studies in the Intellectual Development of Karl Marx* (Ann Arbor, Michigan: University of Michigan Press, 1978), sixth printing, pp. 303–07.
/16/ See, e.g., Richard Bernstein, *Praxis and Action: Contemporary Philosophies of Human Activity* (Philadelphia: University of Pennsylvania Press, 1971) pp. 34–83.
/17/ Gustavo Gutiérrez, *La fuerza histórica de los pobres: Selección de trabajos* (Lima: Centro de Estudios y Publicaciones, 1980) pp. 273–74.
/18/ Ibid., p. 273.
/19/ Schubert Ogden, "The Concept of a Theology of Liberation: Must a Christian Theology Today be So Conceived?," in *The Challenge of Liberation Theology: A First World Response*, eds. Brian Mahan and L. Dale Richesin (Maryknoll, N.Y.: Orbis, 1981) pp. 128–29.
/20/ Dussel, *Etica de la liberación*, 1:91.
/21/ Ibid.
/22/ In discovering him or herself as dominated, the Other discovers and

affirms his or her exteriority, i.e., his or her innate right to be free. By analogy, Rahner and other transcendental Thomists, not to mention Thomas himself, point to the transcendent ground of even explicitly transcendence-denying activity. Lonergan articulates this position by showing how the structures of consciousness are implicitly operative even in the attempt to deny them. See, e.g., Lonergan, *Method in Theology,* p. 336; Lamb, *History, Method and Theology,* p. 379; Karl Rahner, *Foundations of Christian Faith: An Introduction to the Idea of Christianity,* trans. William V. Dych (New York: Seabury, 1978), third printing, pp. 19–23, 31–35, 51–55, 126–33; St. Thomas Aquinas, *Summa Theologica,* 3 vols., trans. Fathers of the English Dominican Province (New York: Benziger Bros., 1947–48), I., pt. 1, q. 49, a. 1–3 (pp. 253–56); I., pt. 1–2, q. 1–5 (pp. 583–615).

/23/ McGovern, pp. 179–80, 188–97.

/24/ Dennis P. McCann, *Christian Realism and Liberation Theology: Practical Theologies in Creative Conflict* (Maryknoll, N.Y.: Orbis, 1981) p. 236.

/25/ Ibid., p. 150.

/26/ Ibid.

/27/ Ibid., p. 157.

/28/ Ibid., pp. 159, 161.

/29/ Ibid., p. 165.

/30/ Ibid.

/31/ Ibid., p. 168.

/32/ Ibid., p. 169.

/33/ Ibid., p. 170.

/34/ Ibid., p. 171.

/35/ Ibid., p. 172.

/36/ Ibid., pp. 157, 177.

/37/ See chapter 3 *supra*.

/38/ Paulo Freire quoted in Matthew Lamb, "A Distorted Interpretation of Latin American Liberation Theology," *Horizons* 8 (Fall, 1981) 355–56.

/39/ McCann, p. 170; Lamb, "A Distorted Interpretation," pp. 356–57. Lamb indicates how behind McCann's distortion of Freire there lies, moreover, a similar distortion of David Tracy's notion of limit-situation. McCann seems to identify Freire's notion of limit-situations, argues Lamb, with Tracy's notion of "limits-*of*" human existence. According to Lamb, a more accurate reading of Tracy would identify Freire's notion more closely with what Tracy calls the "limits-*to*" human existence. As dialectical—*not* paradoxical—human self-transcendence involves precisely our transcending "the limits to our life through the limits of that life as grounded in Divine Mystery" (p. 357).

/40/ Paulo Freire, "Educación, liberación e iglesia" in Paulo Freire, et al., *Teología negra: Teología de la liberación* (Salamanca: Sigueme, 1974) p. 28.

/41/ McCann, p. 157.

/42/ McCann also critiques Jon Sobrino, but not for reductionism, rather for failing to be true to the methodological dicta of "liberation theology," which dicta are "clearly" those of Paulo Freire's theory of conscientization (McCann, pp. 217ff.). Thus, McCann concludes that, unlike either Gutiérrez or Segundo, Sobrino *does* do theology, but that, in order to do theology,

he has to surrender any claims to a liberation methodology. Again, such a conclusion can only be reached after one has imposed an external conceptual framework on the work being critiqued.
/43/ McCann, p. 184.
/44/ Gutiérrez, quoted in Lamb, "A Distorted Interpretation," p. 359.
/45/ Gutiérrez, *A Theology of Liberation*, pp. 236, 21–42. See also Gutiérrez, *La fuerza histórica de los pobres*, pp. 108–16.
/46/ Gutiérrez, *A Theology of Liberation*, pp. 235, 238.
/47/ Ibid., p. 238.
/48/ Ibid., p. 237.
/49/ Hugo Assmann, quoted in Samuel Silva Gotay, *El pensamiento cristiano revolucionario en América Latina y el Caribe: Implicaciones de la teología de la liberación para la sociología de la religión* (Salamanca: Sígueme, 1981) p. 129.
/50/ Gutiérrez, *A Theology of Liberation*, p. 238.
/51/ Ibid., p. 177. I have substituted "human being" where "man" appears in the Orbis English translation.
/52/ Assmann, quoted in Silva Gotay, p. 129.
/53/ McCann, p. 164.
/54/ Actually, triply distorted, since McCann's misreading of Freire results largely from his imposition of David Tracy's notion of limit-concept on Freire's method, which notion is itself misconstrued by McCann (Lamb, "A Distorted Interpretation," pp. 356–57). See also footnote 39, *supra*.
/55/ Gutiérrez, *A Theology of Liberation*, p. 92.
/56/ McCann, pp. 221ff.
/57/ Ibid., pp. 216–17.
/58/ Juan Luis Segundo, *The Liberation of Theology*, trans. John Drury (Maryknoll, N.Y.: Orbis, 1976) pp. 210–11.
/59/ Ibid., pp. 216–31.
/60/ McCann, pp. 222–23.
/61/ Sequndo, *The Liberation of Theology*, p. 109.
/62/ McCann, pp. 223–24; Segundo, *The Liberation of Theology*, p. 109.
/63/ McCann, p. 223.
/64/ Ibid., p. 151.
/65/ Juan Luis Segundo, *Grace and the Human Condition*, vol. 2 of *A Theology for Artisans of a New Humanity*, trans. John Drury (Maryknoll, N.Y.: Orbis, 1973), e.g., pp. 10–11, 14, 58–76.
/66/ Ibid., p. 61.
/67/ Ibid., p. 60.
/68/ Ibid.
/69/ Quoted in ibid., p. 63.
/70/ Segundo, *Grace and the Human Condition*, p. 64.
/71/ Ibid., pp. 58–76.
/72/ Ibid., pp. 66–67.
/73/ Ibid., p. 73.
/74/ Ibid., pp. 66ff.
/75/ Ibid., pp. 72–73.
/76/ Secs. 22, 39, quoted in ibid., p. 73.
/77/ Segundo, *Grace and the Human Condition*, p. 156.

/78/ Ibid., pp. 157–58.
/79/ McCann, pp. 222–23.
/80/ See chapter 2, *supra*.
/81/ See chapters 3 and 4, *supra*.
/82/ See chapter 4, *supra;* Dussel, *Filosofía ética*, 5:90.
/83/ Dussel, *Filosofía ética*, 5:21.
/84/ See chapter 3, *supra*.
/85/ Dussel, *Filosofía ética*, 5:35.
/86/ Ibid.
/87/ Ibid., 5:47.
/88/ Dussel, *Introducción a una filosofía de la liberación*, p. 115.
/89/ Dussel, *Filosofía ética*, 5:56, 57, 89.
/90/ Ibid., 5:55.
/91/ See Dussel, *Introducción a una filosofía de la liberación*, p. 76.
/92/ McCann, pp. 157, 179; see Lamb, "A Distorted Interpretation," pp. 353–55, 358.
/93/ Dussel, *Filosofía ética*, 5:105–6.
/94/ Ibid., 5:57.
/95/ Ibid., 5:92–93; see chapter 4, *supra*.
/96/ Vekemans, "La teología de la liberación," p. 5.
/97/ Ibid., p. 6.
/98/ Ibid.
/99/ For a sobering analysis of the totalitarian instrumentalization of human beings characteristic of this century see Gil Elliot, *Twentieth Century Book of the Dead* (New York: Scribners, 1972).
/100/ Vekemans, "La teología de la liberación," pp. 9ff.
/101/ Ibid., p. 10.
/102/ Ibid., p. 19.
/103/ Ibid., pp. 28, 31–32.
/104/ Ibid., pp. 21ff.
/105/ Dussel, *Método*, p. 287.
/106/ Dussel, *The Church in Latin America*, p. 13.
/107/ Yves Congar, quoted in Vekemans, "La teología de la liberación," p. 29.
/108/ Dussel, *Etica de la liberación*, 2:108–63.
/109/ Enrique Dussel, *Ethics and the Theology of Liberation* (Maryknoll, N.Y.: Orbis, 1978) p. 168.
/110/ Ibid., p. 169.
/111/ Ibid., p. 169–72.
/112/ Dussel, *The Church in Latin America*, p. 13. Here Dussel cites Moses as a paradigmatic Scriptural example of this fundamental openness to exteriority.
/113/ Dussel, *Ethics and the Theology of Liberation*, p. 168.
/114/ Cf. Carlos Bravo, "Fe cristiana y praxis de la liberación," *Tierra Nueva* 20 (January, 1977) 8.
/115/ See chapter 2, *supra;* Dussel, *Método*, p. 224.
/116/ Vekemas, "La teología de la liberación," p. 25; cf. chapter four, *supra* and Dussel, *Etica de la liberación*, 1:142.

CONCLUSION

TOWARD AN INTERNATIONAL DIVISION OF THEOLOGICAL LABOR

Dussel's Contribution

Our aim in the preceding chapters has been two-fold: to set forth the possibility of a non-reductionist, or *ana*-dialectical, Latin American liberation methodology by means of an analysis of the method of Enrique Dussel, and to suggest the concomitant possibility of an analogically liberative North American method. The viability of the second proposal depends, however, on the acceptance of the first, since the blanket imposition of the "reductionist" label on liberation theology would imply an identification of liberative method with, in Dussel's terms, the "closed dialectic."

Within an exclusively "dialectical" liberation, conversion is a theoretical and practical impossibility. Consequently, the liberation of the oppressed can only come about, within such a method, through the destruction of the oppressor.[1] Dialogue is superfluous. Within *ana*dialectical liberation, however, dialogue *is* possible, even if only after a period of intense struggle in which the oppressed seek to regain their rightful humanity. Dialogue is possible precisely insofar as, in conversion to the Other, the oppressors make concrete the already implicit identification between their own liberation and the self-liberation of the oppressed, between their own transcendental irreducibility and that of the oppressed. Dialogue is thus grounded in the prior reality of the identification of the dehumanization of the oppressed with its inevitable correlate, the dehumanization of the oppressor. A genuinely anadialectical Latin American liberation method thus suggests the possibility, as its analogical correlate, of a North American liberative method open to the self-liberation of the oppressed. If the prophet is the one who takes his or her stand with the oppressed over against the system, then such a North American liberative method would be the foundation for what would necessarily and intrinsically be a prophetic theology. Such a theology would unchain itself from the oppressive, totalized system in order to challenge the "divinity" of that system.

The possibility of an analogically liberative North American method thus depends on an understanding of liberation as non-reductionist (vis-a-vis *any* system). We have seen how Dussel neither reduces salvation to liberation nor social liberation to economic liberation. In both cases the dialectic is always open (ana-lectic), thus reflecting the ongoing nature of conversion and liberation. The reduction of salvation to social liberation would imply an atheism, not of the fetishistic Totality, but of the creator God who transcends all Totalities and grounds the exteriority of the person. The reduction of social liberation to economic liberation would short-circuit the multidimensional liberative process by failing to attack the many interrelated levels of domination and failing to acknowledge the impact of the non-economic on the economic. (Liberation is always *practical-poietic*.) The indispensability of economic liberation must be safeguarded without at the same time denying the significance of non-economic forms of liberation. Dussel is able to do this through his analysis of the relationship between praxis and poiesis (see chapter four).

Both of the above forms of reductionism are grounded in a non-metaphysical ontology (e.g., Engels).[2] Within such a world view there is no possibility of exteriority beyond the unidimensional foundation. "Liberation" can thus be only involutive. There is no possibility of genuine conversion to exteriority since there is no exteriority. The "liberation" of the oppressed occurs only "from below" as the oppressors are destroyed and the oppressed become "the sole determinants of their being," i.e., they become another closed Totality. The oppressed become new oppressors.

Dussel's method is the antithesis of such an ontology. For the anadialectical method, grounded as it is not in ontology but in metaphysics (or *trans*-ontology), human beings are intrinsically transcendent and this transcendence, or exteriority, is grounded in divine transcendence. Hence, theology cannot be reduced to politics. Likewise, human beings are intrinsically multidimensional social beings. Hence, liberation cannot simply be reduced to economic liberation. Dussel's articulation of the relationship between praxis and poiesis is a *methodological* formulation of this fact, already made explicit in the dependency paradigm.

His incorporation of the dependency paradigm thus contributes both to the methodological importance accorded poiesis as *sine qua non* of liberation *and* to the methodological recognition of the *inter*-relationship between praxis and poiesis. The dependency paradigm functions as a *safeguard against* reductionism. (This is possible because, unlike the earlier, economistic models, the dependency paradigm acknowledges the multidimensionality of human existence.) Nevertheless, while Frank, Cardoso, Faletto, and others point to the significance of non-economic forms of domination (for Frank, for instance, the determinative criterion of domination is not class oppression *per se* but the metropolis-satellite character of *all* forms of economic, political, and social domination),[3] Dussel articulates that significance methodologically in the praxis-poiesis relationship. At the same time, he grounds practical-poietic liberation in a dialectical retrieval—not a mere rejection—of Latin American history. Furthermore, his notion of sexual, or erotic liberation represents an expansion of the notion of Latin American liberation to include the sexual relationship as both impacted upon and impacting its poietic, or economic mediation. Social liberation would now include sexual liberation.

His critique of the dependency paradigm as in some ways ahistorical suggests one final contribution of Dussel to a non-reductionist, anadialectical Latin American liberation. That contribution is his insistence on a *historical* grounding. Liberation does not arise out of a vacuum but out of the negation of the dominative values of the past *as well as* the recovery of the liberative values of the past. In the context of historical praxis, this means the recovery of those values which have at various moments been embodied in persons like Bartolomé de las Casas who have dared to challenge the divinized system. In the context of theory, it means the recovery and adaptation of the insights of men and women who have attempted to articulate, in various ways and with different vocabularies, the irreducibility of being to the closed Totality.[4]

Lonergan's Contribution

In chapter five we saw how, if Dussel's non-reductionist anadialectical method makes explicit the possibility of an analogically liberative North American method, Lonergan's meta-method emerges as one example of just such an analogue. By formulating the tasks and orientations of a trans-ontological liberative method from a North American perspective Lonergan makes epistemologically explicit and specific the de-fetishization of the dominant Totality and the subsequent conversion to exteriority as the correlates of the self-liberation of the Other. In so doing, he delineates the tasks of the prophet, who challenges the fetishism of the system.

The emergence of a Latin American analectic Totality will be made infinitely more difficult to the extent that it is not accompanied by an exorcism of what Matthew Lamb calls "the demon of mecanomorphic rationality."[5] For Lonergan, this is the task of the "intellectual," but the intellectual so defined, i.e., as everyone in his or her trans-ontological experiencing, understanding, judging, deciding, and acting, is none other than Dussel's prophet, defined as the one who takes a stand with the Other over against the dominant Totality. Lonergan's recovery of the subject-as-subject thus involves a critical, or dialectical, recovery of history as the battleground between authenticity and inauthenticity. Consequently, Dussel's dialectical recovery of history is paralleled in Lonergan's work. In both cases, the recovery is attentive to the priority of consciousness, or praxis, over knowledge and takes cognizance of the suffering wrought when, in conceptualism, that priority is inverted.[6]

The Future

In an address delivered at the "Encounter of Theologies" held at the Theological Community of Mexico in October, 1977, Dussel made the following remarks:

> I profoundly believe that the universality of the theology of liberation will be better understood when the theologians of the different continents discover within their diverse situations what is their specific theoretical labor within a global strategy; that is to say, within an "international division of theological labor," if you will allow the expression. European praxis and theology cannot be the same as those in the U.S. or Latin America; and those procedures in Latin America cannot be identical with those in Africa or Asia. Nevertheless, all must pose the same problems, although historically and concretely the themes, the emphases, and the discourses will differ. Sharing a single world strategic task (the liberation of oppressed peoples, oppressed classes, and the poor), we shall be able to seal an alliance within tactical diversity.[7]

What Dussel refers to here as "tactical" diversity arises from what we referred to above as "perspectival" diversity. In other words, 1) the tactics are diverse because they are grounded in diverse historical perspectives, but 2) like the perspectives, the tactics are complementary insofar as they share "a single world strategic task" and "pose the same problems."

By the "universality of the theology of liberation,'" therefore, Dussel does not mean to imply that "liberation theology" is a univocal term any more than he means to imply that liberation theology is only one among many equally valid ways of doing theology. His method eschews both univocity and relativism; rather, the relationship of Latin American liberation theology to other theologies is one of analogy.[8] Having emerged dialectically from both Latin American historical praxis and Western philosophical and theological theory, it bears the imprints of the latter but extends them beyond their earlier boundaries in the light of the Latin American experience of domination, exteriority, and liberation. Thus, while the theme of liberation is literally as old as Moses, Bartolomé de las Casas, and the Incan descendant Tupac Amaru, it now takes on new meaning.[9]

If Latin American liberation theology has incorporated and adapted those elements of the Western Christian tradition which affirm the irreducibility of both God and the person, then an analogical approach to international theological dialogue would seek to learn from the advances of Latin American liberation theology, respecting its sociohistorical particularity while at the same time recognizing that the particularity is of universal significance. The universality of liberation theology allows it to challenge the various Western theological traditions and to serve as a catalyst for their development in a more liberative direction. By drawing upon the works of scholars like Lonergan, who essays a theoretical formulation of the exigencies implicit in a practical de-fetishization of the Western Totality, North American theologians can develop a method for recovering the meaning of liberation in North American historical praxis. In so doing, they would be affirming the transcendence of God and the human person by denying the divinity of the Euro-American theological Totality.

As we have seen, this is the only avenue open for a genuine "theology," since the rejection of Latin American liberation theology is nothing more than an implicit admission of the univocity, or "divinity," of the established theologies as a closed Totality. The divinized system inevitably becomes an idol, or fetish, to whom human beings and the transcendent God are sacrificed. It is no coincidence, then, that the very charge of reductionism can reflect the reductionist idolatry of the Totality whence it issues, wherein "God" and the person are reduced to mere functional cogs.

The goal of dialogue should not be restricted, as Alfred Hennelly rightly suggests, to "greater harmony or mutual enrichment among theologians. . . ."[10] Such harmony and mutual enrichment will be valid only if they flow from and are directed towards human liberation. To the extent that they evade the issue of liberation, they will merely mask an underlying fetishism.

North America certainly has much to say to the issue of liberation. The United States was founded on the belief—enunciated most concisely in the Declaration of Independence—that, in the words of Thomas Jefferson, "the mass of mankind has not been born with saddles on their backs for a favored few, booted and spurred, ready to ride them by the grace of God."[11] Although it may take the Latin American experience of domination to awaken us to this fact, a dialectical retrieval of North American history can ground an analogically (vis-a-vis Latin American theology) liberative North American theology which would not be simply a foreign import. While, as Hennelly contends, John Courtney Murray and, as we contend, Bernard Lonergan, represent initial steps in the development of an analogically liberative North American theology, much remains to be done. Certainly, as "the Other" within our national borders, Blacks, Native Americans, Hispanics and women will have much to contribute to this task. We need not leave our shores to find the consequences of North American fetishism. These cry out as loudly as do the voices from south of our borders. All of these voices demand liberation and so, demand a recovery of North American liberative values in the wake of the desecration of those values over the last decades by men and institutions who hide behind "liberty" in order to deny liberty—and its spiritual and material preconditions—to others.[12]

In an era dominated (in more ways than one) by capitalist economic monopolies on the one hand and socialist state monopolies on the other, the defense of human and divine transcendence is no longer merely an option; it is the principal and most urgent imperative.[13] And that global defense can be articulated theologically only in the form of analogically-related liberation theologies which proclaim the irreducibility of both God and the person to any system and which, for Christians, express the sacramental significance of the Christ event as God's self-identification with human beings in our irreducibility.

The incarnation of transcendence is an analectical reality precisely because divine *exteriority* becomes incarnate in human *exteriority*. Only if we deny the possibility of human self-transcendence is the incarnation a self-contradictory paradox (rather than analectic), for then there would be no possibility of communication between God and humanity. If human beings are not themselves "internal transcendence," then divine transcendence has no entry into our world and human beings have no way of discovering its presence. God's transcendence would necessarily be reduced to one or another closed Totality.

It is, however, this very denial of human self-transcendence that characterizes the instruments of death fashioned by the competing world systems. It is their common denial of human exteriority that reveals these systems, not as adversaries, but as partners with a common stake in defending the divinity of the global system. And they are willing to defend that divinity to the death—theirs and everyone else's.

This denial of the trans-ontological, or transcendent orientation of the person and, hence, of the person's nature as the sacrament of the transcendent, creator God must be combatted, then, if we as a race are to survive. We must have the courage to proclaim human and divine otherness in all its manifestations. That otherness is human freedom—from all forms of domination and slavery. Consequently, only theologies *of liberation*, cognizant of the many ways in which human and divine transcendence is continually being denied, will be able to provide alternatives to the fetishistic "theologies."

Dussel's anadialectical method provides a methodological grounding for the task of human and divine liberation (yes, God also must be liberated from our clutches) and, in so doing, gives us a way of understanding the "international division of theological labor" as an analogical division whose common goal is—normatively, at least—the affirmation of human and divine freedom. The task of building such an international division of theological labor has only begun. The urgency of the task presses upon us, however, as more and more human beings are sacrificed to the fetishized system (whether capitalist or state socialist).

It is to the affirmation of the transcendent God and the transcendent person that liberation theologies will continue to address themselves. The importance of the task is determined by the magnitude of the goal, and the goal is none other than the freedom of persons to be persons and the freedom of God to be God. May our hearts and minds be equal to this task of liberation. In the words of the Bolivian patriot-martyr Néstor Paz, this is our hope, this the goal of our struggle:

> To be able to see the people
> with hope-filled eyes,
> to be able to say
> get set to be a person,
> to be a person
> to be other . . .[14]

NOTES

/1/ See chapters two and three, *supra.*
/2/ See chapter two, *supra.*
/3/ Frank, "The Development of Underdevelopment."
/4/ See chapter two, *supra.*
/5/ Personal correspondence with Matthew Lamb.
/7/ Enrique Dussel, "An International Division of Theological Labor," *Foundations* 23 (October/December, 1980) 332.
/8/ Dussel, *The Church in Latin America,* p. 20; Dussel, "Supuestos histórico-filosóficos."
/9/ Dussel, "Supuestos histórico-filosóficos," p. 175.
/10/ Hennelly, p. 180.
/11/ Thomas Jefferson, quoted in ibid., p. 181.
/12/ Hennelly, pp. 181ff.
/13/ Personal correspondence with Matthew Lamb.
/14/ Néstor Paz, *My Life for my Friends: The Guerrilla Journal of Néstor Paz, Christian,* trans. and ed. Ed Garcia and John Eagleson (Maryknoll, N.Y.: Orbis, 1975) p. 19. I have substituted "person" for "man," which was the word appearing in the English translation published by Orbis.
/

BIBLIOGRAPHY OF WORKS USED AND/OR CITED

Works by Enrique Dussel

América Latina: Dependencia y liberación. Buenos Aires: Fernando García Cambeiro, 1973.

"Analysis of the Final Document of Puebla: The Relationship between Economics and Christian Ethics." In *Christian Ethics and Economics: The North-South Conflict*, pp. 101–09. Edited by Dietmar Mieth and Jacques Pohier. New York: Seabury, 1980.

"The Bread of the Eucharistic Celebration as a Sign of Justice in the Community." In *Can We Always Celebrate the Eucharist?*, pp. 56–65. Edited by Mary Collins and David Power. New York: Seabury, 1982.

Caminos de liberación latinoamericana I: Interpretación histórico-teológica de nuestro continente latino-americano. Buenos Aires: Latinoamérica, 1972.

"Crisis de la Iglesia latinoamericana y situación del pensador cristiano en Argentina." *Stromata* 26 (1970) 277–336.

Desintegración de la cristiandad colonial y liberación: Perspectiva latinoamericana. Salamanca: Sígueme, 1978.

La dialética hegeliana: Supuestos y superación o del inicio originario del filosofar. Mendoza, Argentina: Editorial Ser y Tiempo, 1972.

Ethics and the Theology of Liberation. Maryknoll, N.Y.: Orbis, 1978.

Filosofía de la liberación. México: Edicol, 1977.

A History of the Church in Latin America: Colonialism to Liberation (1492–1979). Translated and revised by Alan Neely. Grand Rapids, Michigan: Eerdmans, 1981.

El humanismo semita. Buenos Aires: Editorial Universitaria de Buenos Aires, 1969.

"An International Division of Theological Labor." *Foundations* 23 (October–December, 1980) 332–54.

Introducción a una filosofía de la liberación latinoamericana. México: Editorial Extemporáneos, 1977.

"The Kingdom of God and the Poor." *International Review of Mission* 220 (1979) 115–30.

Et al. *Liberación y cautiverio: Debates en torno al método de la teología en América Latina*. México: Comité Organizador, 1975.

With Daniel Guillot. *Liberación latinoamericana y Emmanuel Levinas*. Buenos Aires: Bonum, 1975.

"Marx ante el pasado y el porvenir de la humanidad." *Teología y Vida* 13 (1972) 207–26.

Método para una filosofía de la liberación: Superación analética de la dialéctica hegeliana. Salamanca: Sígueme, 1974.

"Modern Christianity in Face of the 'Other:' From the 'Rude Indian' to the 'Noble Savage.'" In *The Dignity of the Despised of the Earth*, pp. 49–58. Edited by Jacques Pohier and Dietmar Mieth. New York: Seabury, 1979.

Para una ética de la liberación latinoamericana. 2 Vols. (I-II). Buenos aires: Siglo Veintiuno, 1973; *Filosofía ética latinoamericana*. 3 Vols. (III-V). México: Edicol, 1977–1980.

"Para una fundamentación dialéctica de la liberación latinoamericana." *Stromata* 28 (1972) 53–89.

Religión. México: Edicol, 1977.

"La religión en el joven Marx (1835–1849)." *Los Universitarios* 205 (Dec., 1982) 25–31.

"Supuestos histórico-filosóficos de la teología desde América latina." In *La nueva frontera de la teología en América latina*, pp. 174–98. Edited by Rosino Gibellini. Salamanca: Sígueme, 1977.

Social Scientific Works

Amin, Samir. *Unequal Development: An Essay on the Social Formations of Peripheral Capitalism*. New York: Monthly Review Press, 1976.

Booth, David. "Andre Gunder Frank: an Introduction and Appreciation." In *Beyond the Sociology of Development: Economy and Society in Latin America and Africa*, pp. 50–85. Edited by Ivar Oxaal, Tony Barnett and David Booth. London: Routledge and Kegan Paul, 1975.

Cardoso, Fernando Henrique and Faletto, Enzo. *Dependency and Development in Latin America*. Translated by Marjory Mattingly Urquidi. Berkeley, California: University of California Press, 1979.

Cockroft, James D.; Frank, Andre Gunder; and Johnson, Dale L. *Dependence and Underdevelopment: Latin America's Political Economy*. Garden City, N.Y.: Doubleday, 1972.

Dealy, Glen Caudill. *The Public Man: An Interpretation of Latin American and Other Catholic Countries*. Amherst, Massachusetts: University of Massachusetts Press, 1977.

Evans, Peter. *Dependent Development: The Alliance of Multinational, State, and Local Capital in Brazil*. Princeton: Princeton University Press, 1979.

Fishlow, Albert. "Some Reflections on Post-1964 Brazilian Economic Policy." In *Authoritarian Brazil: Origins, Policies and Future*, pp. 69–118. Edited by Alfred Stepan. New Haven: Yale University Press, 1973.

Fleet, Michael. *The Rise and Fall of Chilean Christian Democracy*. Princeton: Princeton University Press, forthcoming.

Frank, Andre Gunder. *Capitalism and Underdevelopment in Latin America: Historical Studies of Chile and Brazil*. New York: Monthly Review Press, 1969.

———. "The Development of Underdevelopment." In *Dependence and Underdevelopment: Latin America's Political Economy*, pp. 3–18. Edited by James D. Cockroft, Andre Gunder Frank and Dale L. Johnson. Garden City, N.Y.: Doubleday, 1972.

———. "Economic Dependence, Class Structure, and Underdevelopment Policy." In *Dependence and Underdevelopment: Latin America's Political Economy*, pp. 19–45. Edited by James D. Cockroft, Andre Gunder Frank, and Dale L. Johnson. Garden City, N.Y.: Doubleday, 1972.

Goulet, Denis. *The Cruel Choice: A New Concept in the Theory of Development*. New York: Atheneum, 1975.

Graham, Lawrence S. "Latin America: Illusion or Reality? A Case for a New Analytic Framework for the Region." In *Politics and Social Change in Latin America: The Distinct Tradition*, pp. 231–48. Edited by Howard J. Wiarda. Amherst, Massachusetts: University of Massachusetts Press, 1974.

Gramsci, Antonio. *Selections from the Prison Notebooks of Antonio Gramsci*. Edited by Quintin Hoare and Geoffrey Nowell Smith. London: Lawrence and Wishart, 1971.

Johnson, Dale L. "Dependence and the International System." In *Dependence and Underdevelopment: Latin America's Political Economy*. Edited by James D. Cockroft, Andre Gunder Frank and Dale L. Johnson, pp. 71–111. Garden City, N.Y.: Doubleday, 1972.

Lall, Sanjaya. "Is 'Dependence' a Useful Concept in Analyzing Underdevelopment?" *World Development* 3 (1975) 799–810.

Morawetz, David. *Twenty-five Years of Economic Development 1950–1975*. Washington, D.C.: The World Bank, 1977.

O'Brien, Philip J. "A Critique of Latin American Theories of Dependency." In *Beyond the Sociology of Development: Economy and Society in Latin America and Africa*, pp. 7–27. Edited by Ivar Oxaal, Tony Barnett and David Booth. London: Routledge and Kegan Paul, 1975.

Parmar, Samule L. "Self-Reliant Development in an 'Interdependent' World." In *Beyond Dependency: The Developing World Speaks Out*, pp. 8–17. Edited by Guy F. Erb and Valeriana Kallab. New York: Praeger, 1975.

Petras, James and Cook, Thomas. "Dependency and the Industrial Bourgeoisie: Attitudes of Argentine Executives Toward Foreign Economic Investment and U. S. Policy." In *Latin America: From Dependence to Revolution*, pp. 143–75. Edited by James Petras. New York: John Wiley and Sons, 1973.

Prebisch, Raúl. *Change and Development: Latin America's Great Task*. Washington, D.C.: Inter-American Development Bank, 1970.

Robinson, Ronald, ed. *Developing the Third World: The Experience of the Nineteen-Sixties*. London: Cambridge University Press, 1971.

Roxborough, Ian. *Theories of Underdevelopment*. London: MacMillan, 1979.

Serra, José. "The Brazilian 'Economic Miracle.'" In *Latin America: From Dependence to Revolution*, pp. 100–140. Edited by James Petras. New York: John Wiley and Sons, 1973.

Stepan, Alfred. *The State and Society: Peru in Comparative Perspective*. Princeton: Princeton University Press, 1978.

———, ed. *Authoritarian Brazil: Origins, Policies and Future*. New Haven: Yale University Press, 1973.

Weisskopf, Thomas. "Depedency as an Explanation of Underdevelopment: A Critique." Paper prepared for presentation at the sixth annual meeting of the Latin American Studies Association, Atlanta, Georgia, March, 1976.

Wood, Ellen Meiksins. "The Separation of the Economic and the Political in Capitalism." *New Left Review*. No. 127 (May–June, 1981) pp. 66–95.

Other Works

Primary

Freire, Paulo, et al. *Teología negra: Teología de la liberación*. Salamanca: Sígueme, 1974.

Gibellini, Rosino, ed *La nueva frontera de la teología en América latina*. Salamanca: Sígueme, 1977.

Gutiérrez, Gustavo. *La fuerza histórica de los pobres: Selección de trabajos*. Lima: Centro de Estudios y Publicaciones, 1980.

———. *A Theology of Liberation: History, Politics and Salvation*. Maryknoll, N.Y.: Orbis, 1973.

Lonergan, Bernard. *Collection: Papers by Bernard Lonergan*. Edited by Frederick E. Crowe. New York: Herder and Herder, 1967.

———. *Insight: A Study of Human Understanding*. Revised edition. New York: Longmans, 1958.

———. *Method in Theology*. New York: Seabury, 1972.

———. *The Subject*. The Aquinas Lecture, 1968. Milwaukee: Marquette University Press, 1968.

McCann, Dennis P. *Christian Realism and Liberation Theology: Practical Theologies in Creative Conflict*. Maryknoll, N.Y.: Orbis, 1981.

Novak, Michael. *The Spirit of Democratic Capitalism*. New York: Simon and Schuster/American Enterprise Institute, 1982.

Segundo, Juan Luis. *Grace and the Human Condition*. Translated by John Drury. Maryknoll, N.Y.: Orbis, 1973.

———. *The Liberation of Theology*. Translated by John Drury. Maryknoll, N.Y.: Orbis, 1976.

———. *A Theology for Artisans of a New Humanity*. 5 vols. Maryknoll, N.Y.: Orbis, 1973–74.

Vekemans, Roger. "Panorámica actual de la teología de la liberación: evaluación critica." *Tierra Nueva* 17 (April, 1976) 5–33.

Secondary

Aquinas, St. Thomas. *Summa Theologica*. 3 Vols. Translated by Fathers of the English Dominican Province, New York: Benziger Brothers, 1947–1948.

Arrom, José Juan. *Certidumbre de América: estudios de letra, folklore y cultura*. Segunda edición ampliada. Madrid: Editorial Gredos, 1971.

Bernstein, Richard. *Praxis and Action: Contemporary Philosophies of Human Activity*. Philadelphia: University of Pennsylvania Press, 1971.

Bravo, Carlos. "Fe cristiana y praxis de la liberación." *Tierra Nueva* 20 (January, 1977) 5–23.

Crowe, Frederick. *The Lonergan Enterprise*. Cambridge, Massachusetts: Cowley Publications, 1980.

Doran, Robert M. *Psychic Conversion and Theological Foundations: Toward a Reorientation of the Human Sciences*. Chico, California: Scholars Press, 1981.

———. *Subject and Psyche: Ricoeur, Jung, and the Search for Foundations*. Washington, D.C.: University Press of America, 1977.

———. "Theological Grounds for a World-Cultural Humanity." In *Creativity and Method: Essays in Honor of Bernard Lonergan, S.J.*, pp. 105–22. Edited by Matthew Lamb. Milwaukee: Marquette University Press, 1981.

Eagleson, John and Scharper, Philip, eds. *Puebla and Beyond: Documentation and Commentary*. Maryknoll, N.Y.: Orbis, 1979.

Elliot, Gil. *Twentieth Century Book of the Dead*. New York: Scribner's, 1972.

Goizueta, Roberto S. "Liberation and Method: The Analectical Method of Enrique Dussel." In *The Pedagogy of God's Image: Essays on Symbol and the Religious Imagination*. Edited by Robert Masson. Chico, California: Scholars Press, 1982.

Hennelly, Alfred T. *Theologies in Conflict: The Challenge of Juan Luis Segundo*. Maryknoll, N.Y.: Orbis, 1979.

Hook, Sidney. *From Hegel to Marx: Studies in the Intellectual Development of Karl Marx*. Ann Arbor, Michigan: University of Michigan Press, 1978.

Lamb, Matthew L. "A Distorted Interpretation of Latin American Liberation Theology." *Horizons* 8 (Fall, 1981) 352–64.

———. *History, Method and Theology: A Dialectical Comparison of Wilhelm Dilthey's Critique of Historical Reason and Bernard Lonergan's Meta-Methodology*. Missoula, Montana: Scholars Press, 1978.

———. *Solidarity With Victims: Toward a Theology of Social Transformation*. New York: Crossroad, 1982.

———. ed. *Creativity and Method: Essays in Honor of Bernard Lonergan, S.J*. Milwaukee: Marquette University Press, 1981.

McGovern, Arthur. *Marxism: An American Christian Perspective*. Maryknoll, N.Y.: Orbis, 1980.

Miranda. José. *Marx Against the Marxists: The Christian Humanism of Karl Marx*. Maryknoll, N.Y.: Orbis, 1980.

Ogden, Schubert. "The Concept of a Theology of Liberation: Must a Christian Theology Today be so Conceived?" In *The Challenge of Liberation Theology: A First World Response*. Edited by Brian Mahan and L. Dale Richesin. Introduction by David Tracy. Maryknoll, N.Y.: Orbis, 1981.

Paz, Néstor. *My Life for my Friends: The Guerrilla Journal of Néstor Paz, Christian*. Translated and edited by Ed Garcia and John Eagleson. Maryknoll, N.Y.: Orbis, 1975.